Forensic Accounting

Forensic Accounting

The Accountant as Expert Witness

FRANCIS C. DYKEMAN
Retired Partner, Price Waterhouse

1807 1982

A Ronald Press Publication

JOHN WILEY & SONS

New York   Chichester   Brisbane   Toronto   Singapore

This publication is designed to provide accurate and
authoritative information in regard to the subject
matter covered. It is sold with the understanding that
the publisher is not engaged in rendering legal, accounting,
or other professional service. If legal advice or other
expert assistance is required, the services of a competent
professional person should be sought. *From a Declaration
of Principles jointly adopted by a Committee of the
American Bar Association and a Committee of Publishers.*

Library of Congress Cataloging in Publication Data:

Dykeman, Francis C.
  Forensic accounting.

  "A Ronald Press publication."
  Includes index.
  1. Forensic accounting—United States.
2. Evidence, Expert—United States. I. Title.

KF8968.15.D94	347.73′67	81-13001
ISBN 0-471-08395-X	347.30767	AACR2

Printed in the United States of America

10 9 8 7 6 5 4 3 2 1

A Word from the Author

The judicial process can seem complex and confusing to the parties involved and to the witnesses. It is frequently characterized by periods of both extreme time pressures and long delays. Huge quantities of often unorganized data need analysis, and traditional accounting controls on the accuracy of the information gathered are usually unavailable.

The judicial process is both an adversary and a decision-making activity. Opposing or conflicting viewpoints are presented by learned attorneys, and the judge and/or jury are called upon to make decisions based upon the laws and facts described to them by the attorneys. Rarely is the art of decision-making open to so great a glare of publicity and to review, analysis, and criticism by others. Not only is the decision of the judge subject to review by higher authority, but attorneys, university professors, and law students can dissect the rationale of the case and the comprehensiveness of the array of facts to which the interpretations of law were applied.

The certified public accountant can frequently make an important contribution to this decision-making process as an expert witness or consultant to the attorneys. Very few demands upon a person in the accounting profession provide greater awareness of personal challenge and contribution than the role of expert witness. To present clear and logical direct testimony and then to defend this testimony under the probe of cross-examination by competent attorneys with no opportunity granted for extensive deliberation or consultation with other experienced associates, is an experience not easily forgotten. These pressures are heightened by the knowledge that the outcome of the case frequently affects the economic welfare of the client and the reputation of an expert witness and the witness's firm. Add to that the stimulation of pitting one's knowledge, background, and opinions against persons determined to prove that you are unqualified to testify as an expert witness and the challenge becomes one that will be long remembered.

Expert accounting witnesses present themselves to the court as leaders in accounting thought, in the use of accounting techniques, and in the application of accounting methodology. This book is dedicated to helping certified public accountants expand their practices and client service opportunities by offering assistance to clients and their attorneys in complex litigation. It will attempt to provide certified public accountants with knowledge about the judicial process as viewed from the perspective of an expert witness rather than from that of an attorney, and to assist expert witnesses in understanding the environment in which they will be operating. It will give them an understanding of the personal and professional abilities required of expert accounting witnesses so that they may determine whether they can serve their clients in this capacity. It will describe how a witness should behave when testifying and how to prepare for the rigors of cross-examination which can become a weapon either in the hands of the witness or opposing counsel, depending upon the relative state of preparedness of the witness and the cross-examining attorney. Problems associated with accumulating, analyzing, filing, and retrieving the huge quantities of data gathered during pretrial activities are described, and examples of how financial, accounting, and statistical information were developed into testimony are presented. The difficulties of communicating with attorneys and among expert witnesses of different disciplines will be illustrated so that the expert accounting witness may avoid the pitfalls brought about by faulty understanding of proposed testimony. Additional services which the certified public accountant may provide the attorney are also described.

The overall objective of this book is to help transform the formidable experience of testifying into an exciting and profitable service by certified public accountants to their clients. It is not possible to acknowledge individually the numerous contributions of my partners and associates in the development of this manuscript. Fortunately, I have worked for many years with a number of energetic and intellectually stimulating thinkers. Although many have contributed, the author alone is responsible for the material presented. I would like to express particular appreciation to my secretary, Mrs. Betty Hutton, for her assistance, and to the members of the Word Processing Department, of Price Waterhouse, Los Angeles, for their diligent efforts in typing this manuscript.

Francis C. Dykeman

Arcadia, California
October 1981

Contents

Impeachment and rehabilitation of witnesses. Cross-examining the opponent's expert accounting witness.

Forensic Accounting

CHAPTER

1

An Overview of the Judicial Process

To the accountant who presents expert testimony, a judicial proceeding can seem slow and inexorable, yet filled with unexpected procedural precautions. The objective of the judicial process is justice to both parties; the judge rules as the principal advocate of this objective, and the attorneys strive to attain justice from the perspectives of their clients. There are frequent delays due to changes in court schedules, yet time pressures can become relentless when time constraints are imposed upon the attorneys by the court.

Although oratory and clever tactical maneuvers by attorneys appear to have some value, the judicial process, by its nature, seems to guard against testimony that is unexpected, argumentative, or emotional. Attorneys for both the plaintiff and the defendant have the right to inspect the opposing party's records and take depositions from its witnesses so that the testimony to be given at the trial is known before the trial commences. Trial exhibits are exchanged between the parties and trial briefs are prepared for the court and opposing counsel so that each party prior to trial knows the opponent's position relative to: the laws involved, the alleged offenses, the facts relied upon, the defenses offered, and the injuries claimed. The courtroom is dominated by the judge, the attorneys lead the proceedings, and the jury usually listens in impassive silence.

This, in brief, is the world into which the expert accounting witness steps.

THE JUDICIAL PROCESS BEGINS

Litigation usually starts when one party, the plaintiff, alleges some action or failure to act by another party, the defendant, which has violated a personal or property right of the plaintiff. The injury is initially described in the complaint prepared by the plaintiff's attorneys. It is filed with the court and copies are forwarded to the defendants. The *complaint* is the legal document that commences the lawsuit, setting forth the statutes and property rights involved, the actions that led to the plaintiff's injuries and, in rather general terms, the monetary value of the damages claimed. The complaint also describes what legal remedies are sought.

Upon receipt of the complaint, the defendant's attorneys may issue either a demurrer to the complaint or an answer. A *demurrer* is an objection to defects appearing on the face of the complaint and pertains to issues of law only. A special demurrer enumerates specific grounds, whereas a general demurrer maintains that there is not sufficient evidence to support the plaintiff's claims. An *answer* is a document filed in reply to the complaint. Its purpose is to deny that certain allegations or parts of them are true, to deny other allegations for lack of information or belief, and/or to admit those that are true. The answer frequently alleges that the actions of the defendant were not the cause of injury to the plaintiff and that the estimates of monetary damages are erroneous.

The complaint and the answer are both subject to change and amendment as the judicial process continues; but they are the initial papers setting out the case, thereby providing the expert witness with an introduction to the issues to be investigated. The expert accounting witness should read and fully understand these documents in order to be able to play an important role in the discussion of the strategic economic position of his client with the judge and jury during the trial.

FACT FINDING AND DISCOVERY

Fact finding starts immediately and lasts throughout the trial. *Discovery* consists basically of prescribed legal procedures by which the attorneys for each litigant attempt to find out, before the trial begins, all they can about the case. Who are the witnesses? What do they know about the facts of the case? Upon what documents are they relying to prove their case? To what facts do the witnesses intend to testify and how did the expert witnesses develop their opinions?

The principal instruments used in discovery proceedings are depositions, interrogatories, and requests for admission. In addition, documents to be presented in evidence may be inspected by opposing lawyers through motions for production of documents and *subpoenas duces tecum.*

Parties may obtain discovery regarding any matter not privileged that is relevant to the subject matter involved in the pending action, whether it relates to the claim or defense of the party seeking discovery, or to the claim or defense of any other party, including the existence, description, nature, custody, condition, and location of any books, documents, or other tangible things, and the identity and location of persons having knowledge of any discoverable matter. It is not grounds for objection that the information sought will be inadmissible at the trial, if such information appears reasonably calculated to lead to the discovery of admissible evidence. Facts known and opinions held by experts may be discovered through *interrogatories,* which require the opposing party to identify each person it expects to call as an expert witness, to state the subject matter and the substance of the facts and opinions to which the expert is expected to testify, and to summarize the grounds for each opinion. Under exceptional circumstances, a party may obtain discovery from an expert witness who does not intend to testify.

Discovery may be made in any sequence. If the original response to a request was complete when made, there is no duty to supplement it except: to include other people having knowledge of discoverable matters, and to identify other expert witnesses and the subject and substance of their testimony; to correct an incorrect response; or to comply with a court order.

To the expert accounting witness, the attorneys' demands for information can seem inexhaustible, limited only by the nature of the lawsuit and the relevance of the information to it. Moreover, at the outset of litigation, the boundaries defining relevance of information are vague and flexible.

The information needs of the plaintiffs and the defendants differ radically, and individual fact-finding programs must be organized to meet these separate needs. Plaintiffs frequently have within their control the *impact data,* that is, the raw data that describe the injuries inflicted upon them by the defendants and the magnitude of the harm that resulted. Such data must be organized, analyzed, and reported in a manner that fully conveys the type and extent of the injury. Plaintiffs frequently need, from information within the defendants' control, facts that prove that the alleged actions were intentionally taken by the defendants with intent to harm the plaintiffs, and were undertaken with expectation of some perceived benefits to the defendants.

The fact-finding problems of the defendants are often more difficult to handle than those of the plaintiffs, for the defendants will usually try to prove that the alleged acts did not cause the claimed injury, but that the plaintiffs were responsible through their own actions for any injury suffered. It is also incumbent upon the defendants to prove that the damages claimed by the plaintiff are exaggerated. Usually such proof is most accessible from the plaintiffs' records.

The investigatory powers of the expert accounting witness are frequently called upon to obtain facts not contained in the adversary's records. Data from industrial and other publications that illustrate policies and operations of the opposing party are searched for relevance; tax records are frequently perused; and speeches, articles, and other available data published by the parties involved are examined.

Searches are made for all relevant information about potential adversary witnesses when they are named. Where such a witness has an accounting background, the opposing expert accounting witness will usually be requested to read anything published by this adversary. Usually, discovery is permitted for only a limited period of time and, as it is performed before many of the legal issues are finalized, the tendency is to copy all available documents. This leads to the enormous problem of organizing, classifying, analyzing, summarizing, and reporting on the documents collected, a job frequently assigned to the expert accounting witness.

When discovery has been completed, the attorneys are in a better position to evaluate their client's case, and their evaluations influence them in seeking a possible out-of-court settlement. If settlement negotiations fail and the case goes to trial, the attorneys are better prepared to argue their client's position. They will not only have acquired the evidence to present at trial but will also know what evidence will be presented by the opposing party, thus reducing the chance of surprise evidence being introduced.

INTERROGATORIES

Neither the plaintiff nor the defendant has in his possession many of the facts that must be introduced into evidence to sustain the allegations in the complaint and answer. Usually, the simplest approach to obtaining this needed information is through the preparation of an *interrogatory,* a series of questions that specifically identifies the information needed and requests the opposing party to prepare the required answers. Both parties must answer these questions as truthfully and completely as possible.

Interrogatories usually provide an introductory level of knowledge about the opposing party and the positions one would expect it to take at trial; they are prepared by the attorneys with whatever assistance is possible from the clients and the expert witnesses. It is usually important for the expert accounting witness to read and study the answers to the interrogatories received from the opposing party.

TAKING DEPOSITIONS

A *deposition* is testimony taken under oath, usually under less formal conditions than in a courtroom, but subject to the rules and regulations of the court as though the testimony were being taken in the courtroom. A notary public or other authorized person administers the oath to the person whose deposition is being taken, with counsel for each of the litigating parties present, and opposing counsel able to ask questions of the witness. A reporter takes the questions and answers verbatim in shorthand or stenotype, and later transcribes the notes. The witness reads and corrects the deposition and signs it. By written stipulation, the parties may agree to take depositions before any person, at any time or place, and upon any notice. The deposition may be read to the court at trial.

Depositions provide an excellent opportunity for counsel to evaluate the opposing expert witnesses and to learn what testimony will be given at trial. While deposition proceedings differ substantially because of differences in issues involved, the timing of the deposition, and the state of completeness of the witness's work, frequently the witness will be precluded from adding anything new at the trial. Thus, a witness must have a substantial understanding of one's proposed testimony and intended trial strategy prior to a deposition hearing. Proposed exhibits must be in reasonably final form and the witness must guard against saying anything that will make trial testimony more difficult than necessary.

Attorneys frequently request that the expert accountant they have employed to assist with the case be present at any depositions of opposing witnesses that relate to accounting matters, in order to help interpret the accounting testimony and raise pertinent questions that will clarify the accounting points at issue, with a view toward strengthening the client's case. Thus, the expert accountant must be alert to detecting errors in fact or technique, as well as ambiguous answers, partial answers, and misleading answers of all kinds. Business and accounting jargon can sometimes be used by unprincipled witnesses to confuse testimony, and it is the duty of the expert accountant to reveal such subterfuge to the attorney.

Since the attorneys are the only individuals allowed to speak directly to the witness, it is customary for the expert accountant to write any suggestions on slips of paper, which are passed to the attorney for consideration and use. In this way, the attorney can note the suggestion without the opposition becoming aware of its content, can drop the suggestion if it is inappropriate, or can work the suggestion into the questions when it can be used most effectively. As the expert accountant becomes familiar with the communication styles of the individual attorneys, the accountant may be able, in many instances, to reduce notes to an almost telegraphic briefness and still achieve full communication. If the attorney is in doubt about the meaning of one of the expert's notes and wishes to discuss some point more fully, a short recess will usually be called to enable the two to discuss the point outside the hearing of the others present.

While the deposition provides advantages to the opposing counsel in that proposed testimony is divulged and the demeanor and ability of the witness are exposed, it is also a valuable pretrial experience for the witness. It gives the opportunity for perhaps the first exposure to opposing counsel under courtroom-like conditions, enabling the witness to obtain an impression of the counsel's probing and analytical abilities and of how rigorous cross-examination may be. It is, of course, also valuable experience in articulating one's proposed testimony. After reading the deposition proceedings, the expert witness can evaluate the strengths and weaknesses of the opponent's position through the evidence developed, and thus assist the attorneys in formulating trial strategy.

ARGUING MOTIONS

A *motion* is an application to the court for an order of the court. A motion may be made at any time that the action or proceeding is pending, whenever the relief sought would be appropriate. The purpose of a motion is usually to reject a claim or portion of it, to challenge the right of a person to testify as a witness, to challenge the use of certain data as evidence, or to clarify the positions of the parties as to the meaning of certain data. Expert witnesses frequently provide the supporting economic, financial, accounting, or mathematical data used in arguing the motions.

USE OF STIPULATIONS

Most trials seem to be conducted under time and scheduling pressures. Therefore, the judge will encourage the parties to clearly define the issues to be resolved at the trial and to agree in advance of the trial to as many of the facts, arguments, applications of law, evidence, procedures, or conditions as possible. Such agreements between the parties are known as *stipulations*. Once a stipulation has been reached, the contents of the stipulation are admitted facts as far as the trial is concerned.

Where any of the stipulations deal with accounting issues, the accounting experts should be consulted by the trial attorneys prior to their agreeing to the stipulation, to avoid difficulties connected with the complexities or ambiguities of accounting theory and practice. For example, in a recent case it was stipulated that only the damage issues would be litigated and that damages would be limited to the excess of revenues received over the costs associated with the services that produced the revenues. Attorneys for both sides assumed that the trial would involve reasonably simple accounting computations of costs incurred for services rendered. But what was meant by the term *costs of services?* Did costs of services include direct costs only, or direct plus indirect costs of the departments in question? Were costs of service departments to be allocated to the departments rendering the service? Were administrative costs to be included? These were only a few of the cost accounting questions that had to be litigated, and what was considered by the trial attorneys to be a simple examination of accounting records turned into a complex and difficult trial.

PRETRIAL CONFERENCES

Pretrial conferences are informal meetings of counsel and the pretrial judge, either in the courtroom or the judge's chambers, for the purposes of determining the matters upon which the parties agree and the genuine issues. Time spent by attorneys in preparing for presentation of evidence is materially reduced, and time for trial is lessened as a result of these conferences. Usually, the attorneys are required to prepare and to submit to the pretrial conference judge, at or before the conference, a joint written statement of the matters agreed upon, and joint or separate written statements of the factual and legal contentions to be made as to the issues remaining in dispute.

At the pretrial conference, or within five days following it, the judge usually makes a pretrial order and the clerk serves it upon the attorneys. The *pretrial order* is a statement of the nature of the case, the matters agreed upon, and so forth. Once filed, the pretrial order becomes a part of the record of the case and takes precedence where there is inconsistency with the other documents filed.

Thus, since much can happen at the pretrial hearing to strengthen or weaken the accounting evidence to be presented at trial, it is important for the expert accounting witness to review the pertinent accounting concepts with counsel beforehand.

IMPORTANCE OF THE TRIAL BRIEF

Prior to the trial, the opposing attorneys may present to the court and to each other, in the form of a *trial brief,* their perspectives on the issues involved, the legal and factual bases for their positions, how and why the actions of the defendant caused harm to or did not injure the plaintiff, and the computations of damages and challenges thereto. The brief is essentially a blueprint of the attorney's case presentation. Obviously, all expert witnesses will play a role in the formulation of the trial brief. The views of experts from different disciplines must be reconciled and presented as a coherent whole, and the experts will be called upon to analyze the opponent's trial brief and suggest how to cross-examine on the issues thus raised.

HOW THE TRIAL PROCEEDS

As the trial begins, the clerk calls the case by announcing the names of the parties and the docket number. The respective parties, assembled in the courtroom, announce readiness for trial. Plaintiff and defendant attorneys each present an *opening statement,* which briefly sets forth the issues involved and what each expects the evidence to be.

The trial addresses three basic issues in separate phases:

1. **Liability:** Whether the defendant has violated a statute or a right of the plaintiff which is actionable in a court of law.
2. **Proximate cause:** Whether the action of the defendant, which is complained of, was the immediate cause of injury to the plaintiff.
3. **Damages:** A determination of the loss sustained by the plaintiff because of the wrongful actions of the defendant.

Counsel for the plaintiff, who usually has the burden of proving the allegations, takes the floor first, introducing the evidence to prove the facts necessary to establish the case. Counsel brings forth the witnesses necessary to establish these facts, as well as the documents that are offered into evidence when they have been identified by the testimony of the witnesses. Each witness, in what is called the *direct examination,* is first questioned by the plaintiff's attorney and then, in the *cross-examination,* by the defendant's attorney. This procedure may then be followed by redirect examination and recross-examination.

Counsel for the defendant subsequently introduces evidence in the same manner, known as the *rebuttal.* Rebuttal testimony is designed to directly refute the evidence previously introduced by the plaintiff. Toward this end, opposing counsel may introduce testimony from an expert that directly refutes the plaintiff's expert testimony. If the original expert has considered and discussed both sides of the question, the impact of a rebuttal witness, whose opinion is based on opposing theories and facts, is greatly diminished.

After all evidence has been received, the trial proceeds to the closing arguments. In the *closing argument,* each attorney is permitted to argue the merits of the client's case based upon the evidence presented.

After closing arguments, the judge instructs the jury as to the law. The jury then retires to consider the case, and when it reaches a decision, the verdict is rendered.

THE JURY

Although in common law and traditionally a jury had twelve members, there is no constitutional requirement for this, and it is not uncommon for state and federal district court juries to consist of six persons instead. Also, in federal district courts and many state courts, the parties may stipulate that the jury shall consist of any specified number fewer than twelve, and that a verdict or finding of a certain specified majority of the jurors shall be taken as the verdict or finding of the jury.

The Seventh Amendment to the United States Constitution preserves the right of trial by jury in civil cases. On the other hand, in criminal cases the accused enjoys the right of jury trial and shall not be denied this right without consent. While the Supreme Court has held that these provisions of the Constitution apply only in federal courts, every state constitution contains a provision similar to the federal one, thereby guaranteeing jury trials in state courts. It is important to note that the federal and state constitutional provisions preserve the right to jury trial in civil cases and do not create this right. Thus, the scope and extent of the right to jury trial must be determined by reviewing the right as it existed at the times the constitutional provisions were written.

In the United States and England, the right to jury trial existed in civil cases for actions at law where the demand was usually for money damages and did not extend to suits in equity where the relief demanded was usually for an order compelling a defendant to perform or refrain from doing an act. In England and in the federal courts in the United States until 1938, there was a clear division between law and equity. This situation changed, however, with the adoption of the Federal Rules of Civil Procedure (1938). These rules specify only one action—a civil action—in which all claims may be joined and all remedies are available. Law and equitable actions are now combined when they come before the court. Thus, when the same case involves both legal and equitable issues, some questions arise when considering the right to jury trial.

In complex civil cases, the right of trial by jury presents unusually difficult problems for the trial judge. The courts recognize that the maintenance of the jury as a fact-finding body occupies so firm a place in history and in jurisprudence that any seeming restriction of the right to a jury trial should be handled with the utmost care. A properly selected panel of veniremen is generally expected to yield an impartial and capable jury. However, at some point, it must be recognized that the complexity of a case may exceed the ability of a jury to decide the facts in an informed and capable manner. When that occurs, the question arises as to whether the objective of fairness is defeated by relegating fact finding to a jury not qualified to determine the facts. In such cases, legal remedies become inadequate and a court of equity is called upon to unravel the facts.

In a recent civil case, the court listed three guidelines for deciding whether a case is so complex that equity jurisdiction will attach and permit the case to be tried without a jury: (1) complicated accounting problems are not amenable to jury resolution. Although such problems often only arise during the damages portion of a trial, they sometimes are present during the liability portion, as well; (2) the jury members must be capable of understanding and dealing rationally with the issues of the case; and (3) the estimated length of the trial may make extraordinary demands upon a jury, making it difficult for the jurors to function effectively throughout the trial.

In most civil cases, however, a jury trial will be held. The jury is selected from the public at large and is called upon to decide the facts in litigation in accordance with the instructions of the judge. In complex litigation, the pertinent facts are frequently enmeshed in masses of data that must be analyzed, classified, summarized, and reported upon in a format understandable to the user, in this case, the jury. Communicating technically complex accounting facts to the jury, which may be composed of people with little or no understanding of accounting, presents a formidable problem to the accounting witness. Effective communication is a difficult art (see Chapter 9), and the expert witness is required to know not only the subject matter of the testimony, but also the most effective manner of presenting such evidence to the jury.

While the competency of the witness is not decided by the jury, the jury does determine the weight that will be given the witness's testimony. Although the technical content of the testimony is of the highest importance, many other factors determine the weight given to accounting testimony. Above all, it is clear that the inability of expert witnesses to express themselves clearly minimizes the value and importance of their testimony.

A person testifying as an expert is intended as an aid to the jury and not as a proponent of either side. Thus, it is necessary to avoid any evidence of bias in presenting testimony and every effort should be made to appear impartial when testifying. Jurors seem to react more favorably to a congenial and pleasant witness and pay more attention to that witness's testimony. Appearance on the witness stand, attention, and direct answering of questions help create a favorable impression. Jurors seem to prefer a witness who faces them and makes them an important part of the proceedings. It is sobering to the expert witness to realize that jurors, in considering an expert's opinion, need not give any weight at all to this opinion in their deliberations. If the jury wishes to disregard the testimony of the expert entirely, it may do so without any explanation.

No authority exists that can compel a jury to bring in a verdict. One unyielding juror can hold out against the other eleven and cause a hung jury. When a jury cannot agree on a verdict, the foreman reports that fact to the judge. A judge can order a directed verdict when he rules that the party with the burden of proof has failed, as a matter of law, to make a prima facie case. Under those circumstances, the judge orders the jury to return a verdict for the other party.

THE JUDGE

Although public criticism has occasionally been directed against judges, the judiciary has traditionally enjoyed a warm public trust. The major functions of a trial judge are: to decide upon litigated issues of law; to instruct the jury on how to resolve the facts in issue; to enforce personal and property rights in equitable actions; and to make effective and efficient use of judicial resources. In performing these functions there is no checklist for the qualities of a good judge, no convenient formula, and not even any agreed upon objective criteria. The demands and pressures of the courtroom require that the trial judges have above average emotional stability, a keen sense of fairness, an even temperament, and intellectual endurance. A judge must have unusual talents for communication, empathy, and patience to deal with jurors and witnesses. Ability to stand pressure, common sense, and knowledge of the community are additional necessary attributes.

Judges are powerful public officials who usually operate within a broad scope during any given trial. Legal rules and procedures are not applied within a vacuum, but must be relevant to a complex and changing society. Cases do not decide themselves. The quality of our justice is a direct function of the abilities of our judges, for in the long run, the law can never be much better than the people who administer and apply it. There is no guarantee of justice except the character, devotion to duty, and performance of the judge, who controls the progress of the trial. Members of the public view the judge as the symbol of the legal order. The public impression concerning the performance of our legal institutions depends almost entirely on the propriety and effectiveness of the functioning of our trial courts. The trial judge is the law for most legal purposes. Whenever a trial judge fails in patience, objectivity, or probity, that failure is observed by the public and impairs public faith in the law, for the proper functioning of the law depends upon public acceptance. Thus, the trial judge is called upon to uphold the integrity and independence of the judiciary, as well as the proper functioning of the law.

Our system is a government of laws. The formulation, application, and enforcement of duties and rights constitute rule by law. Conformity with the law is the substitute for rule by mob reaction. Although there are several tiers of appellate courts to correct on appeal any misreading of the law, in the great bulk of litigated cases the trial judge is the most important and influential participant, since most cases are not appealed. This is true whether or not the case at hand is a jury case, whether or not the legalities of the controversy involve the interpretation of a federal or state statute or a question of common law, and even for those cases that are appealed from the trial court judgment to higher appellate courts. A trial judge's intellect, character, and energy can make a great difference in the decisions the judge hands down. The idea that a judge decides cases on the basis of previous decisions or that judgments are fixed by the rules of the legal system is as inadequate a description of the work of the trial judge as it is of the work of the appellate courts. Even where there is little argument concerning the legal rules that control the dispute between the parties, there are many complex factual situations to which these rules must be applied. No legal code, no amount of statutory directions and judge-made precedents, can furnish explicit and unambiguous rules for the trial judge to follow in interpreting the facts. Where the case involves issues in which the law is unclear, and the judge must choose between the alternatives available, the work of the judge calls upon the exercise of judgment. Only a trial judge with social insight, prudence, and intellectual resourcefulness can measure up to the challenges of such responsibilities.

There is a concept that the decisions of trial judges are provisional and subject to correction on appeal. However, the great majority of controversies are determined as to practical outcome by the rules of law applied and the facts determined at the trial-court stage. While the appellate courts forge precedents for the future and give statutes their authoritative interpretation and effect, the trial courts decide the facts, and in most cases the findings of fact are decisive. The trial court, as the agency for the hearing and determination of disputed issues of fact, holds the important position in the practical administration of justice.

Although it is the function of the jury to determine the facts, the trial judge plays an important role in the determination of disputed issues of facts. Through rulings on questions pertaining to the admissibility of evidence, pointed questions, the occasional disparaging remark, or the use of a harsh or gentle tone, the judge influences the testimonial data from which the jury will draw its inferences as to the truth of the plaintiff's and the defendant's competing versions of the case. A trial judge has a duty to aid witnesses who need help in their efforts to testify. Accordingly, a judge may pose questions to a witness if the witness, in apparent good faith, is unable to comprehend a question, if he has not understood the question, or when contradictory answers indicate that the witness is confused. The stature of the judge is such, however, that there is a tendency on the part of the jurors to give undue weight to any point on which the judge may ask a question and to the answers elicited. Whenever, therefore, the questions posed are within a judge's discretion but outside the judge's scope of duty, either side may claim that the judge prejudiced its case. The trial judge, within certain limits, may also set aside the jury verdict in a civil case and order a new trial of the case when it is evident that the verdict which the jury arrived at was wholly unsupported by the evidence. The most important participation by the judge in jury fact-finding is the *charge* or *instructions to the jury,* in which the judge expounds the law to be applied by the jury in reaching its verdict, telling the jury, in effect, the facts they must find to be true and supported by a preponderance of evidence before they can bring in a verdict for one side or the other.

Where the trial judge can, through an effective personality, maintain a working rapport with the jurors empaneled in the courtroom, the judge becomes the jury's guide and counselor in the jury's discharge of its duty. This achievement requires that the judge exhibit unusual talents of communication in order to translate legal jargon into language intelligible to lay jurymen without endangering the legal soundness of the instructions given to the jury.

The relationships between the trial judge and the attorneys are of crucial importance. The trial attorneys are champions of their clients' causes and are committed to present the legal theory, and the version of the disputed facts that are favorable to the position taken by their clients. The adversary system of court procedure contemplates that the trial of the issues will be conducted by equally competent advocates for each party and a trial judge, who is at least the equal of the advocates. The judge plays the role of an umpire, and this role cannot be performed effectively by a judge who is inferior in intellect or professional skill, lacking in decisiveness, or emotionally insecure in any way. Courtroom decorum has to be maintained with a firm hand, if cases are to be tried fairly and expeditiously, and, as the case proceeds, the trial judge is called upon to make many rulings that influence the outcome of the case. These rulings are generally made under the pressures of the court proceedings and without opportunity for extended research of the formal authorities in the law books. The trial judge who is uncertain in professional understanding or unduly conciliatory in personality, can be dominated by forceful and aggressive trial counsel. If the adversary system is to work effectively, the trial judge must command the respect of the advocates who appear before the judge's court, no matter how powerful or distinguished the advocate may be.

Where the trial judge is arrogant and abusive, the lawyers may find it difficult to develop their cases in an effective and orderly way. Witnesses can become confused or resentful, and the clarity and accuracy of their testimony may suffer accordingly. Jurors can become disinclined to follow the instructions of the judge and both parties may leave the courtroom with the distinct impressions that their claims and grievances have been inadequately heard.

The judge is an expert in the judicial process, but during trial is frequently called upon to understand many different presentations of the technical disciplines of expert witnesses in order to properly advise the jury in its fact-finding role. It is the function of the expert witness to bring to the judge's attention, in an understandable manner, the expert's opinion of the facts that are needed to reach an informed decision. It is the function of the judge to dispense justice in the court-room, for as Benjamin N. Cardozo, the well-known American justice wrote, "Justice, though due the accused, is due to the accuser also. The concept of fairness must not be strained till it is narrowed to a fila-ment. We are to keep the balance true."

The competency of an expert witness is a question of law to be de-cided by the judge. The judge exercises reasonable control over the mode and order of interrogating witnesses and presenting evidence so as to make the interrogation and presentation effective for the ascer-tainment of the truth, avoid needless consumption of time, and protect witnesses from harrassment or undue embarrassment. The judge thus facilitates the orderly introduction of evidence and protects all parties in the action.

On certain occasions, the judge may examine the witness by asking any questions deemed necessary to bring out relevant evidence for the jurors to consider. The judge may ask any type of question as long as a fair examination is conducted, and there is no intimidation of the witness. Either party still has the right to object to either the form or manner of the examination of the witness and has a right to cross-examine the witness. The court has the inherent power to call an expert witness when it seems necessary to overcome conflicting testi-mony by experts already called by the parties in the action.

Judges are required to conform both on the bench and in their pri-vate lives within reasonable codes of conduct. Judges are expected to devote their efforts to the administration of the judicial process and to refrain from the practice of law and from political activities in-appropriate to their judicial office. Judges should avoid financial and business dealings that tend to reflect adversely on their impartiality and should regulate their extrajudicial activities to minimize the risk of conflict with judicial duties. No judicial training is needed to qualify a person for judgeship and no continuing education is required. A number of states have, however, established judicial training centers and judges are expected to avail themselves of these training opportu-nities. Court manuals and guides that describe court administration, case management, judicial problems, the role of the judiciary, courts and the community, and judicial ethics are made available, and experi-enced judges, usually without pay, conduct courses and orientation programs for the newly elected or appointed judges. For judges in mid-career, courses are held to update them on changes in the law and to prepare them for new assignments. None of the programs is compulsory and not all of the expenses are paid. It is recognized, however, that judges who learn everything by experience are reduced to learning by trial and error.

A key requirement of a judge is to be impartial, and the duty of the judge is to the public. Trials are usually open to the public and legal rulings are available for study and evaluation not only by appellate judges, but by the judge's peers, attorneys, law professors, and students. Pressures can be intense when the judge's calendar is full, and when parties to the litigation are uncooperative or unresponsive, fail to keep time commitments, and manage their cases poorly. When called upon to understand complex, technical testimony, the judge must be alert, must possess an active and inquiring mind, and must be able to concentrate totally on the subject matter of the testimony.

THE TRIAL IS OVER

The pressures on the expert witnesses do not end as the trial comes to a conclusion. The time between the end of the trial and the decision by judge or jury is usually a period for reflection. Have the factual problems and weaknesses of the opposing party's position been correctly identified? Have the data supporting the client's position been presented effectively and understandably to judge and jury? At this time, the familiar statement that "a problem does not exist until it has been correctly identified" seems to be particularly appropriate. Judge and jury make decisions, but such decisions, of necessity, revolve around the completeness, clarity, and cogency of the evidence presented. As an expert witness, you recognize that the development and presentation of your testimony has been a function of your ability and was your responsibility.

Although each litigation is unique, the time spent by the expert accounting witness can be generalized in terms of: preparing an analysis of the case from an accounting perspective; assistance in formulating case strategy; analysis of the opponent's exhibits and testimony; analysis and preparation of testimony to support the client's case; and finally, expert testimony. The proportion of time devoted to each of these efforts in a recent case is illustrated in Exhibit 1.

The Verdict

There are several types of verdicts, but the principal verdicts are either general or special. A *general verdict* is one that finds for one party or the other; if for the plaintiff, it also fixes the amount of recovery. To render a general verdict, the jury is supposed to assess the conflicting

Exhibit 1. Distribution of Time Logged on Litigation Services

Activities	April	May	June	July	August	September	Percentage of Man-Hours
a. General analysis	___	___					8%
b. Development of case strategy		___	___	___	___	___	20
c. Analysis of opponent's exhibits and proposed testimony		___	___	___	___		28
d. Analysis and testimony to support client case				___	___	___	39
e. Expert testimony						___	5
							100%

evidence and "find the facts," to which it then applies the law that has been given to it by the judge. How well or how poorly the jury performs this function is difficult to evaluate, since the deliberations of the jury are secret, and the jury is not required to give reasons for its verdict. A *special verdict* is one in which the jury finds the facts, usually in the form of answers to questions formulated by the court, leaving to the judge the task of applying the law to the facts. Thus, the special verdict eliminates the chance of misunderstanding of the law by the jury and minimizes the influence of prejudice and sympathy.

After the verdict has been returned and filed, there is a limited amount of time available within which the losing party may prepare and file motions to the court to set aside the verdict, to grant a new trial, or to grant the losing party judgment notwithstanding the jury's verdict. The court will permit counsel to argue these motions, but if they are overruled, the court will then enter a judgment in conformity with the verdict. From this judgment the losing party may appeal, may negotiate a settlement of the case even at this late date, or may pay the judgment.

2

Trial Attorneys, Cases, Court Systems, and Administrative Agencies

Lawyers are employed by their clients and represent them in legal matters. They have a duty to advocate their clients' positions as effectively as possible within their responsibilities to the court and to the public. As officers of the court, lawyers are subject to the control of the trial judge and can be disciplined to the extent of being disbarred if they misbehave in any aspect of their practice. Lawyers profess adherence to high ethical standards and compliance with the canons of professional ethics. They are expected to aid in the administration of justice and share a responsibility to make our legal system work effectively. The law is a learned profession and ability of a high order is required if one is to meet one's responsibilities in this profession. The lawyer needs to be an advocate, a negotiator, a problem solver, and an expert in dealing with people.

Trial practice is the art of advocating, on a client's behalf, rights to property or liberty. Trial attorneys usually specialize in the fields in which they try cases, and although they have often received public criticism, the highest regard in the law profession has been held for the trial lawyer. The attorneys are the trial strategists: They plan, manage, and control the testimony presented during the trial, and conduct the cross-examinations of the witnesses. It is important that the expert accounting witnesses know as much as possible about these important participants in the judicial process with whom they will associate as litigation team members.

CHARACTERISTICS OF THE TRIAL ATTORNEY

The trial attorney must possess a good knowledge of the law and know how to supplement this knowledge by researching legal questions. The court expects the lawyers on both sides to bring to its attention whatever laws and precedents bear on the matters at issue. The attorney is required to understand the legal decision-making process, to make sound judgments, to have an analytical and agile mind, and to be quick in physical movement. Although it is necessary to be a proficient speaker and even eloquent, the lawyer must be particularly able to express thoughts in the clearest, simplest, and most forceful way. An understanding of human behavior and of human nature is needed, as well as an ability to apply this knowledge under time pressures and during critical situations. The capacity to understand all types of people, not only judges and juries but the variety of witnesses examined during both direct and cross-examination, is essential, as is the capability of dealing with all kinds of actions, motivation, and conduct that cannot be fully explained. A successful trial lawyer must have the ability in the courtroom to gain people's respect, particularly in dealings with the jury, and to influence the judge and jury on the client's behalf, for the principal character in every trial is the client. The trial attorney must know how to clarify the client's position so that the judge and jury will become interested in the case presented on behalf of the client.

Counsel must have a mind that is able to concentrate and to absorb details, having them ready at any moment in the trial. This requires a highly developed memory, not only for immediate details, but also for the background and the history of the subject matter under discussion. Although trained in the law, the attorney will be called upon to gain knowledge in many fields, including the medical, economic, scientific, mathematical, and accounting fields, so as to know as much about the pertinent facts as the expert. People who consider themselves experts in a particular field and more competent than anybody else can frequently be upset as they are being questioned by someone who is as knowledgeable in the areas under examination as they are. Experts like to feel that their fields of knowledge belong to themselves and often show their irritation when they find that the examining attorney also possesses similar knowledge. This irritation often produces an adverse effect upon the jury, and a favorable effect for the attorney who is conducting the cross-examination.

Preparation for trial begins long before the attorney goes into the courtroom, and the successful attorney prepares a case with the utmost care, with the objective of having the greatest persuasive impact on the minds of the judge and jury. Counsel will attempt to turn every fact of the case to the client's advantage, within the limits of truth. Most trial lawyers are keenly aware of the dramatic and have an ability to stage their actions so as to have an impact on the minds and emotions of members of the jury. In preparing a case for trial, the attorney attempts the complete development of all the facts. Every detail is examined and every person who has any knowledge of any fact in issue is interviewed. Statements are taken from all potential witnesses, compared, analyzed, and searched for any possible detail that could be useful. These statements, along with all other listed facts, are compiled in a fact file, indexed by subject matter, indexed by witnesses, and cross-indexed. Where the material so compiled is voluminous, consideration will be given to establishing a computer data base for this purpose. At the same time, the trial attorney researches the law to learn every possible legal subject and question that might be involved in the case. This requires the preparation of many questions of law that may never arise during the trial. The trial attorney thoroughly considers every possible stratagem that could be used by the opposition, and works out defenses against each. Thus, when the stratagem is used during the trial, the attorney is prepared to respond.

Counsel is responsible for identifying, interviewing, and selecting the team of expert witnesses required for the effective presentation of the case, and working with the witnesses in developing an effective presentation of the testimony. The expert witness is expected to bring to the courtroom expert knowledge and the ability to articulate, but the trial attorney is and remains the strategist for the presentation of both the legal and factual aspects of the case, and the attorney cannot shift this responsibility to the expert witness. As an adviser to the court, the expert witness cannot permit domination by the trial attorney, and to be effective, must present only that testimony that is truthful and accurate to the best of his or her knowledge. Usually, the expert witness and the trial attorney develop an effective working relationship.

The trial lawyer must prepare the witnesses for cross-examination by the opposing attorney and develop the information needed to cross-examine the witnesses presented by the adversary. Cross-examination is the most complex art in the whole trial field and the most difficult part of the trial to master (see Chapter 8). The ability to cross-examine is a skill that is difficult to teach, and competence in cross-examination seems to be a function of inherent abilities sharpened by extensive experience in the practice of this art. The skillful cross-examiner seems to be guided by intuition and several basic rules of conduct.

During direct examination, the cross-examiner seldom looks away from an important witness who is being examined by the adversary. Every facial expression, the manner of verbal expression, and the witness's whole bearing all help the examiner to arrive at an estimate of the integrity of the witness. Usually during cross-examination, the attorney is courteous and conciliatory in order to induce the witness to enter into a discussion of the testimony in a fair-minded spirit, which, if the cross-examiner is clever, will disclose the weak points of that testimony. The sympathies of the jury are usually with the witness. Juries are slow to believe that witnesses are guilty of perjury. A good cross-examiner needs to be a good actor for if a damaging answer is elicited, there is need for great self-control. The experienced trial lawyer, instead of appearing surprised or disconcerted, will proceed with the next question as a matter of course. If an unexpectedly favorable answer is received that discredits damaging testimony, the attorney will quickly decide whether to probe further or to terminate questioning on this point, and use the admission during summation when the witness has no opportunity to clarify the statement.

An attorney will usually follow a few basic rules during cross-examination, such as:

1. It is better to have no cross-examination than a bad one. Skip cross-examination entirely if it promises nothing of value, since it can do harm by adding emphasis to damaging testimony and giving a witness an opportunity to elaborate on it.

2. Never ask a question to which the cross-examiner may not know the answer. Concentrate on a few major points and attempt to expose important inconsistencies or omissions in the testimony, thereby impeaching the credibility of the witness.

3. Never ask an adverse witness to give the reasons for doing something, for this usually provides the opportunity for the witness to make a speech unfavorable to the opposition.

4. Always maintain control of the cross-examination. Never give an adverse witness an opportunity to break away from the trend of the examination and take a path of his or her own choice.

5. Question the witness on material testimony that was injurious to the client or made a favorable impression on the jury.

6. If the witness gave previous conflicting testimony and made conflicting statements, take the witness down the path favorable to the examiner.
7. Learn how to terminate cross-examination and exercise restraint during cross-examination.

No substitute has been found for cross-examination as a means for exposing falsehood and for reducing exaggerated statements to their true dimensions. Cross-examination is a mental duel between counsel and witness.

Trial attorneys are skilled practitioners of the arts of listening and of observing and interpreting body movements. Counsel will listen intently to statements, orders, and directions issued by the judge, not only to search for meaning but to gain understanding of the thought processes, preconceptions, and motivations of the judge. The formal statements made by the judge in the courtroom, as well as the informal discussions at the bench and in chambers will be carefully analyzed by counsel to determine how best to present and gain acceptance by the judge of the significant aspects of counsel's case. As evidence is presented, counsel observes the reactions and body movements of each member of the jury in an effort to determine the impact of evidence upon the members of the jury.

In practicing negotiating skills, particularly during settlement negotiations, each attorney evaluates the opponent's contentions, comparing them with personal assessments of what the judge and jury are likely to do, as well as with what might happen if appeals were made to higher tribunals. Settlement proceedings have the benefit of being conducted in private with each party being more flexible and less embittered by the other. If the settlement negotiations are successful, the result is a compromise instead of a judgment, and compromise can frequently be the better part of justice.

Although the lawyer represents the client's interests, there is also a special responsibility to the general public. The lawyer must maintain independence, impartiality, and perspective, and should never forget the public interest in advising clients. Not all trial attorneys possess these characteristics. Many people associate the attorney with the worst aspects of the legal process: the delays inherent in the judicial process, the limitless paperwork, and the injustice of the outcome, at least from the perspective of one party. The adversary legal process is confusing to many people, and at times appears to be a process of competitive distortions with the lawyers participating as the primary characters. Lawyers have failed to find solutions to the unreasonable delays in the legal process and have failed to find new and more efficient ways to provide legal services at lower costs. Many also feel that the legal profession from time to time uses the powers of its monopoly position and specialized knowledge to protect its own interests rather than those of the public that granted them the monopoly. There is widespread concern with the ineffectiveness of the disciplinary procedures against attorneys.

An increasing number of attorneys who appear in court to try cases do not appear to be qualified to do so. Many lawyers have a poor standing in the eyes of the public because of the incompetence, bad manners, and lack of training they display in the courtroom. Many jurors are critical of attorneys for their abuse of witnesses. These failings and abuses result in injury to the public: the waste of time; the needless increase in the expense of litigation; the unnecessary congestion of the court; the clogging of the calendars; the waste of taxpayers' money; and the poor presentation of cases.

TYPES OF CASES

Accounting is a discipline that establishes rules, regulations, and techniques for recording, classifying, and summarizing the results of business transactions and presenting these data to the user in the form of financial reports. As such, the basic objective of accounting is the fulfillment of an important economic function—the communicating of financial and economic facts to a user in a form that has timeliness and contains information that will contribute to the benefit of the recipient. Because accounting deals with business transactions, is the financial language of business, and is used in describing personal wealth and property values, it is used pervasively in litigation. Accounting expertise has been enhanced by working closely with industrial engineers, mathematicians engaged in operations research, and electronic computer specialists. Members of those disciplines frequently work with accountants to improve the use of accounting information in business decision making. Through the application of various analytical techniques that are part of the accounting, industrial engineering, and mathematical disciplines, a body of measurement criteria has been developed that is useful in planning and controlling business activities. These measurement criteria have frequent use in litigation.

ANTITRUST CASES

The philosophy of the antitrust laws is that each individual has a personal and property right to carry on a business of choice. It is not the intent of these laws to interfere with the intelligent conduct of legitimate business operations. The broad concepts and ambiguities that characterize these laws, however, create a vagueness that leads to frequent litigation.

Violations of the antitrust and trade regulations laws can be punished severely as they can result in dismemberment of a company, imprisonment of its officers and employees, cumulative fines, liability for treble damages to parties injured by violations, seizure of goods, and a wide variety of decrees or orders regulating the future conduct of offending firms and individuals. Major antitrust litigation is both long and costly.

The first antitrust bill was the Sherman Antitrust Act, signed in 1890. It outlawed "every contract, combination in the form of trust or otherwise, or conspiracy in restraint of trade." This statute also made it a criminal offense to monopolize or attempt to monopolize any part of interstate commerce.

The statute does not define the type of conduct that is prohibited, except in the general term *restraint of trade*. Thus, the precise meaning of the statute has to be determined by the courts in the process of deciding specific cases. In doing so, the courts generally have held that only those restraints that were "unreasonable" were illegal. The courts have gradually extended the concept of interstate commerce to include anything happening in the flow of interstate commerce, though it happens wholly in one state, and any activity that affects interstate commerce. Certain conduct is illegal no matter what the motive underlying its use and no matter how beneficial to competition the results may be. Among the types of conduct that have been held to violate the statute are price-fixing agreements, group boycotts, agreements to divide markets, and tie-in sales.

The Clayton Act was passed in 1914 to cure certain defects and omissions in the Sherman Act by proscribing certain conduct that had proved anticompetitive in practice. Thus, certain types of acquisitions by one company of the stock of another were prohibited, as were predatory pricing and exclusive dealings. The Clayton Act attempted to reach acts or practices at their outset that might eventually lead to adverse competitive acts, whereas in the Sherman Act, except in the area of per se violations, actual and substantive adverse competitive effects are required.

The Federal Trade Commission Act of 1914 forbids "unfair methods of competition in commerce, and unfair or deceptive acts or practices in commerce." Unfair methods of competition include practices that violate the Sherman or the Clayton provisions and other acts, if they have or are likely to have a substantial anticompetitive effect.

The Robinson-Patman Act of 1936 is an amendment to Section 2 of the Clayton Act and was passed to support two primary objectives: (1) to prevent unscrupulous suppliers from attempting to gain an unfair advantage over their competitors by discriminating among buyers, and (2) to prevent unscrupulous buyers from using their economic power to exact discriminatory prices from suppliers to the disadvantage of less powerful buyers. The act prohibits sellers from discriminating in price unless an otherwise unlawful price discrimination can be cost-justified by the seller, or unless the price discrimination is made in good faith to meet the equally low price of a competitor. It prohibits the seller from paying any brokerage fee, commission, or an equivalent to a buyer or the buyer's agent, and prohibits a buyer from accepting any such brokerage fee or commission. Sellers are prohibited from granting discriminatory allowances and services and facilities to a buyer unless such assistance is made available to other competing buyers on proportionally equal terms. It is unlawful for a seller to provide certain secret allowances to the buyer, and to allow territorial price reductions or sales at unreasonably low prices in order to destroy competition or to eliminate a competitor.

The Miller-Tydings Act and the Wheeler-Lea Act of 1938 round out the federal antitrust statutes. The Miller-Tydings Act provides a limited exception to the antitrust proscriptions against all agreements fixing resale prices. If state law permits, no antitrust liability will attach to a resale price maintenance contract involving a trademarked or brand name product in competition with other similar commodities. This exception is commonly referred to as the *fair trade exception,* and it proceeds on the rationale that certain resale price maintenance contracts should be allowed to protect the goodwill attached to the manufacturer's trademark or brand name. The Wheeler-Lea Act allows the Federal Trade Commission to proceed against unfair or deceptive acts that injure customers without reference to any competitive effect. It declared certain advertisements of foods, drugs, devices, and cosmetics unfair or deceptive acts or practices.

The federal antitrust laws are enforced in three ways: by the Antitrust Division of the Department of Justice, by the Federal Trade Commission, and by private parties asserting damage claims. Each type of enforcing action has contributed to the growth in antitrust law and the number of antitrust cases. The Antitrust Division of the Department of Justice is charged with the enforcement of both the Sherman and Clayton acts and liability may be either criminal or civil.

The Federal Trade Commission is the only agency entitled to insure compliance with the provisions of the Federal Trade Commission Act and has the right to enforce the Clayton Act. Enforcement is civil in nature and hearings are held before a hearing examiner appointed by the commission. An initial decision is prepared by the examiner and appeal of such decision to the full commission is allowed as a matter of right and is a common procedure. The ruling by the commission may be appealed to a court of appeals.

A provision of the Clayton Act permits suit in federal courts for three times the actual damages caused by anything forbidden in the antitrust laws. Any nonconsent judgment in antitrust actions brought by the United States is prima facie evidence of antitrust violations.

Antitrust cases, usually because of their complexity and significance, make use of a variety of expert witnesses. The plaintiff's expert economists in civil cases develop testimony dealing with the market involved, define the product in suit, and describe pricing conditions and competitive forces in the relevant market from both macroeconomic and microeconomic perspectives. The economists attempt to portray what the market conditions would have been "but for" the alleged anticompetitive acts, and how the plaintiffs would have prospered under the "but for" conditions. Mathematical experts quantify through statistical analyses or mathematical models the additional revenues that would have been earned without the alleged anticompetitive acts. Expert accounting witnesses, using economic, mathematical, and accounting data, develop damage models to establish in financial terms the injury sustained because of the alleged anticompetitive acts of the defendant.

The defendants likewise employ a number of expert witnesses. Expert economic witnesses challenge the definitions of markets and products and frequently develop pricing data and descriptions of competitive forces in the market quite different from those described by plaintiff witnesses. Using economic data developed by defendant's economic experts, mathematical expert witnesses may develop testimony through the use of statistical analyses or mathematical models that challenge plaintiff's assertions or restate revenue expectations. The expert accounting witness for the defendant may attempt to demonstrate that any revenue losses were a result of plaintiff's actions not associated with any of the alleged acts of the defendants, and that the plaintiff's damage estimates require substantial correction.

In Robinson-Patman violation cases, much of the testimony by the defendant's expert accounting witness usually attempts to demonstrate that the alleged illegal price differentials make only due allowances for differences in the cost, other than brokerage, of manufacture, sale, or delivery resulting from the differing methods or quantities in which the products were sold or delivered to the purchasers. It may also be shown that the price differentials were made in good faith to meet an equally low price of a competitor, or the services or facilities furnished by a competitor.

Most of the states have also passed antitrust laws and, in general, in applying state statutes the state courts have closely paralleled federal antitrust law as developed by the U. S. Supreme Court under the Sherman Act. The federal antitrust laws do not preclude or preempt state antitrust action in areas of concurrent jurisdiction. In California, the Cartwright Act prohibits all trusts defined as a combination of two or more persons to carry out any of a number of purposes, such as the creation of restrictions in commerce, the limitation of production, or the fixing of prices.

INCOME TAX CASES

The income tax laws have provided a fertile field for litigation, and tax accountants have served as expert witnesses in many cases to help the court to define taxable income, ordinary business expense, and fair property values under the code. A few of the interesting questions on which expert tax accountants have testified are:

1. What are reasonable annual compensations for officers of closely held corporations?
2. Were product prices to foreign subsidiaries developed in fair, arm's length transactions?
3. What is the proper charge against the value of an estate for alimony payable to the deceased's wife until she died or remarried?
4. What part of management fees paid by subsidiaries to their parent company were deductible as ordinary and necessary business expenses?
5. What is the fair value for tax purposes of stock of closely held corporations and for business interests in partnerships and sole proprietorships?
6. What is the tax basis of assets transferred from parent to subsidiary?

7. Should a capital loss be allowed to an individual on property transferred by him to an investment company in which the individual
   taxpayer owned all the preferred stock?

The taxpayer has a number of administrative procedures available
in the event of a disagreement with an agent of the audit branch of the
Internal Revenue Service. If agreement cannot be reached with the
examining revenue agent, the taxpayer will be issued a *30-day letter*
and a complete examination report. Upon filing a protest within that
period, the taxpayer is entitled to a district conference conducted by a
full-time conferee independent of the agent and the supervisor. If the
taxpayer and conferee are unable to reach an agreement at the district
conference, the taxpayer may request a hearing before the Appellate
Division of the Internal Revenue Service. If agreement is not reached
with the Appellate Division, the taxpayer will receive a *90-day letter*.
This is a statutory notice of the proposed deficiency and contains a
statement that, if the taxpayer does not file a petition with the U. S.
Tax Court within 90 days, the deficiency will be assessed against him
or her. Following the receipt of the 90-day letter, the taxpayer may
elect to pay the proposed deficiency, sign the waiver of restriction or
assessment, or challenge the Internal Revenue Service's determination in court.

If the taxpayer takes the dispute to court, there are three federal
tribunals that are available: the U. S. Tax Court, the district court, and
the U. S. Court of Claims. The U. S. Tax Court may be used only in the
case of a deficiency determination, and an advantage of using this
court is that payment of the proposed tax is not required prior to trial.
The taxpayer may pay the asserted deficiency in order to stop the
running of interest during trial. The taxpayer is precluded from
appealing the case to the Tax Court by paying the proposed deficiency
or signing the waiver before the mailing of the 90-day letter. Under the
latter circumstances, the taxpayer must pay the deficiency, file a claim
for refund with the Internal Revenue Service, and sue for refund, if
desirable, in either the district court or the U. S. Court of Claims. It
may be advantageous to sue in the district court, because jury trials
are available and this may be of some importance where borderline
factual issues exist. Also, in some areas of taxation, the taxpayer has
fared better in the district court and the U. S. Court of Claims than in
the U. S. Tax Court. The taxpayer who is not successful in either the
U. S. Tax Court or district court may appeal to the U. S. Court of
Appeals and, if unsuccessful at this level, may seek review directly by
the U. S. Supreme Court.

BANKRUPTCY CASES

Under the Constitution, Congress is granted "the power to establish uniform laws on the subject of bankruptcies throughout the United States." The first act under this power was passed in Congress in 1800 and was repealed three years later. This act applied to traders, brokers, and merchants, and contained no provisions for voluntary bankruptcy. It gave the creditor complete control of the bankrupt's estate. The second act was passed in 1841 and applied to all debtors, contained provisions for voluntary bankruptcy, and allowed a discharge of the unpaid balance remaining after all the assets were distributed to creditors. It gave the court control of bankruptcy, as the court was made responsible for collecting the assets of the bankrupt and distributing them to creditors. This act lasted just over one year. The third act became law in 1867 and was repealed in 1878. It returned to the creditors the right to choose their own trustees subject to the approval of a judge. This act permitted the debtor to escape the stigma associated with bankruptcy by allowing a composition of debts without being adjudicated a bankrupt. The present bankruptcy act is the act passed in 1898, as amended. This act was thoroughly revised by the Bankruptcy Act of 1938, commonly known as the Chandler Act, which added to the law the chapter proceedings. The Chandler Act gave to the courts the power to regulate the disposition of all debtors' estates, individuals as well as business, agriculture, railroads, municipalities, and real estate, whether in liquidation, rehabilitation, or reorganization. The Bankruptcy Reform Act of 1978 drastically overhauled the system, further liberalizing it in favor of the debtor. Chapter 13 was rewritten and now includes sole proprietors of businesses, as well as wage earners. It stops lawsuits and attachments and incoming money can be used to pay incoming bills and permits discharge from debt. The term *bankruptcy law* is used only in reference to federal laws, whereas the term *insolvency law* is used to refer to any of the enactments of the various states. Insolvency laws may be used as long as they do not conflict with the federal laws.

There are many opportunities for accounting services in bankruptcy cases by the accountant who is familiar with the bankruptcy laws and the forms that are required to be prepared in complying with the law. Because many parties are involved and as there are a number of ways of coping with financial difficulties, accountants have many avenues by which they may become involved in bankruptcy and insolvency cases. The retention of an accountant by the receiver, trustee, or debtor-in-possession must be by order of the court, which also issues notice on the amount of fees or the rates to be used. The same accountant may be retained by the various parties, or additional accountants may be employed. Appointment by order for retention through the court makes the accountant a quasi-officer of the court, owing a primary duty to the court. Normally this duty involves reporting to and discussing problems with the trustee in the proceedings. Further, the accountant will be held to fiduciary standards and is bound to act in good faith and with due regard to the interest of the entity imposing the confidence.

The accountant may be called upon to:

1. Establish the financial position of the debtor by performing an audit.
2. Investigate any assets or distribution made by the debtor to the creditors or stockholders before the petition was filed which might be recoverable.
3. Identify the reasons and causes of the business failure.
4. Determine whether any wrongdoing occurred prior to the filing.
5. Render an opinion on the chances for continued operation of the business in the future.
6. Maximize the provisions for creditors in the settlement, while allowing for the relief necessary for the debtor to successfully rehabilitate.

The Securities and Exchange Commission (SEC) is considered to be a party in interest in certain bankruptcy proceedings and may object to the fees of the accountant as being excessive. Most judges accept the SEC recommendations, although they are not bound by them. The SEC's role is to protect the public's interest, and it receives copies of all motions and all papers filed with the court. If the case is a significant one, representatives of the SEC will work closely with the other parties to the proceedings. Their representatives will attend meetings that are held among counsel, trustees, receivers, and accountants, and they will participate in the discussions.

OTHER CASES

Many breach-of-contract cases arise in which plaintiffs allege that the failure of the defendants to meet their contractual obligations caused injury to the plaintiffs. Where the issues of damages are complex, expert accounting witnesses may be employed by both sides of the dispute to estimate the damages and to testify as to these estimates. Such testimony will frequently include the development of estimates of lost revenues, the computation of product costs, and the analyses of fixed and variable expenses so that costs associated with lost revenues may be determined. The expert accountant may not only be asked to prepare direct testimony, but may be requested to prepare questions for use in cross-examining the opponent's expert accounting witness, as well.

Negligence actions usually include accounting presentations of revenue and income losses suffered by the plaintiffs because of the alleged torts committed by the defendants. Accountants for the defendants attempt to refute such studies and may be asked to develop alternate damage estimates. In other types of cases, accounting questions frequently are litigated before administrative agencies and require the testimony of expert accounting witnesses. Rate-making studies have called upon accounting expertise in developing costs under utility commission guidelines and in establishing these costs as a proper basis for utility rates. Stockholder actions challenging an exchange offer have necessitated analyses of past, present, and expected future earnings of properties involved in the exchange offer. And in divorce litigation, no-fault laws and the volatile economy have made the use of actuaries and accountants as common as attorneys, often making the dissolution of a marriage more complicated than that of a corporation.

Criminal actions involving violations of the income tax laws, securities laws, fraud, and theft often require the presentation of accounting evidence to define what has occurred and the impact of the alleged actions. In all criminal trials in federal courts, the Federal Rules of Criminal Procedure require that the testimony of witnesses be given orally in open court. These rules provide for a uniform body of rules of evidence to be applicable in all trials of criminal cases in federal courts. Thus, the federal courts in criminal cases are not bound by the rules of evidence in the state in which the court is held. This differs from the corresponding rule for civil cases, as the rule for civil cases prescribes for partial conformity to state law and results in a divergence in the rules of evidence between various federal district courts. The expert accounting witness should be aware that the Federal Rules of Criminal Procedure and the Federal Rules of Evidence may differ somewhat from similar rules of the various states.

These and many other types of actions continue to expand the use of expert accounting witnesses in litigation.

TYPES OF COURT SYSTEMS

The judicial powers of the federal government and of each state are enforced through their court systems. Each state distributes its judicial powers among its courts as it decides, subject to the federal constitutional limitations, chiefly, the Fourteenth Amendment, which provides that "no state shall deprive any person of life, liberty, or property without due process of law." Thus, there is diversity among state court systems; some are complex and some are relatively simple. The court systems all exhibit, however, certain common traits. All make a distinction between trial courts and appellate courts and all arrange their courts in some sort of hierarchical system.

A chart of the American court system would include crisscrossing and overlapping lines, for legal authority is divided among federal courts, administrative agencies, states, counties, and municipalities. Few states have the same hierarchical court structure; courts with the same name may have different responsibilities in neighboring states, and courts may have names that have no relation to their function. Federal, state, and local courts share jurisdiction or hold their own exclusive mandate. We live in a society that is far more complex and demanding on law and legal institutions than when the court structures were established. New social interests are demanding recognition in the courts and groups that have been silent have found legal spokesmen who are asserting previously unheard grievances. The volume of work imposed upon the courts has greatly increased and so far little has been done to relieve court congestion.

THE FEDERAL JUDICIARY

Federal judges are appointed by the President with the advice and consent of the Senate and generally have lifetime tenure. In the district court organization, the chief judge of a district is the senior person who has administrative responsibilities for the court in addition to his or her caseload. The judges can decide when the courts will operate but usually they have carried a heavy workload. In schematic form, the federal judiciary appears on the following page.

Article III of the U. S. Constitution vests the judicial powers of the United States in the U. S. Supreme Court, the U. S. Court of Appeals, and the district court. A few specialized courts are supplementary, such as the Court of Claims and the Court of Customs and Patent Appeals. The U. S. Supreme Court is the highest court in the federal system and in most instances where cases involve ambassadors or suits

The Federal Court System

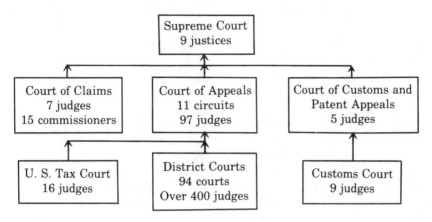

between states, the court exercises original jurisdiction. It then sits as a trial court, but unlike a trial court it does not take testimony in open court but appoints a master to hear the testimony of a witness, and then arranges for the testimony to be put in written form for submission to the court. Most of the work of the court is devoted to review and final settlement of cases that come to it on appeal from lower federal courts, as well as from state courts in cases involving federal questions.

The U. S. Constitution does not define the appellate jurisdiction of the Supreme Court, but has delegated that power to Congress, which has over time both enlarged and restricted the jurisdiction of the court. Congress has invested the Supreme Court with discretionary power to decide whether or not to review a case, but has not given the Supreme Court complete discretion. When a federal court holds an act of Congress to be unconstitutional, or where the United States Court of Appeals holds a state statute unconstitutional or invalid, there is an appeal to the Supreme Court as a matter of right. Also, where the highest court of a state holds a federal law to be invalid, or upholds a state statute that is challenged as unconstitutional, there is an appeal as a matter of right.

Almost all cases reach the Supreme Court through *petitions* for *certiorari,* which, in effect, ask the lower court for the records so that it can review a case and decide it on its merits. The vast majority of cases referred to the Supreme Court are disposed of by the simple denial of the petition. No petition is considered by the justices unless at least one of them believes it important enough, and no case will be accepted unless at least four justices decide in favor of granting *certiorari.*

In the courtroom of the Supreme Court, the attorneys' arguments and the reading of the opinion are conducted publicly. The crucial work on an accepted case, however, occurs in the private research and reflection of each justice and in the conferences that are held by the court as a whole. These group discussions take place once a week in a conference chamber and the decisions are made there with no one present except the justices.

There is one U. S. Court of Appeals for each of the eleven judicial circuits into which the country is divided. There are a different number of judges in each circuit. Any dissatisfied litigant in the federal district court may appeal a case as a matter of right to the appropriate court of appeals. The U. S. Court of Appeals for the District of Columbia reviews the actions of many of the federal administrative agencies, such as the Federal Trade Commission and the National Labor Relations Board.

The United States has been divided by Congress into districts, and a district court has been established for each district. As far as is possible, the individual states are defined as districts, and the more populous states have more than one district. In some districts Congress has appointed more than one district judge. In a vast majority of cases the district court is presided over by a single judge, although there are situations where a three-judge court is convened, such as cases in which it is sought to enjoin the enforcement of a statute of a state or an act of Congress on the grounds that it is repugnant to the Constitution of the United States.

The judicial powers of the federal courts, as defined in Article III of the Constitution, are of three types: (1) those that involve a question of federal law, that is, the Constitution, statutes, and treaties; (2) cases of admiralty and maritime jurisdiction; and (3) controversies involving certain categories of parties, including ambassadors and public ministers, the United States government, a state government, citizens of different states, and foreign states or citizens thereof.

STATE COURT SYSTEMS

Each state has its own system of courts and diversity exists, but all of the court systems involve hierarchical organizations. Every state has *inferior trial courts* to handle minor matters of civil and criminal law. Their civil jurisdiction is frequently defined in terms of a maximum pecuniary figure and criminal jurisdiction in terms of the maximum jail sentence. Such courts go by a variety of names, the most common of which are justice of the peace court or justice court. In more populous areas, such courts are called magistrate's courts, with some specializations, such as police courts which handle minor criminal matters, or traffic courts whose functions are limited to hearing cases involving violations of traffic laws. The inferior courts exhibit certain common characteristics: they are all courts of original jurisdiction; their judicial power is limited; they are not ordinarily courts of record, that is, no detailed record of the proceedings is kept, merely a brief entry identifying the parties, the names of any attorneys, and a final disposition of the case; the procedure is usually informal; and the losing party usually has the right to appeal the case to a higher trial court so as to obtain a whole new trial under more formal proceedings.

Trial courts of general jurisdiction have authority to try all cases, civil or criminal, and their jurisdiction usually begins where that of the inferior trial court leaves off. These courts have different names in the various states, being called courts of common pleas or superior courts, district courts or circuit courts; in New York, this court is called the supreme court. These courts are distributed geographically throughout the state by dividing the state into judicial districts and establishing a court for each one. In large metropolitan areas it is usual to have specialized divisions or departments, such as criminal, civil-jury, civil-nonjury, domestic relations, juvenile, and probate divisions. These courts also act as appellate tribunals for appeals from the inferior trial courts, and to review the actions of state boards and commissions, such as the Public Utilities Commission and the Industrial Accident Board.

In most states there are *trial courts of intermediate jurisdiction,* generally organized on a countywide basis. These courts are usually called county courts and monetary ceilings are established in civil cases to define their jurisdiction. These courts may have concurrent jurisdiction with the inferior trial courts or the superior trial courts when monetary limitations overlap. Frequently this type of court has jurisdiction in some specialized areas, such as the administration of the estates of decedents, minors, or incompetent persons.

Many states, where there is a multiple-judge bench, provide functional specialization by assigning certain judges to particular types of cases at the beginning of the term. Other states solve the problems of specialization by the creation of special courts. There are divorce courts, courts of domestic relations or family courts, and courts of claims, which try civil cases brought against the states. Probate courts, orphans' courts, or surrogate's courts are designed to administer estates.

Technically, an appeal is a privilege that the legislature could grant or withhold in the absence of a specific right to appeal found in the Constitution. Generally, however, provision has been made for the review of a judgment by a court other than the one which rendered it. There are two types of *intermediate appellate courts:* (1) those in which the court is distinct from both the trial court and the court of last resort, and (2) those in which the intermediate appellate court is a branch or division of the trial court. The jurisdiction usually encompasses most appeals, except certain classes of cases that go directly to the court of last resort. These include criminal cases involving the death penalty, cases involving the constitutionality of a state or federal statute, cases involving title to land, civil cases involving an amount in excess of the monetary jurisdiction of the intermediate court, cases involving taxation and revenue, and certain defined criminal cases.

The court of last resort or the *upper appellate court* is usually called the supreme court, but in some states has been called the court of appeals, the supreme judicial court or the supreme court of errors. The function of this court is to review the actions of the lower judicial tribunals of the state, usually by entertaining the appeals of the dissatisfied litigants on a case-by-case basis. In the exercise of appellate jurisdiction, the court does not retry the case on its merits: It reviews the record of the proceedings to determine whether or not the lower court committed error in its procedure or in applying the substantive law to the facts of the case. If there is only a conflict in the evidence, the appellate court will not review the facts of the case, but it may set aside a verdict it feels is unsupported by the evidence. The appellate court can also exercise superintending control by issuing court orders or writs to the lower courts. The principal writs are *mandamus,* by which a lower court is ordered to do something, such as grant a jury trial or a change of venue; *prohibition,* by which a lower court is forbidden to proceed in a case in which it does not have jurisdiction; and *habeas corpus,* by which a lower court is directed to justify its actions in holding a person in custody. The highest courts may also establish rules of procedure that the lower courts must follow.

OVERLAPPING JURISDICTION

The federal and state court systems are superimposed upon the same geographical territory, and thus, in many civil cases the plaintiff has a choice of court—state or federal. Presumably, the plaintiff will bring suit in the court that offers the better advantage. However, when the plaintiff sues in a state court, the defendant may be able to transfer the case to a federal court if the case involves a federal question or if the plaintiff and the defendant are citizens of different states and the defendant is a nonresident of the state in which the suit is brought—provided the amount involved exceeds $10,000.

There are exceptions, however. Certain federal acts give the plaintiff the choice of state or federal court and prohibit the defendant from removing the case. Where there is a conflict of jurisdiction, the same case may be pending between the parties in the state and federal court at the same time. To ease a situation of this type, however, Congress has prohibited federal courts from issuing injunctions against state court proceedings unless the circumstances are exceptional. The federal courts also have adopted the *doctrine of abstention* under which they will frequently stay their proceedings and await the decision of the state court.

ADMINISTRATIVE AGENCIES

The administrative agency first appeared during the last half of the nineteenth century and resulted from the economic conditions that developed during the 25-year period from 1870 to 1895. The model of the modern administrative agency was the Interstate Commerce Commission, established by Congress in 1887 to reduce the abuses that developed in railroading. The Interstate Commerce Act of 1887 did two main things: (1) it prohibited certain railroad practices that were deemed objectionable, such as rate discrimination, rebating, and the charging of unjust and unreasonable rates; and (2) it set up the Interstate Commerce Commission to aid in the enforcement of these prohibitions. Initially the job of the commission was to find the facts, and its orders became effective only if they were obeyed voluntarily; otherwise, they had to be enforced through application by the commission to the federal courts for an injunction. However, with the first chairman of the Interstate Commerce Commission, the commission became a tribunal of justice, following judicial procedure, and this has become the outstanding feature of American administrative agencies. Soon administrative law dealing with the operations of these agencies became one of the major legal developments of the twentieth century.

As modern business life became more complex, Congress created additional administrative agencies, structured similar to the Interstate Commerce Commission, and delegated the power to regulate essential industries to them. These agencies are unique in that they act independently of each of the three branches of the federal government, but combine the functions of all of them. There are seven major agencies:

1. The Interstate Commerce Commission regulates rail, motor, water carriers, and pipelines.
2. The Civil Aeronautics Board deals with air carriers.
3. The Federal Power Commission handles electric and gas utilities.
4. The Federal Communications Commission regulates radio, television, telephone, and telegraph.
5. The Securities and Exchange Commission regulates the investment business.
6. The Federal Trade Commission handles unfair trade practices.
7. The National Labor Relations Board deals with unfair labor practices.

The values involved in the decisions of these commissions exceed many times the annual dollar value of all money judgments rendered by federal courts. The powers of the administrative agencies are broad as they are vested with near life-and-death authority over the businesses affected.

During the second half of the twentieth century, the expanding use of the administrative process to enforce public policy against racial and other discrimination has been one of the more important legal developments. Disability, welfare, aid to dependent children, fair employment practices, health care, environmental protection, and other issues have also come under the protection of the administrative process. This expanding field for the administrative process developed at the very time when it was being increasingly censured as inadequate in its traditional area of regulation.

CHAPTER

3

Qualifications and Behavior of an Expert Accounting Witness

A trial is an exercise in reason. Although truth, facts, statutory definitions of laws and of prohibited conduct, as well as prior court decisions, are the basic ingredients of court trials, reason is employed to assemble, analyze, interpret, and present the facts and to apply statutory requirements. It is the function of the expert witness to assist the judge and the jury in this exercise of reason. Where understanding of the facts underlying a case is limited, the power of reason is restricted and the application of the law to the case being tried becomes uncertain. If reason is to be the life of the law, not only must legal knowledge be argued during the trial, but facts must be clearly identified, analyzed, and described so that the problems inherent in the factual situation may be brought to the attention of the court. Only in this manner can the power of reason be applied to all pertinent facts. It is the effectiveness by which issues are proven by the plaintiff and defended against by the defendant that determines the outcome of the trial.

The individual who undertakes an assignment of expert accounting witness faces a challenging and sometimes harrowing experience. Technical competence will be described by reference to the expert's education, experience, and professional honors and accomplishments, but it will be demonstrated by the expert witness's ability to assemble, understand, and summarize huge quantities of financial data, and testify to the conclusions reached. The professional judgment of the witness will be demonstrated by how carefully this individual distinguishes between significant and insignificant conditions and data. Integrity and openness of mind, too, must be evident in the witness's testimony, so as to avoid challenges of bias. Thus, it is evident that an expert witness needs a number of specific personal characteristics to sustain the rigors of direct testimony and cross-examination.

WHO IS AN EXPERT ACCOUNTING WITNESS?

In most jurisdictions, an expert witness is defined as follows: "A witness is an expert witness and is qualified to give expert testimony if the judge finds that to perceive, know, or understand the matter concerning which the witness is to testify requires special knowledge, skill, experience, or training and that the witness has the requisite special knowledge, skill, experience or training." There is no rigid definition of an expert. Expertise is relative to the subject matter involved, and a witness who has special knowledge, skill, or experience in any craft, trade, or profession may be qualified as an expert in that field in state courts. In federal courts an expert is a skillful or experienced person, or a person having special knowledge of certain subjects or in certain professions.

A certified public accountant may be an expert witness on any subject matter falling within the scope of that individual's experience, training, and education. As most complex litigations require the finding, analyzing, interpreting, and presenting of accounting, statistical, financial, and economic data, the typical experiences of a certified public accountant provide the type of expertise frequently required by attorneys during the progress of a trial. Also, the certified public accountant is experienced in presenting masses of financial data in concise and relevant reports, and in taking and articulating positions on complex questions of accounting principles and reporting formats. The certified public accountant also possesses the knowledge and experience to identify errors in the theories and computations of the opponents; to develop alternative theories and computations which reduce or eliminate the damage claims; to develop additional facts and theories; and to prepare charts and schedules that effectively demonstrate the positions taken by the trial attorneys. With the growing complexity of business affairs, the courts have permitted a more liberal use of expert witnesses in the trial of cases.

Before a person may testify as an expert witness, it must be established that the individual is qualified as an expert in the field in which he or she is attempting to express an opinion. The expert must be prepared to testify to some special knowledge or skill gained through experience and education in a specific field. Usually, opposing counsel will examine the background of the expert witness prior to testimony in an attempt to demonstrate that the witness should not be accepted as an expert. This is known as *voir dire* cross-examination of the expert. The challenges usually relate to the witness's lack of special knowledge and experience or the use by the witness of unreliable information. To overcome such challenges, it must be shown that the witness possesses the ability to interpret, analyze, and evaluate the significant facts on a question which the judge or jury needs assistance to resolve.

Unless there is abuse of such discretion, the decision of the trial court on the qualification of an expert witness will not be overturned on appeal. Usually, any deficiency in the qualifications of an expert witness will show up in the weight given this person's testimony rather than its admissibility. The courts have accepted the accountant as an expert on the subject of accounting and financial analysis, with special knowledge acquired in a particular industry, trade, or occupation which also qualifies that individual as an expert on business and trade practices and on other factors relating to costs and gross profit margins.

There is a distinction between a witness and an expert witness. As a general rule, a witness may only testify to facts and leave inferences or conclusions to the judge or jury. Traditionally, the lay witness could only testify as to what actually was perceived; personal opinion was inadmissible. Since the distinction between fact and opinion is often subtle and one of degree, trial attorneys and judges are constantly struggling with the exclusionary rule applicable to opinions. Hence, the present trend is to permit the lay witness to express an opinion if the subject matter falls within the common experience of most people. Opinion by a lay witness is limited to that which is rationally based upon the perceptions of the witness and helpful to a clear understanding of that witness's testimony.

An expert witness, on the other hand, may testify in the form of an opinion based not only upon those facts perceived by the expert, but on facts perceived by others, as well, and made known to the expert at or before the trial; this may include the evidence or testimony of others. The information must be of a type that is reasonably relied upon by an expert in forming an opinion upon the subject to which the expert's testimony relates. Thus, the expert witness may use previously certified financial statements or books and records of the business, even those not kept by the expert, or a method of accounting commonly used and accepted in the profession, or customs and practices within the business of the party for whom the expert is testifying. An expert may not base an opinion upon any matter that is deemed an improper basis by the constitutional, statutory, or decisioned law of the state.

If expert witnesses do not have firsthand knowledge and have not made an investigation of the facts themselves, the attorneys can obtain the benefit of the experts' knowledge by asking them to assume certain facts and give opinions or inferences based upon these assumptions. All the facts assumed must be a matter of evidence in the case and care should be taken that the expert fully states the facts relied on, and that the facts are from a reliable source and form a permissible basis for an opinion.

SELECTING THE EXPERT ACCOUNTING WITNESS

The trial attorney is responsible for selecting the expert accounting witness. It is the trial attorney who must anticipate how effectively the witness will react in an environment where there are two sides to every question and where the witness will be opposed by an equally competent expert accountant, who can be expected to challenge any direct testimony that is developed. In making this selection, the trial attorney will confer with representatives of the client's auditing firm and will usually be inclined to select a partner of the auditing firm as the expert accounting witness, based on the assumption that the partner selected will have the advantage of being acquainted with: the accounting records of the client; the auditing working papers; the client's business activities; and the industry in which the client operates.

The trial attorney will look for much more, however, than a satisfactory auditing relationship. The individual proposed as expert witness will need to be able to develop the direct accounting testimony needed to support the client's position. How effectively the expert accountant is able to work with the trial attorney and the experts of other disciplines is also anticipated. The expert accountant is expected to work in an unstructured environment and must also be able to work with accounting records which frequently will be disorganized, and with people who will offer only the minimum information necessary to comply with the law. Past experience as an expert witness, although beneficial, is not usually essential, although knowledge of how an expert witness should behave during direct and cross-examination will be important.

At times, the auditing relationship may act as a barrier to using a representative of the client's auditing firm as an expert accounting witness, particularly where the trial attorney is anxious to establish the accounting position of the client as a completely objective one, free from the possible bias in testimony that could arise from the natural desire of the witness to maintain the auditor–client relationship. In such circumstances, a person not associated with the auditing firm would be employed. Also, the facts of the case may require that the expert accountant not be selected from the auditing firm. For example, if expert accounting testimony is needed to defend a client accused of tax evasion, the trial attorney may not want an expert witness who was associated with the firm preparing the tax return. And too, the trial attorney will select the most qualified expert accountant available, regardless of the auditing relationship, as the ability to perform effectively at the trial is more important than any prior business relationship.

PERSONAL CHARACTERISTICS OF THE EXPERT ACCOUNTING WITNESS

The expert accounting witness needs certain key mental attributes which lend weight and seriousness to the information that individual imparts on the witness stand. Following are some of the more important personal characteristics the expert accounting witness needs to call upon in testifying.

Ability to Articulate the Basis of an Opinion

Communication is a complex art, and when it is attempted from the witness stand, usually in an ambiguous situation because of the conflicting facts and interpretations of law presented by the opposing parties, it becomes an extremely difficult undertaking. This difficulty is heightened during cross-examination where words can be used by the opponent to confuse, to win sympathy, to stimulate antagonism, or to bend the listener to the questioner's purpose.

Expert testimony is valuable, however, only when it is understood and acted upon and the responsibility for conveying the message included in the testimony belongs to the witness. The expert must be able to explain and defend opinions in language understood by the layman, based on subject matter that is beyond the common knowledge and experience of the ordinary layman. Thus, the expert must be able to educate the judge and/or jury concerning the expert's specialty as it applies to the case being tried.

A common error committed by the accounting expert is to use technical language in testimony without offering an explanation of its meaning. If testimony necessarily involves technical accounting terms and concepts, means must be devised to explain and clarify these terms and concepts to laymen. It is usually beneficial for the attorney and the expert to discuss the substance of the expert's testimony under simulated trial conditions, including cross-examination. They will then be better prepared for trial, and the expert will have the further opportunity to consider the validity of the opinions and to evaluate his or her ability to articulate the facts and the premises relied on.

The Requisite Knowledge to Form an Opinion

Knowledge is the sum of all one's individual or group experiences, including those insights gained by working with people of other disciplines and skills. For the expert accounting witness, the broad perspective of knowledge should include not only that associated with the auditing discipline, but also analytical, financial, and accounting techniques, computers, and mathematical and statistical procedures. Knowledge must be stimulated by curiosity, which manifests itself in the recurring question, *Why?*, particularly when analyzing the opponent's position and the data supporting it. One must not only know the strengths and limitations of the opponent's position, but why these conditions exist, in order to minimize the strengths of the opponent's position and maximize the weaknesses.

One of the most important and often ignored steps in preparing to testify is acquiring knowledge of the substantive issues. Unless one is aware of the substantive issues, one's investigation and subsequent conclusions may be incomplete and unrelated to them. It is also necessary to know the issues of the case in order to anticipate and respond to cross-examination and avoid answers that are incomplete, confusing, and irrelevant.

The expert must have knowledge of all facts relevant to the subject matter. As a general rule, the fact that the opinion of the expert witness was not founded on all the facts affects the weight given the evidence, not its competency or materiality. Failure to consider all the facts not only diminishes the value of the expert's opinion, but quite often leaves him vulnerable to attack on cross-examination. Not only might the additional facts surprise and confuse the witness, but the expert's authoritative image will be diminished in the minds of the judge and jury.

Ability to Think Creatively

Creative thinking is usually a product of hard work, and the expert accounting witness must be prepared to spend long hours on the assignment and meet the reasonable and unreasonable time demands of the court and the attorneys. To undertake this effort, the accountant needs to be excited by the challenges of the assignment and stimulated by the urge to make a significant contribution toward the resolution of the issues presented. A creative person thinks of a lot of approaches to problem solving, is flexible in dropping one line of thinking and taking up another, has a quality of constructive discontent, and a restlessness of mind, searching for new and better ways of doing things. Such mental attributes are continually employed in developing, evaluating, and preparing proposed testimony.

While the creative thinking process is difficult to define, most thinking classified as creative seems to be the product of an orderly thought process. Although adherence to this process does not assure any specific results, it does seem to fan the spark of creative thinking and to raise the frequency with which the thinking process results in creative ideas. This thinking process is consistent with what is called the *scientific decision-making technique,* for it emphasizes such attributes as the use of empirical data, quantification, explicit assumption, logical rigor, mathematical model building, and prediction and verification. This method of thinking starts with an exploration of the nature of a problem in order to get a clear picture of the real objectives of the study. Information descriptive of the problem and procedures used in decision making and all useful quantitative values are collected and analyzed to determine if a problem-solving structure can be developed. It is at this point that knowledge represented by different disciplines can be used. For knowledge and experience to be a contributing factor, the problem solver should not only be able to retrieve information from memory, but must also be able to combine, blend, restructure, change, and manipulate the individual fragments of knowledge and experience that apply to the problem under study. This is why thought-provoking cues, such as "combine, consolidate, compare, eliminate, rearrange, reverse, substitute, modify, adapt" are useful in the thinking process and why checklists that recall significant questions and stimulate proper attitudes are valuable.

All the alternatives that can accomplish the objective should be examined, including the unorthodox and unpopular ones, and interactions among interesting new combinations of alternatives should be studied. It is probably at this point that the greatest opportunity exists for imaginative and creative thinking. Each alternative should be evaluated against specific criteria dictated by the objectives of the study and the various resources needed to obtain those objectives.

In evaluating alternatives, mathematical models are particularly useful, for they incorporate the study of risks and uncertainties in addition to performing sensitivity analyses. They also display the cost of resources used over a period of time and establish the appropriate present values of benefits developed over time. At this point, the unquantifiable aspects of the problem are considered, prior to selecting the preferred course of action.

Creative people have high energy levels, a sense of humor, and a considerable degree of sensitivity to other people's ideas. They are willing to try new ideas and they tend to absorb from their community and their environment many of the properties and qualities of that environment to a greater extent than do people with less creativity. In general, the creative person is tolerant of ambiguity—ambiguity of ideas, ambiguity of materials, and ambiguity of purposes and goals—but attempts to make order out of it. That reduction of ambiguity, that making of order is a necessary characteristic of the expert accountant who is presented with the volumes of economic and accounting data of the opponent, usually obtained through the discovery process.

Ability to Analyze Huge Volumes of Disorganized Data and Develop Missing Information

During the discovery phase of litigation, when it is necessary to obtain information from the opposing party, that party may avoid giving any assistance beyond the minimum required by law. On the other hand, the opponent may adopt the strategy of inundating the accounting witness with records, reports, and data with the intention of hiding rather than revealing useful information. Obviously, these are not the normal circumstances in which a certified public accountant works. Most clients, in the interest of keeping audit fees down, are cooperative in supplying records, missing information, or explanations as needed.

Under these circumstances, the expert accountant must have a good understanding of accounting systems and procedures in order to know what should be available from the opponent. So too must the accountant be able to analyze the issues involved, organize the data obtained according to the issues, analyze the data using accounting techniques relevant to the problems to be resolved, identifying missing information and discarding useless information, and develop the accounting analyses useful in presenting the client's position during trial.

Stamina and Adaptability to Change

The assignment as expert accounting witness is demanding of time and energy and usually requires complete personal involvement. Time schedules for the taking of depositions, the hearing of motions, and attendance at pretrial conferences are often set arbitrarily, at least from the perspective of the witness, and great effort entailing long working hours is frequently required. Once started, the trial moves forward regardless of the state of preparedness of the parties, and frequently after each day of trial, much time is devoted to reexamining the issues confronted that day, researching unexpected witness testimony, or making changes in trial strategy. A sustaining force, stamina, is needed and this can be generated when the expert is stimulated by the working environment and excited by contributing to the resolution of the issues being tried.

Despite the immense amount of preparation, changes will frequently be made in the evidence to be presented: issues will be dropped from the trial, witnesses will be excused, and trial strategy will be modified. The expert accountant must be able to respond to change and to adjust the accumulated evidence to meet the requirements of change.

BEHAVIOR OF AN EXPERT ACCOUNTING WITNESS

Technical competence, good professional judgment, integrity, and an open mind are expected to be demonstrated by the expert accounting witness, on the witness stand. Prior to taking the stand, the expert accounting witness should obtain from legal counsel background information and general advice on the procedures to be followed while testifying. Usually, the attorney will prepare the expert witness for testimony by running through the kinds of questions that will be asked. This assures that the expert witness has a chance to acquire adequate background on the questions that will be asked, and also gives the attorney an opportunity to see how the witness's answers will affect the case.

This preparation is ethically and legally proper, and the expert witness should never feel that there is anything inappropriate in having discussed one's testimony in advance with the attorneys who employed that expert. In fact, it is necessary in the interests of better preparing the case for trial. One can, without hesitation, acknowledge this to opposing counsel if asked. This is not to say that the expert's testimony will be furnished by the employing attorneys or distorted to suit their ends. The expert must remain responsible for answers under oath and must maintain professional integrity in so answering.

There are certain rules of conduct that should guide the expert witness, and a brief list follows.

1. Be punctual and make definite arrangements with the attorneys as to the time and place of testimony.

2. Become familiar with the layout of the courtroom. Learn what facilities are available for presenting evidence other than oral testimony from the witness stand. Are blackboard facilities available, may slides be used, and can photographs of tables, graphs, charts and financial statements be shown?

3. Try to get a feel of the trial in action, if witnesses are not excluded from the courtroom. Observe the conduct of the judge, jury, and opposing counsel.

4. Be fully prepared on the testimony you expect to present.

5. Make certain you understand a question before answering it.

6. Answer questions as directly, concisely, and honestly as you can.

7. Address the jury as much as possible, rather than the observers in the courtroom.

8. Maintain a courteous and professional attitude throughout your testimony.

9. Layman's language, rather than accounting jargon, should be used, as jurors do not understand technical accounting terminology.

10. Examine thoroughly all notes and memoranda on the case. All material needed during the presentation of evidence should be available in the courtroom.

11. Don't answer ambiguous or equivocal questions without obtaining clarification.

12. Don't volunteer information beyond that required to answer each question.

13. Avoid the appearance of quibbling or being evasive.

14. Avoid attempts at humor; they are almost always out of place and harmful to the testimony.

15. Be courteous to the opposing attorney.

16. Relax on the witness stand; it contributes to a keener mind.

17. Don't engage in personal exchanges with the opposing counsel, no matter what the apparent provocation.

18. Be interested in what is being said and do not appear bored with the proceedings.

19. Speak loudly enough at all times for the jurors to hear every word.

20. Speak slowly enough for the stenotypist to record the testimony.

21. Do not hesitate to pause before answering, when that is necessary to give adequate consideration to the question.

Under the rules of law, an attorney can ask only one question at a time and the witness need not answer the question if he or she does not understand it or there are words in the question that need explanation. In such instances, the witness has a right to ask the court or the attorney to explain the question or to clarify the question or any of the words that were used. If asked a question, the witness need only answer the question asked, without elaborating.

An attorney cannot compel a witness to change answers or testimony; a witness is on the stand to tell what one knows and to give an opinion based upon reasonable certainty. Confidence in oneself and in the correctness of one's testimony is important. The rules of the court do not permit an attorney to defame a witness, to go far afield from the subject of the case, or to embarrass a witness. When the expert witness becomes familiar with the pertinent data before taking the witness stand, testifies only to facts found by the witness or made known to the witness by others, bases opinions on sound accounting doctrines, and has a basis for those opinions in reasonable accounting practices and procedures, cross-examination should not present a problem.

The role of expert accounting witness is frequently more difficult than necessary because of a rather general misunderstanding of the nature of accounting and of the terms used in its applications. To some degree, persons with no particular accounting background underrate the extent to which judgment must enter into any accounting determination, and consequently may rely too heavily on published material of general application without fully appreciating its limitations in particular circumstances or even what it actually means. Great patience is often required to communicate to the layman the difficulties involved in the art of accounting.

Giving expert testimony from the witness chair, under oath, is one important way the expert accounting witness can assist the client to obtain fair and equitable decisions under the law. While rewarding in the feeling of professional accomplishment it provides, expert testimony can be physically taxing because of the high demands it places on mental alertness and professional judgment. Thorough preparation makes it easier to meet these demands, and is, therefore, a must for the certified public accountant who hopes to successfully serve as an expert witness.

BE PREPARED FOR LONG ASSIGNMENTS

Antitrust cases are not only complex but are also prosecuted over long periods of time. Recently, 15 years of antitrust litigation ended in a federal court in Pittsburgh as the Justice Department and gypsum makers formally settled criminal price-fixing charges. The criminal case preceded the civil cases against the gypsum makers. Many attorneys have criticized the terms of the settlement as being potentially harmful to private antitrust plaintiffs, who haven't had their "day in court," as in law, private individuals claiming treble antitrust damages can use a government conviction to establish immediately a civil case against the guilty party. The length of the gypsum antitrust litigation is not unique in major antitrust cases.

Antitrust investigations were instituted against broad-spectrum antibiotic drug manufacturers in 1953 and legal proceedings were finally concluded in 1980. During this period, the defendants paid huge settlement fees to numerous plaintiffs and incurred significant attorneys' fees, expert witness fees, and major business costs in terms of the time and expenses of corporate executives. Ultimately, in the criminal and civil cases prosecuted by the federal government and a state, the defendants won verdicts on both the criminal and civil issues. In reports of the attorneys' for the defendants and the special master employed to distribute the settlement fees, the history of this difficult case was described.

In 1953, the Federal Trade Commission began an investigation into the business, conduct, practices, and management of corporations engaged in the production, sale, or distribution of antibiotic drugs, and completed this investigation in 1958 with the issuance of an Economic Report on Antibiotic Manufacture. In 1959, Senator Kefauver's Judiciary Subcommittee on Antitrust and Monopoly started an investigation into the ethical drug industry, including manufacturers of broad-spectrum antibiotics, and in 1961 a report entitled "A Study of Administered Prices in the Drug Industry" was transmitted to the full committee.

During July 1958, the Federal Trade Commission issued a complaint charging American Cyanamid Company, Charles Pfizer & Co., Inc., Bristol-Meyers Company, the Upjohn Company, and Olin Mathieson Chemical Corporation (Squibb), with unfair methods of competition and unfair acts and practices in the sale of antibiotics, in violation of Section 5 of the Federal Trade Commission Act. In October 1961, the hearing examiner filed an initial decision exonerating all defendants from any violation of the Federal Trade Commission Act and dismissed the complaint. The matter was then heard by the full commission which in August 1963 filed its opinion disagreeing with that of the hearing examiner, and found: that Pfizer had obtained the Conover patent on tetracycline through misrepresentations and withholding of information from the Patent Office; that Cyanamid's conduct before the Patent Office was the same as Pfizer's; that it was not proven that a conspiracy existed between Pfizer and Cyanamid before the Patent Office, or any other conspiracy among the five defendants to exclude others; that there was no misconduct before the Patent Office by Bristol, Squibb, or Upjohn; and that the five defendants had conspired to fix the prices of tetracycline.

The order of the commission was appealed, and in June 1966, the U. S. Court of Appeals for the Sixth Circuit ruled that the participation of the Federal Trade Commission chairman in the proceedings had been a denial of due process to the defendants, in view of his former position as counsel for the Kefauver Subcommittee. The Court held that the order of the commission on Patent Office misconduct was not supported by substantial evidence, expressed no opinion on price fixing by the defendants, and remanded the matter to the commission for consideration without participation by its chairman. On remand, a new hearing examiner ruled that there was substantial evidence to support a finding of misconduct by Pfizer and Cyanamid before the Patent Office, and when the matter was again presented to the commission for consideration without participation by its chairman, the commission concluded that Pfizer and Cyanamid were guilty of fraud before the Patent Office, as a result of which the Conover patent was issued. The Commission again required compulsory licensing of the patent, but as the commissioners were equally divided as to price fixing, the charges of price fixing were dismissed. Pfizer and Cyanamid appealed the commission's order. In September 1968, the Court of Appeals ruled that the evidence supported the findings of misconduct before the Patent Office and justified the compulsory licensing order of the commission. At this point, the Federal Trade Commission proceedings terminated.

In 1961, a criminal indictment was returned by a grand jury in the Southern District of New York naming Pfizer, Cyanamid, Bristol, Squibb, and Upjohn as co-conspirators, charging that pursuant to a conspiracy, the co-conspirators had misled the Patent Office to obtain a patent on tetracycline and had used the patent to exclude competition and to fix prices. Trial took place during November and December 1966, and the jury returned a verdict of guilty on all counts. In April 1970, the U. S. Second Circuit Court of Appeals reversed the judgments of conviction for errors in the trial court's charge to the jury. The circuit court did not determine whether the evidence was sufficient to support the convictions, nor did it decide any of the questions of patent law presented to it. The U. S. Supreme Court affirmed the circuit court decision and the case was retried without a jury. On November 30, 1973, the judge found each defendant not guilty on all counts of the indictment, and this ended the federal criminal proceedings.

Following the December 1967 jury verdict in the criminal proceedings, more than 140 civil actions were filed against the defendants claiming treble damages on account of alleged antitrust violations in the sale of broad-spectrum antibiotic drugs. A large number of these actions were brought as class actions and in November 1968 all the broad-spectrum antibiotic cases filed throughout the United States were transferred to the Southern District of New York for coordinated pretrial discovery. In February and May 1969, the defendants made a written offer of $100,000,000 in settlement of all claims of the 50 states, their counties, cities, and political subdivisions and agencies, and any other government entities (excluding the Federal Government), arising out of their purchases or payments for broad-spectrum antibiotics, as well as the claims of wholesalers, retailers, and individual consumers arising out of such purchases, including the claims of states as *parens patrie* on behalf of their citizens, or on behalf of classes including the states as consumers and all other consumers in the states.

The offer of settlement was accepted by all the states except California, Kansas, Hawaii, Oregon, Utah, Washington, and North Carolina. Following the election of these states not to participate in the settlement, the nonsettling cases were divided into four categories: city, county, state, and United States Government cases; farm cases; miscellaneous cases; and hospital cases. A new federal judge was named to continue on these cases. Throughout the years 1971, 1972, and 1973, extensive discovery was carried out by the parties. Teams of economists, statisticians, and accountants for both parties analyzed the many hundreds of thousands of documents deposited by the defendants in the document depository. The plaintiffs copied nearly a quarter of a million documents which they felt were useful, and transferred those documents to their depository for further review. They summarized the testimony and exhibits which had been offered and received in evidence in the prior Federal Trade Commission and criminal proceedings, which exceeded 20,000 pages. Meanwhile, the case was transferred to the District of Minnesota.

During 1971 and 1972, the court retained an expert economist and a statistician to review the economic and statistical reports of the plaintiffs' experts and to mediate informal meetings between the economic, statistical, and accounting experts of both parties. The informal conferences with the various experts resulted in an exchange of views and some clarification of the economic and damage issues among the parties. Revised damage studies were submitted and the defendants filed extensive responses.

During September and October 1973, plaintiffs' and defendants' counsel met frequently and continued to explore the possibilities of settlement of these actions. On October 17, 1973, a Memorandum of Agreement was signed by counsel for all of the parties in each of the states, with the exception of North Carolina, terminating the state cases, and in March 1974, the court accepted the proposed settlements as fair and adequate to the parties involved. The North Carolina case was transferred to the Eastern District of North Carolina and was tried by a judge, sitting without a jury, during the Summer, Fall, and Winter of 1973. In the Summer of 1974, the judge entered judgment for the defendants on all counts and dismissed the North Carolina action with prejudice. The United States Government case was tried in Philadelphia. In August 1980, the federal district judge in Philadelphia ruled that Pfizer was not guilty of the charge that the tetracycline patent had been obtained fraudulently and in September dismissed the charge of conspiracy in establishing prices.

HOW THE EXPERT ACCOUNTING WITNESS IS EVALUATED

There is no test for determining when an expert should be used, other than a common-sense inquiry as to whether the untrained layman needs enlightenment by those having a specialized understanding of the subject involved in the dispute. Where an intelligent evaluation of the accounting issues is difficult or impossible without the application of specialized accounting knowledge, the most common source for this knowledge is the expert accounting witness. The initial criteria for evaluating the performance of the expert accounting witness, therefore, will be concerned with determining how effectively the witness used accounting knowledge to organize, analyze, and interpret the accounting data made available to him, and how intelligently the witness applied general and cost accounting theories, methods, and techniques in developing direct testimony and in cross-examining the opposing accounting witnesses.

The accounting witness will be called upon to work closely with the trial attorneys, and in complex cases with representatives of other disciplines. How successfully the accounting witness contributes to the pooling of knowledge from these different sources in arriving at a coordinated legal position to be taken at the trial will help to distinguish between what is outstanding and what is merely satisfactory service to the client. How willingly the accounting witness responds to the changing time pressures upon the trial attorneys, and to the need to work under flexible time schedules, which sometimes demand long hours, sometimes frequent delays, and sometimes uncertain time demands, will help to determine how important a member of the litigation team the accounting expert was.

The accounting witness will be evaluated on the ability to work in an ambiguous environment. Rarely is it a clearly defined case: the facts are usually in dispute and are frequently interpreted differently by each party, the techniques of analysis and presentation of data can be subject to bias and judgment by the sponsors of the study, and different sets of facts can be used to support conflicting positions. Accounting data provided by the opponents under discovery proceedings will be as complete as required by law, but generally will not be organized to facilitate examination and understanding. Within this environment, the most important contribution the accounting witness can make will be the direct testimony and answers given during cross-examination. As an expert accounting witness, one is expected to convey accounting facts and information to the jury and the judge in a manner that will permit these decision makers, who may not be familiar with accounting, to understand the essential accounting facts that are needed for an informed decision. Demeanor while on the stand, ability to clearly and concisely communicate the technical accounting matters that are involved, and ability to withstand the rigors of cross-examination will weigh heavily in others' assessment of the accountant's performance as an expert witness.

REWARDS FOR SERVING AS AN EXPERT ACCOUNTING WITNESS

The pressures and demands upon an expert witness are significant. Consequently, when a favorable decision is handed down and the expert witness has played a major role on the successful litigation team, the feeling of satisfaction that is experienced is rarely equalled on other assignments.

Yet, there are other rewards, as well. Services as an expert witness provide many opportunities for individual intellectual expression because such services are generally performed in an unstructured environment under work plans that are developed to meet the unique requirements of the litigation. Frequently, the work performed by the expert accountant requires the joint participation of experts in economics, mathematics, and statistics and it is both stimulating and educational to study with and/or to oppose recognized experts in other disciplines, as well as those in one's own field of endeavor. Communicating with and matching wits against learned attorneys are stimulating challenges.

We live in a society that is far more complex and vastly more demanding of legal solutions than it was at any previous period. Litigation has grown and will continue to grow at an accelerated pace, and because of its increasing complexity, the services of expert witnesses will be needed with increasing frequency. Thus, the opportunities to develop one's practice by serving attorneys as an expert accounting witness will increase with the passage of time.

Service to clients and nonclients in so sensitive an area of concern as litigation can add to the stature of the individual and the reputation of that individual's firm. Many of the assignments require huge amounts of time and consequently, fees for professional services can be large. Moreover, litigation provides the opportunity to the truly competent expert accountant to demonstrate one's unique abilities and professionalism.

CHAPTER

4

Working in an
Ambiguous Environment

The lawmaking process has produced a vast amount of law. Congress
and state legislatures enact thousands of statutes each year, which add
to the existing statutory compilations. The great volumes of administrative agencies' regulations exceed the statutes of Congress and state
legislatures. In addition, there are several million American judicial
decisions. All these constitute law in the United States.

In general, the answer to such a huge volume of law has been codi-
fication by the American Law Institute. This approach has attempted
to clarify and simplify the law and to adapt the law to social needs by
reducing the uncertainty and complexity of American law.

The accountant, who accepts the assignment as expert accounting
witness, must be prepared to work in an environment of ambiguity.
Not only do existing statutory and case laws create uncertainties, but
ambiguities exist in the application of the different technical disciplines called upon in complex litigation to analyze and present facts to
the judge and jury. To be an effective member of an interdisciplinary
team of expert witnesses in such cases, an understanding of the limitations of the various analytical techniques used in the several different
fields of knowledge and applied to the facts at issue will be of benefit to
the expert accounting witness in preparing and presenting his testimony.

AMBIGUITIES IN THE ADMINISTRATION OF THE LAW

Uncertainties seem to have been created from the inception of law-making. Basically, the legislator's approach is to develop generalizations that include all possible kinds of actions or conditions. The generalizations aim to relate a variety of instances with common factors. Even at the lowest level of understanding this process can be ambiguous, for the difficulty of defining an action or a prohibition so that it is used in the same way by everyone is much greater than might be anticipated.

Most legal systems are a combination of statutory and case law. The statute is written to control or influence some type of condition, but because the same event can occur in a variety of circumstances and in many different ways, some approach has to be taken to organize the statute to make it cover this wide range of situations. This usually leads to an involved statute, including numerous qualifications. Even under these circumstances, the statute may fail to relate in many ways to the complexities of the real conditions.

Statutory ambiguity leads to case law, or law by precedent. *Case law* attempts to provide examples of previous rulings to clarify the statutes. However, the difficulty of relating the facts and their interpretations in previous cases to present cases limits the application of case law. The gulf between law and real-life situations is accentuated by the rules and conventions which are followed during court trials. Thus, certain questions may or may not be asked: rules of evidence control the testimony that is admissible and the form of reply that is acceptable. Long delays may result in the death or disappearance of key witnesses or the distortions of memory among those taking part. These practices contribute to the already difficult problems of relating complex factual situations to generalized statutes.

More and more, both plaintiff and defense attorneys are seeking to associate past decisions with the facts of their cases through the use of quantitative studies which require the pooling of interdisciplinary talents: economists, accountants, statisticians, computer specialists, and attorneys. While such testimony is aimed at reducing uncertainty, this testimony adds additional levels of complexity to case law and places additional emphasis upon the resolution of ambiguities. For example, it is not unusual to use an interdisciplinary team to testify to the key issues in monopoly cases, which typically boil down to evidence regarding power over prices and power over entry. An infinite variety of quantitative analyses can be undertaken to support or refute such power. Power over entry can be inferred by demonstrating analytically the economic profits earned by current market participants over long periods of time, during which no significant entry occurred. This evidence, however, is merely inferential since economies of scale, high levels of risk, long start-up periods, and random fluctuations in commodity prices may also explain the observed conditions. Power over prices can be demonstrated by statistical comparisons to similar product or geographic markets or by examining pricing patterns. The absence of such power can be demonstrated through sophisticated statistical techniques designed to show the random character of price movements over time.

Where testimony is presented by expert witnesses of different disciplines, such testimony must be coordinated and directed toward specific trial objectives. This requires that each expert witness understands the strengths and limitations of the proposed testimony of his trial associates, particularly where reliance is placed upon such information. While coordination of testimony is the responsibility of the trial attorney, the interdisciplinary team members have the obligation of understanding the testimony of each other, must be cognizant of the barriers to effective understanding, and must overcome them. Where the expert witnesses fail in attaining this objective, case law adds additional complexities to the administration of the law.

THE CHANGING NATURE OF THE LAW

Concern with the administration of the law seems to be as old as the law. The courts are preeminent in the legal process and the judges are the dominating figures in the courtrooms. Thus, much of the criticism dealing with the administration of the law has been directed against the judges and courtroom procedures. On the one hand, critics who oppose change frequently state that many judges are inclined to create and expand the principles of law rather than interpret them, and that judges incorporate their individual understandings of economic and social concerns in their decisions. Other critics feel that the law does not respond rapidly enough to the main movements of the society that it regulates. These critics feel that each society has its own values, which should be reflected in the objectives that the legal order seeks to advance. The critics state that the purposes of law are reached by accepting certain interests, establishing the boundaries within which they shall be recognized legally, and endeavoring to secure those interests which are within the limits defined.

In 1906, at the annual meeting of the American Bar Association in St. Paul, Minnesota, Mr. Roscoe Pound, a young attorney at that time, expressed his dissatisfaction with the administration of the law by stating that: "Our system of courts is archaic . . . our procedures are behind the times . . . our courts have seemed to obstruct public efforts to get relief." The courts "have been put in a false position of doing nothing and obstructing everything." The courts' "time is frittered away on mere points of legal etiquette. . . . Putting courts into politics . . . has almost destroyed the traditional respect for the bench." Pound also listed the defects in the law as: (1) the mechanical operation of legal rules; (2) the difference in the rate of progress between law and public opinion; (3) the individualist spirit of the common law; (4) the doctrine of contentious procedure; and (5) the deficiencies of judicial organization and administration. Theodore Roosevelt described judges as irresponsible lawmakers who delegate to themselves the power to decide whether or not people are to have certain laws in the interest of social justice. Franklin D. Roosevelt threatened the members of the U.S. Supreme Court with his court-packing plan of 1937, and although the court reform bill was defeated, a significant reversal in the Supreme Court's attitude toward the New Deal program occurred shortly thereafter.

The dilemma in the administration of justice seems to originate with the basic demands placed upon the law. The law must be stable so that the public can engage in personal and commercial endeavors with a reasonable expectation of what their rights and duties will be. However, nothing is more certain in our society than the principle that there are no absolutes. Thus the law must be flexible to accommodate the changing interests, needs, and demands of the public. There is no accepted calculus of change to determine when change will begin or how rapidly it will proceed once it has started. Law in the United States, however, has undergone a remarkable process of change.

Law consists of a system of social rules which establishes standards of conduct enforceable by officials of the courts. The sources of these standards are either legislative command, custom, rationalized precedent, or a sense of morals or equity. The enforcement of the law depends on popular agreement with its basic rules. The function of law is to adjust or balance conflicting human wants so as to achieve the expectations of the public with a minimum of friction and waste. Law is conceived as a restraint upon the power of men, and the history of law in the United States records the attempts to cast legal institutions and doctrines into structures that meet the needs of the changing times. These efforts have not always been successful, but where failures have occurred, judges, lawyers, and legislators have attempted to develop new principles better adapted to the changed conditions of the day. In this process, courts frequently have turned to economic, business, and scientific literature, not merely for helpful analytical techniques, but to seek to understand evidence in terms of academic and market theories.

The law in the United States was taken from the precedents of common law and equity known to the authors of the Constitution. The origins of common law were the royal courts established in England following the Norman conquest; the law was common, since it applied throughout the realm. It was based upon principles set forth by judges in their decisions, and not upon specific laws or statutes. It was judge-made law resulting from case decisions. The source of common law was custom. Where these customs were well known, the judge acted to maintain order. As the ways of the community became more complex, with the development of towns, technology, and legislation that raised many questions, judges became engaged in the business of making laws.

In England the king was the fountain of justice. If justice could not be obtained in the common law courts, the disappointed party had an opportunity to obtain justice by appealing directly to the king who, not skilled in law, turned to one of his advisers, usually his secretary or chancellor. The early chancellors were clergymen, not learned in common law but in Roman and church law, and in giving relief, the chancellor acted on ethical grounds. Gradually the task of giving relief from inadequacies of the common law became so heavy that the chancellor came to have a separate court, which became known as the court of chancery or equity.

As contrasted with common law, equity was flexible rather than rigid. The chancellor was often able to take into consideration all the circumstances of a case instead of following hard and fast rules to arrive at a decision. Chancellors could give commands to defendants instead of only to sheriffs; they could exercise preventive jurisdiction by issuing injunctions against a threatened wrong, and could deal with a case having many sides, settling the rights of all parties against each other.

In the United States, the common law and equity developed separately from the English law from which they were taken. Common law was not adopted in its entirety in America, but only those portions which were applicable to the needs of the new country. Colonial law attempted to recognize and protect the natural rights of man: the rights to life, liberty, and property. Property rights were considered to be as important as personal rights.

The adoption of the Constitution of the United States in 1789 established the forms of government for the nation and the states. Article 1, Section 8, known as the *Necessary and Proper Clause,* created vast federal authority. Among other powers, it gave Congress the rights to levy and collect taxes, to provide for the common defense and general welfare of the United States, to regulate commerce with foreign nations and among the several states, to borrow money, and to establish uniform rules on the subject of bankruptcies.

Early decisions of the U. S. Supreme Court under John Marshall (1801–1835) gave the nation the powers needed to govern effectively, and insured the supremacy of the federal government in dealing with state powers. The Marshall Court established the U.S. Supreme Court as the final arbiter of federal–state conflicts and the federal courts as paramount in deciding constitutional questions. The federal courts were enabled to invalidate state legislation and to overrule the decisions of state courts on matters of constitutional interpretations. The Taney Court, following the death of Marshall, construed the powers of the national government somewhat differently and attempted to avoid projecting the national government into the internal activities of the states. The Taney Court declared a moderate version of the states' rights creed. The supremacy of federal over state law was retained, but the scope of federal activity was curtailed.

From 1789 to 1860, American law was essentially judge-made law. By means of court decisions, judges established a legal system to meet the needs of the new nation and performed a legislative role in a broad sense. In reshaping the common law into American law, concepts of what best served public interests, and prejudices of the judges all had as much influence in forming the American version of common law as did the legal concepts the judges decided to apply.

The American law during this period tended to favor individual initiative and recognized the desirability of individual action and decision. It encouraged risk-taking involved in business ventures. The burden was imposed upon the injured party to show why the law should shift the loss to the one who caused the injury. Liability was attached to cause rather than the act. Damages were assessed as the natural and proximate results of a wrongful act and did not include, as did the English courts, the total results of an unlawful act.

The American law of damages was based upon the need to protect individuals against the risks undertaken in improving productivity. There was a desire not to add to those risks inherent in the business situation; if those in business were to be held responsible for all damages however remote, it was believed that they could not operate in the marketplace with the required safety and that the result of such responsibility would be to harm important business ventures. To encourage business, risks were reduced by the *doctrine of proximate cause,* which limited the claims for damages to those which were the effective producing causes.

In employer–employee relations, the fellow-servant rule held that an employer was not liable for the injuries caused by a fellow employee. This was another example of the individualism of the nineteenth century law. It was believed that individuals were free to follow the calling of their choice, and as such, assumed the risks of their chosen occupations, including any harm that might occur to them from the negligence of fellow workers.

The nineteenth century provided for freedom of action through the expansion of contract law. The law put individual conscience, needs, and judgment first. Legal consequences were attached to individual conduct and everyone was required to abide by the results of free choice. The important objective was the maintenance of the transaction entered into freely by the parties. It was in the field of contracts that the judges developed new branches of law, such as the laws of negotiable instruments, sales, factors, agency, insurance, banking, and the development of corporation law. The corporation became a legal person. The decisions, which permitted corporations to operate on a nationwide basis as natural persons, were powerful factors in economic expansion.

The Civil War significantly changed federal–state relations, and the passage of the 14th Amendment to the Constitution of the United States proved to be the basis for significant modifications in American public law. It took many years, however, for these changes to be realized. Gradually the focus of public law moved from safeguarding federal power and property rights to advancing individual rights. The 14th Amendment stated: "No state shall make or enforce any law which shall abridge the privileges or immunities of citizens of the United States; nor shall any state deprive any person of life, liberty, or property, without due process of law; nor deny to any person within its jurisdiction the equal protection of the laws." For a time following its passage, the 14th Amendment served to support the individualistic and business needs of the nation. Gradually minorities turned with increasing success to the federal government and the federal courts to enforce their individual rights against states and individuals.

The due process clause of the 14th Amendment initially was considered to be a restriction upon the power of Congress to interfere with the rights of property. It also was used to protect corporate enterprises from governmental interventions aimed at controlling the misuse of corporate power. Abuses of the freedom to contract and the inequality of bargaining power between capital and labor, however, led to demands upon the legislature to protect employees by legislating minimum standards governing the conditions of employment. Soon laws were passed regulating hours of labor, forbidding employers from interfering with union marshals, prohibiting imposition of fines on employees, and requiring payment of wages in money. These laws were invalidated by the courts based upon the freedom of contract doctrine. Additional benefits were allowed to corporations. As corporations were recognized as persons under the 14th Amendment and came under its protection, corporations were free to contract, consolidate, and combine with other corporations.

During the second half of the nineteenth century significant social, political, and economic alterations occurred. Railroads changed the restrictions of geography and time. New technology expanded business ventures and markets. It was a time of great energy, imagination, and ambition. During this period, the government attempted to promote the growth and development of industry. Markets and investments grew and competition expanded. Most often, competition ended in consolidation and the great trusts were formed.

Toward the end of the nineteenth century the public reacted adversely to the many abuses by business. In 1887, the Interstate Commerce Commission was created by Congress to limit the abuses that had developed in the railroad industry. In 1890, the Sherman Antitrust Law was passed to regulate the combination and consolidation of corporations. In 1917 and 1919, the Supreme Court permitted workmen's compensation laws disallowed in 1909, on the theory that such laws deprived employers of their properties without due process of law. Economists discussed concepts of marginal utility and presented complicated theoretical conditions of competitive equilibrium. Some economists favored laissez-faire and others thought the involvement of the state essential to progress. One economic school started to focus attention not on the individual or the firm but on the industry. More economic concepts became available for the court to choose among.

The economic collapse of the 1930s led to major changes in American law. With the economy in deep trouble there was a need for the use of federal powers as businessmen and the individual states had found the problems beyond their abilities to manage. Initially, the Supreme Court invalidated most of the important New Deal legislation on the grounds that any legislative extension of federal powers over the existing economic order was unconstitutional and not considered to be socially desirable. After 1936, the Supreme Court revised its approach to the application of government powers and regulatory laws were not invalidated on due process grounds. This reflected a substantial change in judicial thinking. The Supreme Court returned to a constitutional concept that the judiciary was not empowered to enforce its social and economic beliefs rather than the laws passed by the legislative bodies. New Deal laws, the growth of administrative agencies, factory and workmen's compensation laws, and the concept of the welfare state came into existence.

During the second quarter of the twentieth century, the U. S. Supreme Court started to emphasize personal rights over property rights. Equality was interpreted to mean equality of opportunity in the marketplace. After the Civil War, limitations were placed on state powers by the federal constitution and gradually the Supreme Court began to provide protection for individual rights at the level of state government through the due process clause of the 14th Amendment. This was accomplished by the incorporation of certain guarantees of the Bill of Rights within the 14th Amendment due process clause.

The result of these changes of attitude by the U. S. Supreme Court was to emphasize the welfare of the community at the expense of individual rights of property and contract. The law began to be used as an instrument to help people get to where they wanted to go. Courts refused to enforce contracts consented to by both parties which they considered unequal or unfair where one party unconscientiously took advantage of the other. The concept of status, which meant the attachment of legal consequences to the position of the party concerned became important, and the law tended to be influenced by relationships and duties, not isolated individuals and rights.

In recent years the pendulum seems to have started to turn in the opposite direction, as there appears to be an increasing concern with the misuse of centralized powers. In 1946, Congress enacted the Federal Administrative Procedures Act, which was a regulator of procedures in many agencies. It provided minimum standards of administrative procedures and was evidence of a congressional desire to halt the process of administrative expansion. Previously, Congress had made broad delegations of government authority to the administrative agencies and administrative law had become one of the important legal developments of the twentieth century. The recent decisions of the Supreme Court have shown concern for the interests and prerogatives of states. Conflict has arisen between the recognition that states mean something in the federal system and the belief that a primary role of the federal government is to provide protection for civil rights against state abuse.

UNCERTAINTIES IN ECONOMIC ANALYSES

Economic analyses frequently aid in the decision-making process in antitrust cases, not by providing a set of conclusions, but by presenting a willingness to look beyond the apparent conduct of the parties and to question whether the alleged behavior of the parties could be predicted under the axiom of profit maximization. It asks whether such conduct can be explained on the basis of profit maximization, or alternatively, only as an irrational or random event. If specific conduct is explained as not profit-maximizing behavior, there is need to examine the circumstances in detail and to demonstrate why the firm behaved in that way. Economics offers a general or overall blueprint describing how the various elements of the economy fit together in a consistent whole. In particular, it provides an analytical system for appraising the factors which both promote and restrain the degree of competition. Economic analysis, however, does not provide a road toward certainty in litigation.

An important purpose of economic theory is to explain and predict the economic behavior of societies and men, and the value of economic theory is that it permits concentration of a few important relationships. Economic theories thus are simplified representations of the real world in which less important or less complicating factors are held constant or assumed not to exist, so that major points and relationships can be made more visible. Theories are proposed explanations or hypotheses; they are not immutable truths unless and until all available evidence has corroborated them.

Economic theory is frequently difficult to relate to the real world of business events because simplifying assumptions are often made when developing the theory, and important aberrations and exceptions to theory may be ignored. Economic theory cannot always be verified or refuted by controlled and explicit empirical testing, and economic laws may hold to be true only on average, with considerable dispersions of exceptions around the average.

Economic analyses can create unnecessary problems for interdisciplinary team members where such studies are inundated with economic jargon familiar only to the economist. While some of the jargon is necessary to attain precise meaning, in certain instances the precision may have to be sacrificed for understanding, particularly if the jargon creates misunderstanding. At times, unwarranted extensions of economic theory seem to be made on the grounds that what is accurate for an individual firm is accurate for all firms or, in the reverse, what is applicable to all firms is applicable to individual businesses. Often economic reasoning seems to be based more upon what should be, according to the concepts of the investigator, rather than what is. Under these circumstances factual information is at a minimum, many relevant characteristics of the problem are ignored, and the theories are far too general and underspecified.

Preconceptions or biases of the researcher in economics, as in other disciplines, can lead to problems in coordinating testimony of the interdisciplinary team members. Initiating an inquiry on an issue with a preconceived answer in mind and then attempting to develop supporting evidence for the preconception leads to testimony of little value. Care must be taken to insure that objective information is obtained and that all available information is critically evaluated.

The power of change and development in economic theory continues as old schools of economic thought fragment and new groupings appear. Courts are involved in these developments. Any judicial expectation of gaining certainty through contemporary economics will fail because economics itself evolves. Economic theory is linked to a particular view of the world and to a set of convictions about what is important. In choosing among economic theories, courts are making social judgments and are not expressing unchangeable rules.

BIAS IN STATISTICAL SAMPLING PLANS

The principal object of any sampling procedure is to secure a sample which, subject to the limitation of size, will reproduce the characteristics of the population, especially those of immediate interest. Whether or not a sample will give results which are sufficiently representative of the whole depends primarily on whether errors introduced by the sample process are sufficiently small not to invalidate the results for the purpose for which they are required. Random sampling errors which arise from the sampling process itself are not of great concern because it is recognized that the sample cannot be exactly representative of the whole, and that the average magnitude of the sampling errors, which depends on the size of the sample, the variability of the data, the sampling procedures adopted, and the way in which results are calculated, can be determined if a proper process of selection is adopted.

Sampling can give unsatisfactory results if faulty methods of sample selection or an inappropriate sampling design are followed. Following are the conditions which can give rise to bias in sampling.

1. Failure to define the characteristics of the problem with sufficient precision to provide an adequate basis for sample selection.
2. A deliberate rather than a probabilistic selection of a representative sample.
3. A haphazard procedure for sample selection, which depends upon some characteristic which is correlated with properties of the end which are of interest, and which allows the investigator his desire to obtain a certain result.
4. Substitution of available data when difficulties are encountered in obtaining information.
5. Failure to cover the whole of the chosen sample where no second attempt is made to include samples which are difficult to obtain. (Nonresponse to sampling questionnaires thus requires careful analysis, interpretation, and follow-up so that alternate means of attaining the required information are used).

If bias exists, no fully objective conclusions can be drawn from the sample. At best, the sample must be considered a judgment sample, which is subject to a greater variety of attacks in cross-examination than a probabilistic sample would face. The bases for the sample selection, the biases of the statistician, the limitations of the statistical analyses, and the restrictions on the use of the statistical conclusions would be probed vigorously by opposing counsel where judgment sampling is applied.

MATHEMATICAL UNCERTAINTIES

Mathematical models are being used extensively in establishing damage claims. A model is a representation of the subject of inquiry and is used for purposes of explanation, prediction, and control. It is intended to facilitate determination of how changes in one aspect of the modeled entity (the alleged injury in damage models) affected other aspects of the model (the revenue or profits of the injured party). Because the model is expressed in mathematical terms, computations can be made of the impact of different assumptions or changes in inputs to demonstrate how these changes affected the outputs of the models.

Where graphs are used to represent quantitative relationships between properties of classes of things, how a change in one property will affect another property can be measured. Care must be exercised, however, not to assume that, because a change in one property can be measured by a change in a second property, a causal relationship also exists. For example, in a recent case the plaintiffs, a class of pharmaceutical consumers, included in their damage claim against the defendant drug manufacturers not only the alleged illegal overcharges for merchandise included in the sales prices of pharmaceuticals but also the mark-up applied on this merchandise when resold at retail by pharmacies. The basis for this assertion was that mark-up was added directly to the merchandise cost as a percentage of the purchase cost and that perfect correlation could be shown graphically between mark-up dollars and merchandise costs. The defendant was required to demonstrate that while mark-up dollars were measured by merchandise costs as a convenient method for establishing selling prices at retail, mark-up dollars were caused by operating costs and profit objectives of the retail pharmacy, and that if merchandise costs were not used as a basis for allocating operating expenses and profits to product sales, some other allocation method would have been devised, such as a fixed add-on cost per prescription. A mark-up computation based upon a fixed cost per prescription obviously would have no measurable relationship to varying merchandise costs.

Mathematical models also can fail to represent reality adequately, and thus lose some of their potential usefulness. Some of the ways in which this can occur are:

1. The model may assert a dependency of the effectiveness of the system on one or more variables which, as a matter of fact, do not have such an impact.

2. Conversely, the model may fail to include variables which have significant effects on the system.

3. The model may inaccurately express the actual relationships which exist between the measures of effectiveness and one or more of the pertinent independent variables.

4. Inaccurate or improper data may be included in the model. In certain instances, past information may exist, but because of the dependence on so many other changeable factors, a great deal of uncertainty may exist as to the meaning of the data. In such circumstances, premises have to be assumed whose consequences are not known. The model may incorporate objective data and intuition of the model builder and the model will aggregate both into an overall result. Estimates may be used, in the absence of reliable data, which prove to be inaccurate.

AMBIGUITIES IN ACCOUNTING

Accounting results, which because they are stated numerically give the appearance of precision, nevertheless call for the exercise of judgment in many accounting determinations. Competent accountants may obtain somewhat different results from the same data because of the frequent need in accounting determinations to select among equally acceptable accounting principles, methods of analysis, techniques, and procedures. Different estimates of costs are possible when studies are made by different but equally competent cost accountants. Also, accounting terminology is not sufficiently precise to avoid careless usage, and this can lead to faulty understanding of accounting reports.

Few words in the lexicon of accounting and law give rise to as much misunderstanding as the simple term *cost*. Much of the dispute associated with damage claims centers around distorted estimates of costs. A key contributor to this confusion is the body of cost jargon in widespread use by accountants, economists, and statisticians. Much of this language is introduced into legal proceedings during the discovery phase when the depositions of the expert witnesses, or of employees of the plaintiff or defendant are taken. The combination of loosely used terms, overlapping meanings, and elaborate distinctions encountered in the testimony in many cases involving damage claims are not suited to clear communications of the positions of opposing parties who wish to resolve differences and negotiate settlements.

Part of the ambiguity arising from the term *cost* results from the different ways in which costs can be viewed and the number of terms used to describe costs. Costs can be viewed as follows:

1. **In terms of behavior:** That is, how do costs change as the volume of output increases or decreases (variable, semi-variable, fixed, programmed)?

2. **By traceability:** How closely can the costs be traced to specific actions (direct, indirect)?

3. **By responsibility:** What functional areas were responsible for the cost expenditures (manufacturing, selling, general, administrative)?

4. **By timing:** In what period were the costs incurred (current, future, past)?

5. **By compilation:** How were the costs calculated (actual, average, standard)?

6. **By objects:** What objects were used to accomplish the results derived from the costs incurred (material, labor, supply, service)?

7. **By payment:** When were the costs paid (paid, accrued, deferred)?

The term *cost* has many meanings:

Burden cost. The same as indirect cost. However, burden is sometimes used to designate only those indirect costs associated with the factory or manufacturing plant.

By-product cost. The costs directly identifiable with a secondary product that resulted during the production of the primary product or products. The costs of production of both the primary and secondary products are usually charged only to the primary product, since it is usually not possible to determine separately the cost of production for the secondary product. The only costs that can usually be identified directly with the by-product are those occurring after production, such as handling and storage, packaging, shipping, and selling costs.

Controllable cost. A cost which some person in the organization is responsible for controlling and which that person has the authority and ability to control. Variable costs are often designated as controllable costs on the assumption that they can be controlled on a day-to-day basis, whereas fixed costs are assumed to be noncontrollable because they cannot usually be changed except over the long term.

Estimated cost. A cost that is based on estimated factors (quantities, objects, prices, etc.), as compared to an actual cost that is based on known factors. It may be necessary to calculate an estimated cost for a past output or accomplishment when the specific cost factors are not available to make an actual cost calculation. Estimated costs may also be calculated for anticipated future outputs or accomplishments.

Full cost. The same as total cost. Includes all of the costs connected with a particular output or accomplishment.

Historical cost. The actual cost experienced in the past to perform a particular output or accomplishment.

Joint cost. A cost incurred in the concurrent production and/or distribution of two or more closely related products. The assignment of portions of a joint cost to each of the related products is arbitrary. For example, many costs of operating a refinery are joint costs, and are allocated to the several products obtained, and cannot be identified with any one of the products except by some arbitrary relationship.

Marginal, differential, or incremental cost. The amount which represents the difference between costs at two different levels of output.

Noncontrollable cost. A cost which is not assigned to some person in the organization for direct control, and which is not, therefore, controlled on a day-to-day or short-term basis. Fixed costs are often designated as noncontrollable costs on the assumption that they cannot be changed except over the long term.

Out-of-pocket cost. Usually a cost paid for directly in cash. However, the term is also sometimes used to imply variable costs for which payment is normally made currently, as compared to fixed costs for which payment has usually been made in an earlier period. Because of the ambiguity surrounding the term, it is probably better avoided and a more specific description used, such as "costs paid for directly in cash", or "variable costs", depending on the meaning intended.

Overhead cost. The same as indirect cost. However, overhead is sometimes used to designate only those indirect costs associated with the factory or manufacturing plant.

Period cost. A cost that is consumed by the passage of time rather than by the amount of activity or output.

Program cost. A cost directly connected with a program of activities aimed at accomplishing a particular goal, such as an advertising program, a maintenance program, and so forth.

Prime cost. The cost of direct labor and direct materials associated with a particular product.

Sunk cost. A past cost that is not relevant to decisions about specific current or future economic events.

Economists do not agree with accountants as to what is included by the term *costs,* and their definitions go further than those of accountants. To an economist, the return to a factor of production is economically important regardless of how it happens to be owned. Thus, implicit cost elements, such as the return for the labor provided by the owner himself (implicit wages) and returns to the land and capital provided by the owner (implicit rent and interest) are included in the economist's concept of costs. The economist also includes opportunity costs as part of the concept of full competitive costs. Opportunity costs are the costs of alternative output or accomplishment that would have been possible if the chosen output or accomplishment had not been selected. The concept of opportunity costs is difficult to handle and makes a complicated area in litigation more trying.

Recently, in an attempt to conclude certain litigation as quickly as possible, it was stipulated that the amount of lost revenue would be agreed upon and that damages would be based upon the lost revenue as agreed, less the costs of the services required to produce the lost revenue. Attorneys for both sides and the judge believed that the cost of services rendered could be developed quite simply and that the trial of this one issue could be concluded in several days. Expert accounting witnesses were employed by both sides and the question of what was intended by the term *cost* immediately surfaced. Each side defined and argued for a concept of cost that suited its own position. After several weeks of litigation and extensive direct and cross-examination of the expert accounting witnesses, the trial judge arbitrarily selected a level of cost that he felt was equitable and rendered a judgment that was satisfactory to neither side. In hindsight, it was apparent that great care should have been taken in defining the term *cost of services rendered* in the stipulation.

AMBIGUITIES IN BUSINESS DECISIONS

Many court decisions seem to accept the simplifying assumption that decision makers in business know all relevant cost and demand functions and that profit maximization is a matter of calculation rather than judgment. Generally, however, business decisions are not that precise. They are usually based upon information supplemented by the knowledge, experience, judgment, and interpretive ability of the individual proposing a decision or a course of action. Information costs money, and when decisions must be reached, uncertainty about some factors inevitably remains. There are problems inherent in developing accurate knowledge about conditions outside the company, and the extent of knowledge and understanding of competitors' plans, actions, and strategies is problematic. This uncertainty can have a substantial impact upon the use by the decision maker of information generated inside the company. It is not only difficult to anticipate reactions of customers and changes in the economic and political environments, but delays in obtaining these data reduce their importance. External information on what actually did happen in the marketplace may be vague and incomplete.

There usually are unsolved problems in understanding cause-and-effect relationships within a company. While an information report may illustrate a favorable or unfavorable operating situation, available information may not be sufficiently precise to allocate responsibility for this condition among a multiplicity of possible causes. There are uncertainties in predicting how information will be used, how it will be interpreted, and what actions will be taken on it. All too often, these reactions become evident only when a considerable period of time has elapsed after the event and thus become confused with reactions to many other situations. Firms need not try to optimize everything.

Many seem content as long as profits are adequate and market shares are stable. The existence of firms of great size and high levels of concentration makes the use of discretionary powers inevitable. On questions involving investments in research and development, competitive strategies, product design, plant location, levels and styles of advertising, pricing strategies, and legal strategies, the profit maximization solutions will rarely be precise. Such decisions will be market tested only if other firms in the same market adopt different strategies. Even then such questions may be tested only over such a long period of time and in connection with so many other decisions that no clear market assessment of any one decision may appear. The concept of profit maximization is important in the analyses of business behavior by economists and such analyses can be faulty unless the limitations of the business decision-making processes are understood and included in the studies of business behavior.

5

Developing and Managing Accounting Information Used in Litigation

The civil justice system depends upon the willingness of both litigants and lawyers to try in good faith to comply with the rules established for the equitable and efficient administration of justice. When those rules and established procedures are manipulated or violated for the purposes of delay, unfair advantage, confusion, or harrassment, the system breaks down, and in contravention of the fundamental goal of the Federal Rules of Civil Procedures, the determinations of civil actions become unjust, delayed, and expensive.

Abuse of the judicial process occurs most often during discovery. Unreasonable demands for information and refusal to provide discovery prolong litigation and make it more expensive than is necessary. Misleading information can be given, material facts can be suppressed, and fabrication can occur. Frequently, where they do not believe in good faith that a valid claim exists, parties will nevertheless file complaints in order to gain access to discovery which is used not to find evidence to support their claim but to discover whether they have a claim at all. The reluctance to evaluate the merits of a case before trial and the great potential for the invasion of privacy that the discovery system permits make this kind of abuse costly and contribute to the overburdening of the judicial process. Because the large proportion of cases are settled before trial, pretrial costs account for the largest percentage of litigation expenses, and measures that reduce such costs would make litigation available to many additional people needing judicial relief.

Discovery remains, however, the major opportunity for obtaining the needed information beyond the control of the party seeking the data. During the discovery process, vast quantities of data are frequently obtained from the opponents and are reviewed, copied, analyzed, classified, summarized, and filed for retention until needed. Large amounts of data dealing with the lawsuit are also obtained from the client's records and such data must be handled in a similar manner. During the early stages of a lawsuit, it is difficult to be selective in the accumulation of data, for the issues are not clearly defined and discovery is terminated at an agreed upon date. Therefore, the tendency is to accumulate as much data as possible within the time constraints.

Care, however, must be exercised in the selection and accumulation of data, for data alone, regardless of volume, do not necessarily constitute information, and frequently the case will suffer from an overabundance of irrelevant information rather than a lack of relevant information. Too much information hides an issue rather than lending weight to it. Where there are too many conflicting, duplicating, or unnecessary data with too many analyses and excessive detail, the results usually are superficial perusal of the data and much wasted effort and frustration.

ORGANIZING THE DATA DEVELOPMENT EFFORT

Early in the proceedings, a decision should be made by the trial attorneys on who will be responsible for accumulating needed information and how this information is to be managed, particularly where several expert witnesses of different disciplines are members of the trial attorneys' team. Frequently, the role of the accounting team member will be to accumulate, analyze, and present data to the team members for their examination and use in developing relevant testimony. Where the accounting witness is called into a legal situation while the information relating to it is still current, the assistance that can be given to team members is usually more complete, and therefore more useful. Not only can accounting witnesses identify and preserve useful accounting documents and files, some of which may not be readily evident to a nonaccountant, but they can also identify the need for economic and quantitative data useful in model building, as well as supplementary information (such as scrap tickets, weight slips, photographs of damage, and names of employees familiar with the details of transactions or calculations) to support or corroborate key information.

Where the expert accountant is called in months or several years after the event or events giving rise to the litigation, it is usually necessary to do considerably more analytical work in seeking to establish pertinent accounting information. This work must often be done under time pressures because of impending trial dates. Much of the additional work arises because the individuals who could have given first-hand information regarding the details of the transactions have frequently left the jobs they held and cannot be located. In addition, the files or documents needed to substantiate transactions often have been totally or partially destroyed, or cannot be located. Under these circumstances, considerable thought must be given to alternative sources of information, and to synthesis of missing information from fragments that can be located in the available records. Sometimes missing information can be obtained more easily from suppliers' or customers' files than from the records of the litigants.

Because class action and antitrust suits frequently are instituted several years after the subject events have taken place, the accounting witness will probably have to work with old information. Under these circumstances, one needs to devote all the creativity and imagination one can muster to reconstruct information from the data available. Lack of enough supporting detail may prevent satisfactory completion of a specific analysis, and an overall calculation may have to be resorted to based on general relationships. For these reasons, it is important that the accounting witness be given the opportunity to assess the information needs and availabilities as early as possible, thus avoiding considerable time consuming and sometimes fruitless digging in the archives.

In the discovery phase of litigation, it is sometimes necessary for the expert accountant to work in the offices of the opposing party. When this is so, it is obvious that considerable tact and perseverance are required to seek out the information that is needed, for the opposing party may avoid giving any assistance beyond the minimum required by law, and will usually volunteer nothing considered to be useful.

Needless to say, a well considered plan for obtaining the information needed is a prerequisite when entering a hostile office to obtain information; not only should the information be specifically identified, but the most likely source for obtaining it should be clearly in mind. Payroll information, for example, may be obtained from payroll registers, social security reports, earnings records, personnel rate files, cancelled checks, time cards, or other sources. The expert accountant should find out what are all the available sources of information in order to assure oneself of the correct information by crosschecking among these different sources, as well as to be aware of the completeness and accuracy of the opposing party's information. Attorneys can demand information by court order, but time and costs can be saved if the information can be obtained without the formal intervention of the court.

The expert accountant has a special responsibility for the proper identification and control of relevant accounting information. A checklist of questions which the expert can use to advantage in fulfilling this responsibility follows.

1. Has a line of communication been established with the trial attorney so that accounting information needs are revised as changes are made to the issues to be tried?

2. Has a meeting been held with all key accounting employees to discuss and evaluate accounting information needs and to assign responsibilities and authorities for obtaining and controlling the information?

3. Has the form "Schedule of Accounting Information Used in Litigation," Exhibit 2, used for documenting the logic for identifying needed accounting information and for providing the details for controlling that information, been prepared for each type of information that might be needed? Use of these forms should be helpful in evaluating the need for accounting information, and in identifying and controlling information so that it is available to support litigation needs.

4. Have all the organization's records and documents supporting the litigation been identified, labeled, and physically controlled to assure that they will be available when needed?

5. Have copies been made where necessary to assure availability of the information?

6. Has all needed analytical work been started?

7. Are adequate working papers being prepared to support all needed analytical work?

8. Is any information needed from outsiders, such as suppliers, customers, sales agents, trade associations, and so forth?

9. If so, has a control schedule for this information been prepared and is action under way to obtain the needed information in the form needed and by the time needed?

Exhibit 2. Schedule of Accounting Information Used in Litigation

Instructions: This form is intended as an aid in identifying and controlling account-ing information that could be useful in obtaining a fair decision in litigation. The fol-lowing questions should be asked by the person preparing the form: What types of accounting information are likely to be useful in this litigation? Why will they be useful? Who knows most about this information? Where is the information available? For each type of information that can be separately identified, a separate form should be prepared.

WHAT

Type of information:

WHY

Reason for usefulness:

WHO

What are the names of the individuals having direct participation in the recording, processing, and reporting of the accounting information described above?

	Name:	Title:	Dept.:
1	Connection with information:		
2	Name:	Title:	Dept.:
	Connection with information:		
3	Name:	Title:	Dept.:
	Connection with information:		

More WHO

What are the names of individuals having direct knowledge of the physical or technical background events on which the accounting entries are based?

	Name:	Title:	Dept.:
1	Connection with information:		
2	Name:	Title:	Dept.:
	Connection with information:		
3	Name:	Title:	Dept.:
	Connection with information:		

78

Exhibit 2   (Continued)

	What records and reports contain the accounting information that is important to the case, and who has custody of the records?			
WHERE	1	Title or description of document:		Period covered:
		Location and individual in charge of custody:		Page and/or volume #:
		Type of preparation: ☐ Handwritten ☐ Computer output ☐ Typewritten ☐ Other		Source documents used for preparation:
	2	Title or description of document:		Period covered:
		Location and individual in charge of custody:		Page and/or volume #:
		Type of preparation: ☐ Handwritten ☐ Computer output ☐ Typewritten ☐ Other		Source documents used for preparation:
	3	Title or description of document:		Period covered:
		Location and individual in charge of custody:		Page and/or volume #:
		Type of preparation: ☐ Handwritten ☐ Computer output ☐ Typewritten ☐ Other		Source documents used for preparation

There is a special responsibility for maintaining working papers in an orderly and understandable manner when they are used in litigation. Because the working papers are often submitted as supporting or corroborating evidence, their condition can reflect favorably or unfavorably on the outcome of the case. It is essential, therefore, that all schedules be indexed and cross-indexed to provide a key to the flow of supporting information. In addition, all schedules should be signed and dated by the persons who have prepared them, and should indicate the sources from which the information in the schedules was obtained. An orderly, indexed set of working papers carries an implication of accuracy and professional competence and lends support to the case. Anything less than this tends to reduce the credibility of the information supplied by the working papers.

Juries do not come to their tasks equipped with the jargon of accounting nor with the training of accountants in specialized analytical and financial reporting techniques. As a consequence, the information compiled by the expert accountant must be evaluated by the trial attorneys to determine how likely it is to be understood in the courtroom by lay jurors. If the information is crucial to a just decision in the case, the attorneys will wish to use it, and will attempt to make it more easily understandable by breaking it into smaller elements and using exhibits to graphically portray its significance. However, sometimes highly valid technical accounting data are thought to be too complex for jurors to understand and are not presented as evidence. Thus, it is desirable to bear in mind how understandable, and therefore how useful the litigation support information sought will be. Also, as the work progresses, the expert accountant should attempt to develop suggestions for exhibits that the attorneys can use to clearly present the information in court, if they wish to do so.

SOURCES OF ACCOUNTING INFORMATION USED IN LITIGATION

The sources of much of the accounting data used in litigation are the internal records of the parties involved. These include all types of accounting and operating records—those that are formally prepared from accounting and operating records, as well as analytical reports which attempt to dissect available information and focus upon specific problems. Some of the more important reports and data frequently used include the following:

Financial

Annual financial reports to stockholders.

Annual financial reports to the Securities and Exchange Commission.

Monthly financial and budgetary reports to management.

Long-range and short-range profit plans.

Consolidated company and divisional financial results of operations.

Cash flow information.

Departmental budgets illustrating actual versus budgeted results.

Capital expenditure programs and costs accumulated thereunder.

Cost accounting data for each product.

Break-even points.

Maintenance-tooling-plant engineering cost reports.

Research and development expenditures versus programmed expenditures.

Various financial ratios including; inventory turnover rates, return on investment, working capital ratios, aging of accounts receivable, overtime percentages.

Sales and income analyses.

Special financial analyses including product profitability studies, distribution cost analyses, various expense and expenditure reports.

Cost–profit–volume relationships.

Capital asset surveys.

Internal audit reports.

External financial, statistical, and economic data.

Marketing

Long-range goals and short-range objectives of the marketing activity.

Estimated market size and share of market by product.

Sales trends and sales forecasts.

Marketing plans and programs.

Sales budgets and shipping plans.

Departmental expense budgets.

Capital expenditure programs.

Advertising, promotion and technical service programs and costs and results thereof.

Marketing distribution methods compared with competitors, health of dealer organization.

Order influx and current backlog.

Customer calls and results achieved versus planned programs.

Customer order history data and new account analyses.

Customer complaints, returns, and lost order reports.

Reactions of salesmen to company products.

Salesmen effectivity reports.

Product pricing, costing and profitability data.

Product performance compared with customer needs.

Significant new product developments.

Major activities of competitors.

Competitive product evaluations.

General economic conditions and trends.

Manufacturing

Long-range goals and short-range objectives of the manufacturing activity.

Manufacturing capacity, programs, and production schedules.

Physical characteristics of existing facilities and technological status.

Inventory investments and inventory turnover.

Economic lot sizes of items purchased and/or manufactured.

Obsolescence of inventories.

Material usage and variance analyses.

Employee efficiency data.

Scrap and rework costs.

Maintenance problems and costs.

Quality control data.

Space and equipment utilization.

Purchasing budgets.

Purchase price variances.

Evaluation of vendors.

Make or buy study results.

Savings achieved by buyers.

Logistics of plant engineering and improvements in plant machinery.

Product costs and direct labor productivity.

Manufacturing departments' expense budgets.

Capital expenditure programs.

Cost reduction results.

Impending problems.

Research and Development

Research goals and opportunities.

Research proposals for product improvements, new products, new processes.

Research projects: accomplishments, technical status, costs, time status.

Research personnel: qualifications and experience.

Research costs as a percentage of sales.

Research accomplishments.

Employee Relations

Employee turnover, age, distributions, skills.

Employee requirements, availability and shortages.

Lost time, accidents.

Absenteeism.

Wage and salary administration reports.

Overtime costs.

Employee opinion reports, morale and attitudes.

Employee appraisals.

Union grievances, status of labor negotiations.

Data sources other than the parties' records are also researched for relevant information. Data in the financial press, comments and reports of security analysts, speeches by company executives to the financial community, and comments by bankers and loan officers are useful sources of information. External information can also provide data on the overall economic environment and the specific economic trends and conditions having a direct impact upon the parties. Trends in the specific marketplace may be important and may indicate the actions and preferences of customers, activities of competitors, and the results of new product developments. Attention should be directed toward identifying the key success factors of the parties, as such factors can vary by industry and by company. For example, in the automobile industry, the success factors revolve around styling, the effectiveness of the dealer organization, and manufacturing cost control. In the food processing industry, new product developments, good distribution, and effective advertising are of great significance. In the life insurance field, the development of agency management personnel, the control of clerical costs, and innovations in types of policies issued are critical factors. In antitrust proceedings, knowledge of the key success factors of the plaintiff may enable the defendant to demonstrate that failures in these areas were the proximate cause of the injury suffered by the plaintiff rather than the alleged actions of the defendants.

HOW COMPUTERS ARE USED TO MANAGE A LITIGATION DATA BASE

As soon as practical, a decision must also be made by the trial attorney on how information is to be managed. Modern litigation has created a problem in the handling, storage, and retrieving of information in complex cases. Complex litigation can generate a large volume of paperwork because of the multiplicity and changing natures of the issues, the approach to discovery which calls for the accumulation of massive amounts of records, and the inherent growth in the size and complexity of business records. The manpower and time necessary to review, analyze, and construct a strategy from this large base of documents have become so large as to make this a major problem in the preparation and management of modern litigation.

This problem of information management has forced many trial attorneys to turn from the previous methods of using homemade notebooks or card systems to the use of the computer to solve the problem. The computerization of a file, however, does nothing more than can be done manually. Computers have vast capacity for absorbing, holding, manipulating, and reproducing information. Computers do what lawyers do manually—receive the evidence, sort it, classify it, find its common denominator, match it, index it, remember it, state conclusions from it, and reproduce everything from it on demand. But computers can hold vast amounts of information and can digest it and come up with required answers much more quickly than a manually operated system can.

By far the greatest expense of an information management system in complex litigation is the cost of the people needed to screen documents, to identify the relevant ones, and then to prepare them for access, either by putting them into a filing system or by preparing coded indices. If one were to rely on people instead of computers to manage the information in a complex case, there would be a constant problem of keeping enough people who are knowledgeable about the case and intelligent enough to be of help. Large clerical projects using skilled people often have high turnover rates because of inadequate pay and the dull nature of the work. One advantage of the computers is that they do not have morale problems. The use of computers adds a small cost at the start of the litigation which is recouped over time by decreasing the cost of retrieving information. The trial attorney must, however, identify what information will be needed during pretrial and trial and ensure that the lure of the computer does not lead to loading into the retrieval system volumes of marginally useful material.

While one can envision an exciting use of a computerized data base during trial by producing the key document which will impeach an important witness, the greatest use for a computerized information system is during the pretrial phases of litigation. It is in the taking of depositions and in answering interrogatories that this type of information system will usually be most useful. The computer offers instant retrieval with a minimum likelihood of error, and permits a retrieval based upon an almost infinite combination of criteria impossible under a manual system. Furthermore, documents may be searched under names or terms, or combinations of them, which may not have been deemed significant at the time the data base was created. Thus, the sooner one can establish a working system the greater the benefit.

There are two basic techniques by which a computer can manage information. In the *index* method, the computer can be programmed to store and manipulate some form of manually prepared index or digest of the data—presumably sufficiently extensive to permit identification of all the documents in the file on a particular subject, as well as the characteristics and contents of these documents. Second, the computer can store the entirety of the basic documents themselves, and be programmed to permit research and retrieval on the basis of the words appearing in them. The second approach is called *full text* and is usually the more powerful analytical tool of the two, as every word of the document can serve as an index for the identification of relevant documents. Its disadvantage, however, includes the time and cost in putting the entire text into the computer. In addition, although the documents may be prescreened to determine their relevance, there is no paring down, abstracting, or keywording of the text, and the searcher may find that the use of ordinary words as indices will turn up a number of useless documents.

It is also possible to have a combination of the full-text and index methods by accompanying the entry of the text with key words for more precise reference. This has the advantages of both methods, but, since it requires both prior evaluation of the contents of documents and the entry of the entire text, it can be expensive.

Once material has been converted to a computer data base, two forms of output are available to the searcher—computer indexes and computer search and retrieval. For a full-text data base, a computer index may take the form of a traditional keyword-in-context index, in which all words in the data base are cited except for user-defined common words. The indexes include the context in which words were actually used and a citation to the original source material. In the case of material coded on forms, computer indexes may address a particular field on the form, citing for each unique entry in the field the information found on the coding form on which the field and entry appear. Computer indexes are both cost-effective and relatively easy to introduce compared to alternative methods of processing because of their similarity to traditional hard-copy indexes.

As the volume of material increases, computer indexes frequently give way to computer search and retrieval systems. Access to the computer data base is usually on a real-time basis, and instead of asking for total access to a defined body of material in a single output, users request more specific information from a system; that is, instead of requesting an alphabetical index to all authors, the searcher might ask the computer to locate and retrieve all material authored by a specific individual. More specific inquiry is also possible; for example, the computer may be asked to locate all material authored by a specific individual between certain dates and dealing with a specific issue. These location and comparison tasks are accomplished by the computer through the And and OR (Boolean) logic available in most systems.

A number of vendors have developed sophisticated, generalized data manipulation and retrieval systems which are now on the market. These vendors have experience and they have learned most of the difficult lessons about cost control and performance of computerized information management systems used in litigation. Consultants are available to assist trial attorneys in selecting the system most suitable to their needs.

HOW COMPUTERS ARE USED IN LEGAL RESEARCH

Computers are used not only for the filing, sorting, storing, and retrieving of evidentiary materials, but also to keep track of time spent by the legal staff on cases, for bookkeeping functions, docket control, and legal research. More than two dozen firms offer information management systems and litigation research, and most litigation of even moderate proportions now involves the use of the computer by one or both parties. The Lexis system offered by Mead Data Control, Inc., of New York, and the Westlaw system offered by West Publishing Company of St. Paul, Minnesota are used by many attorneys for litigation research.

Digital computers are used in litigation research to search through large collections of legal documents for those containing words, phrases, and numbers specified by the researcher. A researcher can retrieve, for example, all cases containing the word *discoverable,* the phrase *offer of proof,* or the numeric expression *809 US 80.* A researcher can quickly assemble cases in which the opinion is authored by a particular judge by searching for all cases having the judge's name. The researcher sits at a special terminal in his office and searches through legal documents stored in a central computer. The special terminal includes a keyboard similar to that of a typewriter, a display device similar to a small television set, a printer, and a special telephone. The researcher places the system in operation by dialing a special telephone number, and the computer responds, by typing a special identification number on the keyboard. This number identifies the researcher for billing purposes and prevents unauthorized access to the central computer. If a user is interrupted, a sign-off key is pressed and the work done may be stored until the time research is continued. A number of options are available to users, including one where as many as 30 attorneys may join in an agreement to share the use of a terminal. Costs of the services are separately maintained and separately billed. The consortium of users shares the installation costs and the monthly charges for equipment and communication.

Available legal materials are organized into "libraries," and the user can obtain the names of the libraries on the video screen. By transmitting the name of the library one wishes to search, the user has available all the materials stored on the computer files for that selected library. A user may select a new library by pressing the change-file or change-library key. Following are the materials presently compiled into libraries.

1. A general federal library consisting of all reported decisions of the Supreme Court of the United States from 1938 to the present, the Courts of Appeal from 1945 to the present, the District Courts from 1960 to the present, and the United States Code.

2. A federal tax library consisting of: the Internal Revenue Code and Regulations, the Cumulative Bulletin since 1954, all tax decisions from the federal courts from various dates differing from court to court complete to the present, and legislative history materials related to the 1954 Code and subsequent tax legislation.

3. A federal securities library, consisting of the relevant statutes and regulations, cases, and no-action letters.

4. A federal trade regulation library, consisting of federal court cases and Federal Trade Commission decisions.

5. Libraries of the statutory and case law of Arizona, California, Florida, Illinois, Kansas, Kentucky, Massachusetts, Michigan, Missouri, New Jersey, New York, Ohio, Pennsylvania, Texas, and Virginia.

When decisions are handed down that substantially change the law, the relevant library files are updated so that the latest cases are available.

An example of a computerized litigation research effort follows: An expert accounting witness is subpoenaed by the opposing attorney to turn over working papers developed during an investigation of antitrust charges asserted against the attorney's client. The expert witness wishes to know from the employing attorneys whether this information is privileged.

The witness's employing attorney will dial the computer on the data phone at the terminal, using an identity number to show authorization as a user. The attorney will then instruct the computer to perform a search of the files on recent antitrust cases on issues involving privileges of expert witnesses and confidentiality of working papers. The search may be organized as "Expert Witness, Confidentiality, W/10 Privilege*." This commands the computer to search for cases in which the words *expert witness,* or *confidentiality* appear within 10 words of the word *privilege.* The computer will then list within seconds the recent cases which meet these specifications. If the user wishes to further restrict this listing, the additional command "And Accountant" may be given. This tells the computer to select from the computer listing the cases mentioning accountants. The user may then command the computer to print the selected cases on the terminal screen, and may read the printout of the cases or note the citations and read the summaries of the cases listed. The final step is to command the computer to search for all references to the selected cases to see if they have remained valid law or have been modified by subsequent decision.

It is generally believed that computer-assisted research is faster than conventional methods. Browsing through materials selectively displayed on a screen is much faster than searching for the required books, taking them down from the shelves, and reading the printed page. Computer-assisted research improves on the certainty, accuracy, and thoroughness of legal research. A full-text, interactive system will usually locate cases or other materials entirely pertinent to the problem that will not be cited in any index or digest. Doing research with computer assistance frees the lawyer from the inherent limitations on all indexing, as there is no need to tailor one's thinking and research to the logic and judgment of the indexes. Search specifications are tailored to one's own research problems, and the computer follows the exact instructions and searches directly in the texts of the legal materials themselves. The search covers not merely an edited version of the materials and cases but the full text, free of summarizations, omissions, or abridgements, and including dicta, footnotes, or whatever else the materials may contain. The lawyer who wishes to retrieve cases which are directly comparable to the one being managed can establish very narrow specifications for the search, or generalized specifications for a broader search, in which much more reference material will be made available.

In 1971, the National Center for Automated Information Retrieval, a national organization of lawyers and certified public accountants, was formed to encourage the development and implementation of computer-assisted legal research. Members of this organization have contributed to the work of identifying and defining the kind of legal materials that should be made accessible by computer and have sponsored meetings of lawyers and judges to advise them about its activities and to hear their views about what should be done in the area of computer-assisted legal research.

THE DISCOVERABILITY OF WORKING PAPERS

The expert accounting witness is usually employed by the trial attorney and communicates with the litigant through counsel. While the rules on discoverability are not completely settled, in most instances, federal judges seem to be increasingly lenient in allowing discovery. To maintain some confidentiality, trial attorneys will classify reports to them from expert witnesses as "attorney work products" and argue that such reports are used in devising litigation strategy or in revising previous approaches, and as such are not subject to review by their opponents. Trial attorneys will usually accommodate each other on this point, particularly where each side uses expert witnesses and both face the same problems of disclosing present or previous strategic positions and the detailed analyses made prior to arriving at these positions.

The expert accountant may use working papers to refresh his memory during direct testimony or when responding to cross-examination. Any papers taken to the witness stand may be examined and used by opposing counsel. When the accountant is testifying to results prepared through the use of computer facilities, the overall computer flow diagrams, memory layouts, and descriptions of computer systems are subject to discovery. It is doubtful that an opponent could compel the delivery of the detailed coded computer program so that the opponent could avoid the effort of developing an equally useful computer system for the manipulation of its own data or the recasting of its opponent's data.

Working papers prepared by the expert accountant are subject to discovery and cannot be classified as "attorney work products." Working papers are discovered through the use of a *subpoena duces tecum*, which calls for the production of all papers, notes, articles, and writings of the expert witness as applied to the case being tried. The timing of the *subpoena duces tecum* is usually agreed upon between opposing counsel. As a subpoena of working papers should be expected, it is incumbent upon the expert accountant to insure that no extraneous material is contained in the working papers and that only information which is developed during the study to support the conclusions reached is included. Materials descriptive of studies which were made but were not used as being irrelevant to the strategy decided upon, or were discarded after more useful information had been attained should be destroyed. Data descriptive of erroneous concepts, incorrect analyses, or revised positions should be excluded so as to avoid unnecessary examination or embarrassment when explanations are asked of such studies. It is too late to destroy any working papers, no matter how incorrect or embarrassing, after the summons has been served. The expert witness should review and receive approval from counsel concerning the working papers to be submitted prior to complying with the subpoena. Any questions relative to compliance with the subpoena should be also resolved with counsel.

The rules of discovery of working papers limit the freedom of action of expert witnesses in the use of such papers. Witnesses will be required to rely upon memory while testifying if they do not wish to disclose to the opposing side the contents of written reference material used. Written communications with the attorneys, unless they are classified as "attorney work products," are discoverable by the opposition and it is important to discuss with counsel what should be in written form and when such writings should be prepared. Strategic trial decisions may require that certain communications be oral rather than in written form, or that studies be postponed, or that the delivery of a report be purposely delayed to prevent premature disclosure to the opposition. Errors or omissions in working papers are particularly significant, as they provide an excellent opportunity to discredit or embarrass the witness during cross-examination. Poorly organized working papers can be used by opposing counsel to demonstrate the ineptness of a witness, who may fumble through the working papers to recall requested information.

CHAPTER

6

Preparing and Presenting Direct Testimony

Expert accounting testimony is valuable only when it clearly and factually presents and explains the pertinent financial and accounting issues in a manner understandable to the judge and jury. The testimony must be consistent with the trial strategies outlined in the trial brief and with the testimony presented during depositions. The expert must be able to explain and defend his opinions in language comprehended by the layman, and it should be remembered that the expert is testifying on subject matter that is beyond the common knowledge and experience of the judge and jury. An expert is, therefore, charged with the responsibility of educating the audience concerning one's specialty as it applies to the case being tried. Education is a difficult process.

The essence of the process of preparing testimony is to foresee all possible problems, to bring them to the attention of counsel, and to prepare in such a manner as to approach the act of testifying with confidence that you are possessed of all the relevant facts and have reached conclusions that are completely defensible. Preparing to testify starts with the acceptance of the assignment as expert accounting witness.

One of the most important and often ignored steps in preparing to testify is acquiring knowledge of the substantive issues. Unless you are aware of the substantive issues, your investigation and subsequent conclusions may be incomplete and unrelated to the issues. It is also necessary to know the issues of the case so that you can anticipate and defend your position on cross-examination, avoiding answers that are incomplete, confusing, and irrelevant. It is necessary to read the complaint and the answer, and to review the attorneys' general legal strategy prior to beginning an investigation of the facts which will form the basis for the expert testimony.

The expert must have knowledge of all facts relevant to the subject matter. As previously stated, the fact that expert witness opinion was not founded on all the facts affects the weight given the evidence, not its competency or materiality. Failure to consider all the facts not only diminishes the value of an expert's opinion, but quite often leaves one vulnerable to attack on cross-examination. The expert can become surprised and confused by the additional facts, and the expert's image is also diminished in the minds of the judge and jury.

Albert Einstein once commented that "imagination is more important than knowledge." Nowhere is this more true than when the expert is seeking information in the office of the opposing party. In these circumstances, as Einstein observed, imagination may be initially more important than the information itself, since without imagination it is unlikely that an expert will discover all of the accounting evidence needed or available.

HOW TO PREPARE ACCOUNTING TESTIMONY

The discovery phase of the judicial process is characterized by a painstaking effort to obtain all relevant documents, records, and reports of the opponent concerning the issues to be tried. These documents must be rigorously analyzed from the various perspectives of all the expert witnesses. In the liability phase of the trial, financial and accounting information may be used by the plaintiff to demonstrate that an injury was suffered as a result of the alleged illegal actions of the defendant. The defendant may attempt to demonstrate through financial and accounting data that such injury was the result of management plans and activities or economic conditions not associated with any of its actions. In the damages phase of the trial, extensive use is usually made of accounting data by the plaintiff to demonstrate what profits would have accrued, but for the alleged illegal actions of the defendant, whereas the defendant will also use accounting data to refute these allegations.

Much of the information developed by the expert accountant will be in the form of accounting exhibits prepared for the court and the attorneys. These exhibits are not audit reports of the expert accounting witness, but are the results of accounting analyses of data made available to the witness and presented to the court in the most illustrative format possible. As such, the expert accounting witness makes no representation of the accuracy of the accounting data contained therein other than that such data were correctly copied from the books and records of the parties involved. In the analysis of such data and in the preparation of accounting reports used as testimony, the expert must comply with accepted accounting principles, methods, and techniques. Otherwise this testimony can be attacked and seriously damaged. The purpose of accounting reports used in testimony is to impart knowledge with the expectation that such knowledge will inform the decision makers of the concepts presented by the expert accounting witness. In this projection of information and attitudes, the expectation is that the recipients not only will understand the testimony, but will arrive at the conclusions articulated by the witness. As such, the accounting reports have motivational impact. In imparting information to the judge and/or jury and in attempting to motivate them, it is essential that the rules for effective communication be observed within the legal framework for presenting evidence in a court of law.

In preparing accounting evidence as testimony, it is necessary to observe a number of basic rules of communication. Perhaps the most important consideration is to use terminology which the judge and jury understand. Accounting is a technical discipline, and as such includes jargon which has significance only to an accountant. As the judge rarely has extensive experience in accounting, and the jury may have none, technical accounting language must be avoided and language understandable to the audience must be used. Within this framework, the witness has many options in presenting data. If data are more easily understood when presented as graphs or as operating statistics, these formats should be used rather than presenting financial data in the columnar form so typical of many accounting reports.

One should avoid using too much information, for this only confuses and conceals the points to be made. Frequently, there are not only too many conflicting, duplicating, or unnecessary reports used as evidence, but too many analyses and too much detail, as well. This usually leads to superficial understanding of the testimony and consequently, much frustration and wasted effort.

However, essential information which highlights the basic issues being tried and has a major bearing on the outcome of the trial must be included in the accounting testimony. Frequently, effective accounting testimony cannot be limited to a recitation of costs or other performance criteria that can be expressed quantitatively or included in the accounting system. Qualitative data, such as appearance of competitive products, reputation for service of competitors, strength of competitive dealer organizations, preferences of customers, customer complaints or suggestions, and so forth, can be as important to the outcome of the case as quantified accounting data.

Experts should differentiate information needed for different purposes and should not expect reports to serve multiple purposes. The accounting reports used in testifying must be accurate, logical, and clear. Unless information given can accurately describe an event or situation, expert witnesses subject themselves to loss of credibility during cross-examination.

From the Plaintiff's Perspective

In preparing accounting testimony as expert witness for the plaintiff, the information developed will usually be based upon the books and records of the plaintiff. In this endeavor, the expert accounting witness operates within a friendly environment. Accounting methods and procedures will be explained by financial executives of the plaintiff, the cost accounting records will be produced and described, and financial plans, budgets, and forecasts will be provided, where available. The major role for accounting testimony will be designing and explaining the accounting model used in the quantification of the alleged injury suffered.

Quantification models describing the alleged injuries can vary in complexity, depending upon the issues presented, the magnitude of operations involved, the state of the financial and accounting records made available, and the quantity of records to be researched and analyzed. The usual approach to the quantification of the alleged injury is the establishment of what the financial position of the plaintiff would have been but for the alleged illegal acts of the defendant, and a comparison of the but for position with the actual financial position of the plaintiff to establish the difference as a measure of damages.

The plaintiff has available a number of accounting and mathematical techniques which can be used to establish the but for position. Usually, the simplest approach focuses upon the use of accounting measurements. Any financial forecasts of profits that were prepared prior to the alleged injury can be used to demonstrate what the profits would have been, but for the alleged injuries caused by the defendant. These forecasts, when compared with actual results which reflect the alleged actions of the defendant, can be used to demonstrate the loss caused by the defendant. Also, simple comparisons can be made between financial returns for periods prior to the injury and those of the period of injury, and the differences can be used to estimate damages. In other circumstances, where lost sales can be demonstrated as a result of the alleged injury, damages may be computed as a function of the profit attributed to the lost sales plus the amount of fixed costs normally attributed to such sales. In these circumstances, the expert must be able to prove that the method used to establish fixed costs attributed to lost sales is reasonable.

There are a number of mathematical techniques which the expert accounting witness can use to quantify damages, such as the following.

1. **Model building** The development of a mathematical representation of the business area being investigated which can be subjected to mathematical investigation and manipulation. Thus, if the mathematical model can portray the situation that actually occurred, variables can be inserted into the mathematical model representative of what the situation would have been but for the alleged injury by the defendant. The mathematical model can be used to establish the profit or income that would have been received but for the actions of the defendants.

2. **Simulation** A mathematical technique by which the real problem is replaced by a theoretical counterpart. A probability distribution is assigned to the theoretical counterpart equivalent to the existing situation before the injury. What would have happened but for the alleged actions of the defendant can be anticipated by drawing a sample of these events from the probability distribution by means of a random number table. By mathematical manipulation of these variables, an estimate of the profit or income that would have accrued can be made.

3. **Discriminant analysis** The use of mathematical procedures to measure the relative importance of characteristics deemed to have been impacted by the actions of the defendant.

4. **Linear programming** The development of mathematical expressions dealing with the interaction of many variables which are subject to certain restraining conditions initially expressed as inequalities. Iterative techniques are used to solve these mathematical expressions. Variables that identify the alleged illegal actions of the defendant can be changed to demonstrate the impact of such actions.

5. **Statistical sampling** A means of obtaining information about a population which is too large for each member to be individually treated; inferences about the characteristics of the overall population can be drawn from a properly chosen representative sample.

In complex antitrust actions statistical sampling is frequently the only practical approach to the analysis of the large volumes of transaction data.

6. **Curve fitting**   A method of fitting an algebraic function to the observed relationship between two or more variable quantities in order to represent the relationship graphically or analytically. The results are useful for estimating quantitative changes in the dependent variables which can be associated with the alleged illegal actions of the defendant.

7. **Dynamic programming**   An extension of linear programming used for developing an optimal overall estimation when the interactions among the individual optimal component policies affected by the alleged illegal actions of the defendants were such that they yielded a less than optimal overall result.

8. **Bidding strategy and the theory of games**   A theory and technique useful in competitive situations in which the effectiveness of decisions made by one party is dependent upon the decisions made by another party. The method consists of using historical data or predicted actions of an opponent, in addition to one's own past experience, to arrive at decisions which will maximize total expected results. Where sales practices and techniques were changed to meet the alleged illegal sales practices of the defendants, the impact of such changes can be measured by use of these techniques and a basis for damage claims can be established.

Fortunately, most computer service bureaus offer to their clients packaged mathematical programs to perform the sizeable number of computations required to accomplish these mathematical procedures. An expert witness making use of such programs should be in a position to explain the mathematical theories and calculations used in the computer programs where such programs are incorporated in the testimony.

In presenting testimony based upon the use of mathematical models, it should be remembered that a mathematical model is necessarily a simplification of reality and is a process of abstraction and simplification. All attributes of the actual phenomenon are rarely included in a model, for it would become too unwieldy. Instead, judgments are made about which of many possible details are most relevant and attempts are made to capture them through an appropriate formulation of premises and definitions. This process of selection suggests that at least two preliminary considerations must be kept in mind when evaluating the appropriateness of a particular model: the precise purpose for which it is intended, and the decision maker for whose use it was formulated. However, the simplification inherent in the formal model is also the source of its power and utility, as it will often lead to insights that would otherwise be obscured and overwhelmed by the complexity of the data.

Technical mathematical models have been accepted by the court as evidence in estimating damages. While the burden of proof falls upon the plaintiff in proving the amount of damages, the court does not require a precise estimate, but will accept a reasonable computation on the grounds that a plaintiff, after being injured by a defendant, should not be denied recovery because conditions caused by the defendant prevent a precise estimate of damages. However, the more easily understood the damage model is, the greater the likelihood the court will accept this mathematical model as a reasonable estimate of damages.

In preparing evidence for direct testimony, the expert witness should strive for brevity, simplicity, and clarity in presentation. For example, in attempting to quantify the amount of sales volume lost at a soft drink plant through an illegal 19-day stoppage of work during August, the expert analyzed sales statistics and other available data for a period of years using multiple regression techniques. These analyses demonstrated that population growth, proportion of teenagers in the population, type of residents, and weather influenced changes in sales volume. When adjustments were made for long-term trends in population growth and characteristics of the population, it was found that more than 90 percent of the monthly changes in soft drink sales were associated with variations in the monthly highs of temperature. This is demonstrated in graphic form in Exhibit 3, which compares the number of cases of soft drinks sold in each month with the average high temperature for that month.

By concluding that during a short-term period, temperature was a major determinant of sales, and by presenting evidence that during the month of August, when the alleged illegal stoppage occurred, the average high of the daily temperatures was 80 degrees, the expert witness concluded that, but for the alleged illegal work stoppage, 93,000 cases of soft drinks would have been sold. Lost sales volume was estimated as the difference between the estimated volume of sales (93,000 cases) and the actual volume of sales (31,000 cases).

From the Defendant's Perspective

Preparation of expert accounting testimony for the defendant is a burdensome and complex undertaking, for many of the facts demon-

Exhibit 3.   Effect of Temperature on Sales.

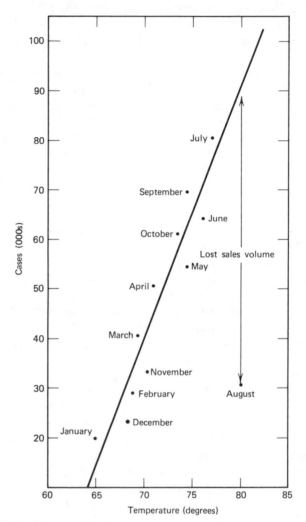

strating proximate cause and the extent of the damages suffered are included in the records of the plaintiff. If the plaintiff is in bankruptcy as an alleged result of the behavior of the defendant, the plaintiff's records can be in a state of disarray. Under these circumstances, considerable thought must be given to the organization of the approach toward the analysis of available records, the synthesis of missing information from fragments that can be located in the available records, and the interpretation and presentation of these data. Where discovery of accounting information occurs in the office of the plaintiff, a presumably hostile environment, extreme tact and a well organized plan for accumulating the needed information is essential.

The major function of the defendant's expert accounting witness is to refute the financial and accounting claims of the plaintiff and, if desired by counsel, to develop alternate and more favorable damage estimates. Thus, the defendant expert should become thoroughly familiar with the issues involved and with the financial and accounting theories and proposed testimony of the plaintiff. To accomplish this, the defendant expert witness should not only study the proposed financial testimony of the plaintiff, but should also become familiar with the financial and accounting records, methods, and procedures of the opposing party.

Recently published annual financial reports present not only significant financial and accounting data about the company as a whole, but also describe the major products and significant operating divisions or organizational entities of the company. Comparative accounting data for periods up to 10 years are usually included. The letter to the stockholders from the chief executive officer describes the results of operations for the year, compares these results with budgets and operating plans, and discusses reasons for attaining or failing to attain business objectives. Frequently, these comments, written prior to the institution of the lawsuit, contain statements of reasons for success or failure to attain business plans and objectives which are quite different from those asserted in the lawsuit upon which damage claims are based. Such data may provide a basis for challenging the financial and accounting theories of the plaintiff or may provide a direction for investigation of the assertions of the plaintiff.

Long-range and short-range profit plans of the plaintiff provide useful background information about how the plaintiff intended to manage company operations during the period in dispute. Such reports may include information useful in challenging the plaintiff's assertions that the defendant's alleged illegal acts were the sole cause of the failure of the plaintiff to attain planned results.

In many cases, damage claims demand reimbursement for additional costs incurred by the plaintiff because of the alleged illegal acts of the defendant. To understand such claims, it is frequently necessary to understand clearly the general and cost accounting systems of the plaintiff. While answers to interrogatories and deposition questions will provide some information about them, copies of the accounting and cost accounting manuals can provide clearer perspectives on these procedures. To avoid confusion and misunderstanding in interpreting the accounting information made available, not only are current accounting manuals required, but where changes in accounting procedures have been made, the accounting manuals for the entire damage period must also be obtained.

The monthly financial reports to management generally present the results of operations, highlight the major activities of the period, and explain significant deviations from plans and budgets. These reports are usually structured to present, first, the broad company-wide perspectives, then the financial results by divisions, and finally the detailed operating results of each department. Much of the accounting analyses made to support or challenge damage claims are prepared from accounting information developed at the departmental level of operations. At the departmental level, the available accounting information should include: departmental income and expense items compared with planning and control data; the status of departmental capital expenditures and operating programs; key production, sales, or operating statistics; cost accounting reports and summaries; labor distribution and efficiency reports; various expense summaries and analyses; planning and forecast data; and technical reports.

In addition to researching plaintiff's records, external sources of information about the plaintiff should be investigated. The financial press, speeches by company executives before financial groups, reports of security analysts or commentary by loan officers may portray the problems of the plaintiff in a manner different from the allegations in the complaint and may provide bases for direct testimony of the defendant expert accounting witness which contradicts the assertions of the plaintiff.

All of the accounting methods, procedures, techniques, and mathematical methods useful in the analyses of data that are available to the plaintiff's expert accounting witness in preparing direct testimony can also be used by the defendant's expert accountant. The defendant also has available the use of the facilities of computer service bureaus. Brevity, simplicity, and clarity of presentation of the evidence are as important to the defendant expert accountant as to the plaintiff's expert witness.

From the Perspectives of Both Parties

Litigation frequently arises when, because of the alleged illegal conduct of the defendant, the plaintiff claims to have been unable to manufacture and sell quantities of certain products which were to be introduced into the market. Where the manufacture of such products requires complex manufacturing processes and the use of extensive marketing and distribution operations, and where such products have not previously been sold by the plaintiff, the development of accounting testimony to support or to challenge the damage assertions of the plaintiff presents formidable problems to the expert accounting witnesses for both parties. Existing accounting records will be of limited value to the accountants in estimating lost revenues and expected costs of production, distribution, and administration. In such circumstances, recourse will usually be made to any available sales forecasts, production plans, marketing and distribution concepts in an attempt to estimate what revenues would have been realized and what costs would have been incurred, but for the alleged illegal acts of the defendant.

In a recent case of this nature, the plaintiff instigated litigation on the grounds that it had been precluded from manufacturing and selling newly designed computer systems because of the alleged anticompetitive acts of the defendant. In planning to build and market the computer equipment and to determine the economic feasibility of undertaking this venture, the plaintiff had prepared a 10-year sales forecast and used this forecast as a basis for estimating lost revenues on lost sales. Material requirements had been defined and manufacturing routing sheets had been prepared describing in some detail the manufacturing processes and labor hours required to manufacture the computer equipment. Hourly labor rates and anticipated inflation in these rates for the 10-year period had also been estimated. The plaintiff decided that sufficient plant and equipment capacities already existed to manufacture the forecasted quantities of computer equipment and as a result, only variable overhead would be incurred. Variable overhead costs were estimated on the basis of existing variable overhead rates for the manufacturing departments involved in the manufacture of the proposed computer equipment. Warehousing needs for the distribution of computer equipment throughout the United States were identified and manpower costs for all selling and distribution activities were estimated. It was determined that very little additional administrative costs, which were considered to be fixed in nature, would be incurred for the manufacture and sale of the proposed computer equipment.

On the basis of information of this nature, the plaintiff expert accounting witness developed for damage claim purposes an estimate of the lost profits on lost sales of computer equipment. Such computations, while arithmetically accurate, were admittedly imprecise estimates of lost profits on lost sales, but it was asserted that the results were reasonable estimates of loss for damage claim purposes.

During discovery, the expert accountant for the defendant obtained copies of the sales forecasts, product designs, manufacturing routing sheets, labor standards and hourly rates, variable overhead analyses, and the selling and distribution cost studies. As previously noted, no accounting or cost accounting records dealing with the manufacture of computer equipment by the plaintiff were available, as operations had not commenced. Oral explanations of the documents by plaintiff's representatives while complying with discovery requirements were disjointed and incomplete.

To obtain some understanding of computer manufacturing and marketing functions, it was necessary for the defendant expert accountant to study these activities and the accounting methods used at the premises of other computer manufacturers. The documents received from the plaintiff were then examined in detail. The accuracy of the plaintiff in forecasting sales was tested by reviewing its past sales forecasts for products which had been manufactured and sold. Estimates of available financial resources of the plaintiff were established and compared with the financial investments required to manufacture and sell the quantities of computer equipment estimated in the sales forecasts. Reasonable doubts were established that the plaintiff had the financial or personnel resources needed for the proposed program, and studies were prepared to demonstrate that the plaintiff had no reasonable expectation of acquiring these resources in the near future. The details of the estimated costs to manufacture the computer equipment as prepared by the plaintiff were studied and compared with costs of other manufacturers of similar computer equipment. The use of variable manufacturing costs only was challenged on the basis that the plaintiff did not appear to have sufficient manufacturing and distribution facilities available to handle the production and sales of the quantities of computer equipment included in the sales forecast. These challenges served to reduce the damage claim substantially.

Upon the completion of damage studies, the expert accountants for both the plaintiff and the defendant usually prepare detailed reports for the trial attorneys describing their findings and the type of testimony they feel qualified to present. These reports are carefully studied by the trial attorneys and read by the expert witnesses of other disciplines where the case is sufficiently complex to require a multidisciplinary team of expert witnesses. Meetings of expert witnesses are held to determine how the proposed accounting testimony coordinates with the proposed testimony of the other expert witnesses. Such meetings offer the members of each discipline an opportunity to hear, challenge, debate, and revise where necessary, the proposed testimony so that a clever opponent is not given the opportunity to contradict the testimony of one expert through the statements of another expert who is testifying on behalf of the same party. Such meetings also allow the interdisciplinary analysis of problems, the focusing of different perspectives on similar problems, learning experiences for all participants and opportunities for trial attorneys to gain a broad understanding of the technical business issues involved in the trial. Frequently, new ideas for research are generated by the discussions and lead to studies and greater depth of analysis of the problems.

These meetings, which focus the minds of trial attorneys and expert witnesses on imaginative problem solving, also furnish the expert accounting witnesses with a sounding board to evaluate the soundness of their proposed testimony and forewarn them of possible future challenges to their testimony by the opponents. They can determine how to respond to the issues and develop a coordinated approach for testimony. If the meetings are periodically organized as brainstorming sessions to further stimulate the creative talents of the expert witnesses, such techniques can improve communications among the expert witnesses and broaden the outlook of each member of the interdisciplinary team.

HOW COMPUTERS CAN BE USED TO DEVELOP DIRECT TESTIMONY

Computer analysis encompasses a broad range of techniques that can be applied by both plaintiffs and defendants to virtually any kind of case, for both liability and damage issues. When used as an analytical tool, computer techniques can be applied to demonstrate quantitatively the merits of a party's position on a litigated substantive issue. Also, where the issues involve the manipulation of huge quantities of numerical data, various types of analyses and but for or what if types of conditions can be applied to the data to restructure the evidence or premises of the plaintiff or defendant. When changes are made to these conditions, new tabulations can be readily produced by the computer to demonstrate the impact of the changes in assumptions.

In price fixing cases, the computer has been used to uncover facts dealing with liability issues. Computer analyses involving comparisons of prices over time, and from one geographic market to another have addressed the questions of parallel behavior over time and whether conditions in one geographic market (alleged to be anticompetitive) produced anticompetitive prices in other geographic markets not having that condition. Price comparisons from market to market can be used to develop evidence of predatory pricing. Where one competitor in a multibrand market alleged predatory pricing on selective brands in selective geographic markets, the computer was useful in analyzing, tabulating, and displaying data. Direct competition, market domination, and effective competition through alternative products are issues that can be demonstrated and presented quantitatively. An infinite variety of quantitative analyses can be undertaken to support or refute power over prices and power over market entry.

Quantitative analyses help to evaluate the available evidence objectively. Computer capability is valuable in tracing the ultimate impact of many interrelated events and conditions where manual calculation of such issues would be inefficient, even if theoretically possible. The computer can assist the witness who employs scientific approaches to uncover underlying relationships. Transaction patterns can be examined to test for the presence of systematic bidding, and historical prices can be reviewed to determine whether price behavior deviated from normally expected relationships. Other computer techniques examine the behavior of market participants in light of their historical behavior to identify whether there are any abrupt, sudden, or suspicious changes. Simulation models can be developed to test many different assumptions when forecasting earnings and cash flows under alternative operating and financing plans.

Damage calculations frequently provide opportunities for effective use of computer analysis. When huge volumes of financial data must be organized, analyzed, compared, and tested under varying assumptions, computers can perform these functions quickly. One situation may involve forecasting, interpolating, and projecting revenues from partial information under changing premises. Another kind of damage analysis might require the assessment of damages to a plaintiff who has been put out of business by the actions of an alleged monopolist. Here, the existence of hard data will be spotty, and revenue forecasts, expense estimates, relationships and profit projections will be less certain. In such instances, it is necessary to examine the effects under several scenarios and assumptions, an examination that would be significantly hampered without some form of computer-based model to process the various possibilities. Computer simulation models specifically designed to process various inputs systematically offer a cost-effective and worthwhile approach to producing such damage estimates.

HOW TO PRESENT ACCOUNTING TESTIMONY

In presenting direct testimony, expert accounting witnesses have a difficult job. They must exercise all of their professional judgment and skill to maintain an unbiased and fair presentation of the accounting facts. The concept of fairness should be a guiding principle, and expert accounting witnesses must make a conscious effort to remain objective in their evaluations of information and in their presentations of testimony. Counsel and the expert should discuss the substance of the expert's testimony under simulated trial conditions, including mock cross-examination. The experts and the attorneys will then be better prepared for trial, and the experts will have the further opportunity to consider the validity of their opinions and their ability to articulate the facts and premises upon which they rely.

Direct testimony, whether given at deposition hearings or in the courtroom, is communicated through responses to questions of counsel. For oral testimony to be effective, it is as important to understand how information will be received and acted on by the judge and jury as it is to know what information to present. It is the human reaction to the testimony that determines what action will be taken on the information imparted. Since action is the product of human behavior, all that is known about human behavior should be employed in exercising the art of communicating accounting data through direct testimony.

Accounting testimony will frequently be presented as exhibits in the form of financial statements, cost accounting analyses, graphs, charts, and accounting schedules. Copies of these exhibits are provided to the judge and jury, as well as to opposing counsel, so that they may more closely follow and more easily remember the testimony of the expert. Usually, the attention of the expert witness is directed by counsel to enlarged copies of these exhibits placed in the courtroom near the witness and within view of judge and jury, and testimony is taken from the witness to explain the exhibits. Upon request, the judge will generally allow the witness to leave the jury box and approach the exhibits to point out the area of the exhibit under discussion. The witness is also permitted to explain the meaning and conclusions to be drawn from the exhibits. It is at this point that the ability of the witness to articulate, to explain, and to communicate assumes great importance.

A common error committed by expert witnesses is using technical language in testimony without offering explanations of the meaning of such language. If the testimony must necessarily involve technical accounting terms and concepts, a means must be found to explain the testimony in language understandable by a layman.

Where necessary to explain a technical concept, the judge may allow in evidence a simple hypothetical example of the concept under discussion. For example, during a recent trial it became obvious to the expert accounting witness that the jury was having difficulty understanding the behavior of fixed and variable costs and the proposition that the plaintiff, because of the illegal acts of the defendant, was entitled to recover lost profits plus the amount of fixed costs normally allocated to the lost sales. After consultations between the judge and counsel for both parties on why a hypothetical example was needed to explain the complex accounting issues, the expert accounting witness was permitted to describe a simplified situation not associated with the factual events of the trial. This situation revealed how costs and profits of a small retail store which sold pocketbooks was affected by the discontinuance of operations. For purposes of this presentation, it was assumed that during month number one, the retail store sold 1000 pocketbooks at $20 each, cost of each pocketbook was $10, salesmen were paid $5 for each pocketbook sold and rent was $1000 per month. It was further assumed that the retail store, because of the alleged illegal acts of the defendant was unable to sell anything during month number two, that salesmen—because they were paid on a piecework basis—received no salary, but that rent for the store of $1000 was paid. The simple profit-and-loss statement shown in Exhibit 4 illustrates the concepts under discussion.

The expert accounting witness described how various costs behaved because of changes in volume of sales, and why it was necessary to identify costs as fixed or variable to anticipate such cost variations. It was also noted that damages, as the results of the alleged injury, were not only equivalent to the loss of profits on the sale of pocketbooks ($4000), but that recovery of the fixed expenses that had to be paid ($1000) by the plaintiff to remain in business was required in order to compensate the plaintiff adequately. With this hypothetical example as background material, it was possible to explain more clearly than would have been possible otherwise, the more complicated accounting analyses made to present the loss suffered by the plaintiff in the actual case.

Exhibit 4.   ABC Store Profit-and-Loss Statement for Periods 1 and 2

	Month 1	Month 2	Behavior of Costs
Sales of pocketbooks	$20,000	$ –0–	
Costs of pocketbooks	$10,000	$ –0–	Variable
Salaries	5,000	–0–	Variable
Rent	1,000	1000	Fixed
Total costs	$16,000	$1000	
Profit (loss) before taxes	$4,000	($1000)	

In testifying, the expert witness need not rely on memory, particularly when dealing with voluminous records from which a number of schedules and exhibits have been prepared. Such schedules and exhibits used in presenting testimony, along with the underlying data supporting that testimony, should be indexed so that they can be found quickly. A witness who cannot readily turn to the appropriate schedule and supporting data during both direct and cross-examination will give the impression of being unprepared and unfamiliar with the facts.

Documents used by witnesses to refresh their memories with respect to any matters to which they testify must be produced at the hearing at the request of the adverse party, and unless the documents are produced, such matters will be stricken from the record. If such documents are produced, the adverse party may inspect them, cross-examine the witness concerning them, and introduce into evidence such portions as may be pertinent to the testimony of the witness.

Expert witnesses' demeanor when testifying should be those of impartial witnesses who are simply and unemotionally stating professional views; they should not become advocates or be emotionally involved in the case. They should be respectful, courteous, and conservative in language, and yet at the same time offer their opinions with conviction. Witnesses should speak slowly, distinctly, and firmly, as everything that is said on the witness stand is being taken down by a court reporter. All the qualities and the behavioral traits of an expert witness discussed in Chapter 3 are called upon at this time.

Examples of Direct
Testimony

Current decisions are more closely related to case facts than to abstract rules or rigid formulae. Courts more frequently seem to base their decisions on the premise that the business environment is a constantly changing process whose elements shift over time and differ from industry to industry and company to company. The following case studies describe how facts, developed after careful examination of business records by expert accounting witnesses, were used as direct testimony.

THE INVESTOR WHO DID NOT INVEST

The plaintiff complained that the defendant violated the antitrust laws and that such anticompetitive activities resulted in the plaintiff's bankruptcy. Financial analysis of the plaintiff's records revealed that prior to acquisition of the company by current management, the company had been successful as a manufacturer and distributor. Present management had, however, purchased the stock of former majority stockholders by offering excessive prices. This acquisition was paid for by depleting available company cash and by using cash acquired by selling manufacturing facilities. The company thus was forced to purchase their products from a competitive manufacturer at costs significantly higher than prior manufacturing costs. Naturally, profits declined and soon significant losses occurred.

At trial, the issue of the proximate cause of bankruptcy centered upon the determination of whether bankruptcy resulted from the depletion of company cash and unprofitable product sales resulting from the high costs of manufacturing company products, or the anticompetitive behavior of the defendant. Also, the validity of computing damages based upon prior financial results when the plaintiff was both manufacturer and distributor was challenged as not being applicable to the existing situation where the plaintiff was a distributor only.

The issues in this case were resolved in favor of the defendant.

DO EXHIBITS LEAD OR MISLEAD?

The plaintiff complained that, but for the anticompetitive behavior of the defendant, sales and profits for the years in suit would have been substantially higher than those realized. To substantiate this claim, the plaintiff prepared several exhibits which portrayed sales and profits for a number of years prior to the claimed anticompetitive behavior of the defendant. By the use of statistical regression techniques, the plaintiff developed trend lines and projected these data into the periods covered by the suit. By comparing projected sales and profits with actual sales and profits, the plaintiff estimated the sales and profits lost as a result of the alleged behavior of the defendant.

Initially, the plaintiff's damage exhibits were quite convincing. However, after careful review of the plaintiff's financial and statistical records, the exhibits were found to be both incomplete and inconsistent. It was shown that numerous changes in corporate, division, and marketing structures had occurred and that selective rather than complete financial and statistical data formed the basis for plaintiff's exhibits. While there was an acceptable rationale for the selective use of data, when all marketing activities of the plaintiff were considered, the sales and profit trend lines as corrected by the defendant expert accountant and projected into the damage period were significantly different from those presented by the plaintiff. These adjusted damage estimates were placed in evidence by the expert accounting witness for the defendant.

In this instance, while the trial judge permitted the introduction of selective data by the plaintiff, the more complete analyses of plaintiff's activities as developed by the defendant were also allowed, and the jury was required to determine which set of analyses more accurately described the situation.

WHAT IS THE COST OF A CLERICAL PROCEDURE?

The plaintiffs complained that the defendant, a savings and loan company, failed to pay interest on monthly deposits made by the plaintiffs as advance payments for taxes and insurance premiums on property purchased by the plaintiffs from funds that the defendant had loaned to the plaintiffs; these deposits were known as impound funds. The defendant alleged that the costs of handling the funds deposited, paying the taxes and insurance when due, and accounting for these activities offset any interest to which the plaintiffs may have been entitled. It was stipulated between the parties that damages would be equivalent to the amount by which interest at an agreed rate on the deposits exceeded the costs of these clerical functions. As the amount of funds on deposit each month for the entire class of plaintiffs was known, and the interest rate was agreed upon, interest amounts that could have been earned on the totals deposited were computed simply. The problem to be litigated was: What were the costs incurred in handling these deposits?

Upon reviewing the clerical procedures followed in accounting for these impound funds, it was recognized that an initial objective of the defendant was to demonstrate to the court that impound processing was a complex clerical function rather than a simple process of debiting and crediting an account for each payment and disbursement. It was decided that a flow chart (Exhibit 5) describing the major activities and departments involved in impound processing was needed to portray these activities and to demonstrate the interrelationships among the departments involved in this clerical process. A series of questions to be used in direct testimony was also prepared to introduce the flow chart into evidence and to describe the impound-processing activities by reference to the flow chart.

The flow chart identified the departments or cost centers involved in the direct furnishing of impound services (loan origination and processing; loan service; central files; data processing; financial division; and cash and securities management) and studies were made of the direct labor and overhead costs of these services. A work measurement study of the direct labor activities in loan origination and processing, loan service, and central files was made by applying industrial engineering techniques. Each of the major activities in these departments was broken down into individual tasks, and records were maintained of the working hours required to complete these tasks. After referring to payroll records, working hours were converted to payroll costs. Data processing activities were separately analyzed by computer specialists

Exhibit 5. Impound Processing.

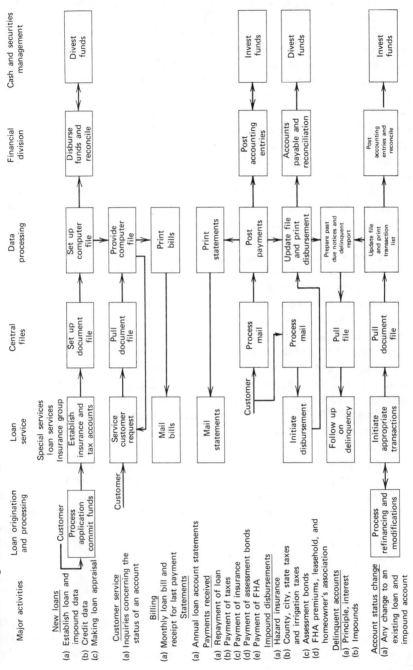

111

to arrive at costs of systems and programming, operations, keypunch, terminals, communication lines, forms, and billing. Accountants studied the labor costs incurred in the finance division and in cash and securities management. Total overhead costs were accumulated for each of the above departments, overhead as a percentage of departmental labor was calculated, and these percentages were applied to the direct labor estimates for impound services to calculate overhead costs for each of these departments. The costs of other indirect-service departments and general corporate overhead were allocated to the departments performing impound services, and all costs were totalled to arrive at an estimated cost of impound processing for the year in question. This total cost was then compared with the estimate of interest earned on impound funds to determine the damage amount, if any. A series of questions to be used in direct testimony was developed to introduce this cost study into evidence.

During direct testimony, an effort was made to distinguish between: direct costs, indirect costs, prime costs, joint costs, byproduct costs, variable costs, fixed costs, semivariable costs, and incremental costs, and to describe the methods and approximations used in arriving at the estimated costs of this clerical activity. During cross-examination, opposing counsel attempted to limit the term *cost* to a compilation of direct labor costs of the impound activity, excluding overhead allocations, and challenged many methods used in the cost computations. Opposing expert accounting witnesses offered different concepts of cost accounting, concentrating instead on direct costing, and also challenged the overhead calculations.

During closing arguments, the defendant attorneys submitted to the court their conclusions on the clerical costs of the impound activities, as shown in Exhibit 6.

The judge accepted the cost studies and cost accounting methods of the defendant but decided, without explanation, that the amounts claimed for administrative and corporate overheads were not reasonably related to the processing, accounting, and disbursing of impound payments for members of the class. The clerical cost of handling impounds for the class members was therefore established as $717,482 ($969,721 − $252,239).

WHAT IS AN EXECUTIVE WORTH?

This case involved the question of what is reasonable compensation for the chief executive in a closely held corporation. The taxpayer, a closely held company in the food industry, paid its president, who

Exhibit 6. Clerical Costs of Impound Activities.

Direct labor		
Loan origination	$ 36,237	
Loan service	188,232	
Central files	12,953	
Electronic data processing	104,196	
Financial division	39,130	
Security portfolio	2,064	
Total direct labor		$382,812
Other direct costs		
Loan service	$ 14,210	
Electronic data processing equipment	48,442	
Key punch	3,024	
Communications	9,435	
Forms and supplies	12,327	
Bill and receipt	23,781	
Total other direct costs		111,219
Operating divisions overhead		
Loan origination	$ 13,186	
Loan service	127,776	
Electronic data processing	74,037	
Financial and security portfolio	8,452	
Total operating division overhead		223,451
Administrative and corporate overheads		252,239
Total costs		$969,721

owned 95% of the company's stock, $180,000 as annual compensation. The court had already indicated in a prior suit on earlier years' compensation that it would allow only $120,000 as deductible compensation, but the taxpayer (the corporation) claimed that for the year in question the $180,000 was in no way unreasonable under the circumstances.

The problem was to determine how to support this contention, and the burden of proof was on the taxpayer. The expert accountant called in by the taxpayer's attorney considered that any such support should, if possible, rest on certain objective analyses: first, as indicated by the company's growth and profits, how effectively this chief executive managed the company (it had been indicated that the president was, in effect, "the management" during this period); and second, how the litigated compensation compared with compensation of other chief executives in companies of similar size in the food industry.

Subsequent testimony discussed the following in regard to acceptable concepts of compensation and the profitability of the company under this president's management.

First it was determined that salary was only part of what is termed "total compensation." Total compensation was defined to include salaries, bonus, retirement, and stock option values. It was concluded that invalid comparisons of total compensation of executives might be made if only salary were considered, particularly where some but not all executives received substantial fringe benefits in their pay packages.

Second, the Chief Executive Compensation Study (Exhibit 7) of a leading research agency was introduced into evidence to demonstrate the variability of executive compensation. This exhibit was also used to show that the food industry was not a typically high-paying industry. Noting that executive compensation was not an exact science, but one based upon many comparisons and indications of what is being done in industry in general, it was shown that the importance of such statistics was to determine the range of compensation paid to the chief executive of the business represented in the study. Though the range was quite wide, it was based upon experience tables.

Next, it was explained that the compensation ranges depended upon two things: the industry, and the size of the company. The average compensation paid to chief executives in the food industry for companies whose annual sales were $19 million to $20 million was approximately $165,000 (Exhibit 8). The average compensation figures illustrated in Exhibit 8 were published by a leading research association, the figures having been compiled from responses by businessmen to questionnaires soliciting compensation information. To obtain an accurate range, it was suggested that 15% above and below the average was proper. This would cover 80% of the compensation cases reported by the chief executives included in the study. Thus, the range for the food industry with sales of from $19 million to $20 million worked out to be from $140,000 to $190,000, with the average being $165,000. Such information was used as a starting point for determining where the salary of a particular executive should fall within that range.

The sales growth of this company was then compared with the growth of the food industry in general. The company's sales increased seven times during the period when the growth of sales in the food industry was rather nominal. This demonstrated strong management and not a fortuitous increase of sales in a fortunate industry. This situation implied that the compensation of the chief executive of this company should lie in the upper part of the salary range.

Exhibit 7. Chief Executive Compensation Comparison (Food Industry to Specific and General Industry).

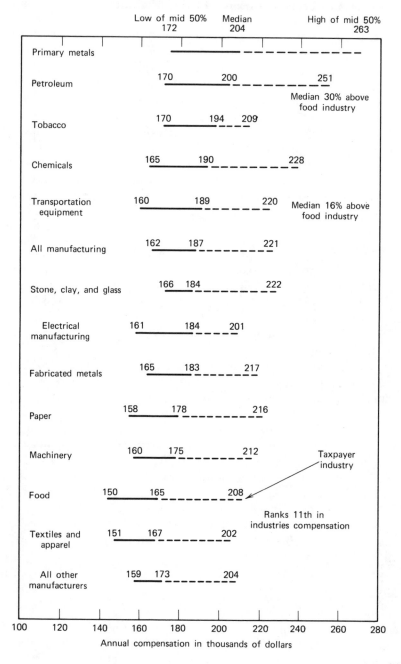

Annual compensation in thousands of dollars

Exhibit 8.   Comparison of Compensation—Food Industry (Total Compensation for All Types of Payments).

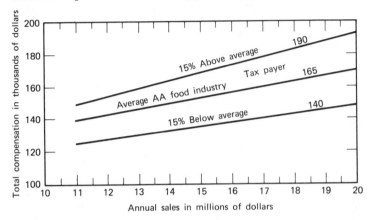

Annual sales in millions of dollars

Another question investigated was: How much of the sales increase was reflected in an increase in profits? The results of this study showed that profits increased from approximately 2% of net sales to nearly 5% of net sales, indicating that management under this president had not only increased sales, but had also increased its rate of profit.

The next question studied included a review of the records to determine if the company had been lucky, or if the growth of profits had been a result of good management. The growth of net profits after taxes as a percentage of sales of the company was compared with that of other companies in the food industry with $19 million to $20 million of annual sales, and with all companies in the food industry regardless of their size. The results showed that the company's net profit rose from 1.9% to 4.8% of net sales, whereas companies of the same size in the industry for this period of time fell from 3.9% of net sales to 3%, and the industry as a whole remained static at 2%. The expert accountant testified that profit comparisons were major indicators of the effectiveness of management. A similar type of comparison was made for return on investment, or how wisely had the president used his assets to make profits for his company. The company earned a 23% return on investment. Competitors of the same size received 7.2%, and for the industry as a whole, the investors received 4.4% on their investment. This indicated an extremely advantageous use of assets.

To summarize the facts presented in this case:

1. Sales of the company increased in volume above the periods involved in the previous litigation. Sales doubled in seven years, and increased seven times the average increase of the industry.

2. Net income after taxes rose from roughly 2% of sales to approximately 5% of sales during the years in question.

3. The ratio of net profit after taxes as compared to sales was the highest in the industry.

4. The return on investment rose from 13.4% to 23% in three years.

5. The taxpayer's wage policy showed that during a five-year period there had been 22 pay raises for wage-earning employees based upon a contract containing a cost-of-living provision.

6. The taxpayer packed and sold more food of its particular kind than any other packer on the West Coast.

7. Comparison of net profit after taxes as a percentage of sales with other companies in the food industry having the same range of annual sales for these years showed: (a) the taxpayer's net profit after taxes as a percentage of sales rose from 1.9% to 4.8%; (b) companies of the same size fell from 3.9% to 3.0%; (c) the industry as a whole remained at about 2.0% of sales.

All of this indicated unusually strong management.

Finally, a comparison of the salary paid the taxpayer's president with the salaries paid to presidents of corporations in the food industry having comparable sales showed that the average yearly compensation paid was $165,000, with the range extending from $140,000 to $190,000.

After considering these facts and other testimony, the district court upheld as reasonable the $180,000 as compensation for the year in question.

IS THE PLAINTIFF WITHOUT FAULT?

The plaintiff developed a packaging product which, if successful, threatened to obtain a major share of the packaging market enjoyed by the defendant. The plaintiff complained that because of unfair anticompetitive activities of the defendant, including coercion of potential plaintiff customers through market dominance and the use of discriminatory pricing, the plaintiff was unable to realize the market potential of its new and unique product.

In an attempt to estimate the potential market share lost by the plaintiff, production and sales records of the plaintiff were examined. In certain sales correspondence it was noted that the plaintiff may have been using, with a number of customers, marketing tactics similar to those of the defendant. Several questions also arose as to the pricing practices of the plaintiff.

Discussion of these findings with the defendant attorneys led to a conference between the plaintiff and defendant attorneys and an amicable settlement of the case.

WHAT IS THE VALUE OF STOCK OF A CLOSELY HELD COMPANY?

The decedent left 100 shares of stock in a closely held company which had 1000 shares of outstanding common stock. In the estate tax return filed by the executors, the stock was valued at $700 per share and upon examination of the return, the Commissioner of Internal Revenue asserted a value of $950 per share and assessed the estate a deficiency tax on such basis. The additional tax and interest was paid by the plaintiffs, who then instituted suit for refund of the sum paid. During the previous five-year period there were only four sales involving stock of this company. The book value per share was $1100 and net income per share for the past five years averaged $104 per share. Dividends averaged $20 per share.

Expert witnesses for the plaintiff asserted that the valuation of $700 per share was high because of lack of marketability, low dividend payout, and the fact that a minority interest would have no voice in the management of the company. A formula computation wherein: five-year average dividends were capitalized by 6%, average earnings for the five-year period were multiplied by 10, 50% of the book value was computed, and the total of these three factors was divided by three, was used to demonstrate that the value placed on the stock was high.

The expert witness for the government presented the names of competitive companies and the price–earnings ratios at which the stocks of these companies sold. On the basis of the average of such price–earnings ratios, this witness concluded that the book value per share established by the commissioner was reasonable.

The court held that the dividend factor was a material element in the valuation of a minority stockholder's interests and that the record of the dividends paid was poor for the earnings record. The court agreed to the relevance of the price–earnings ratio test but rejected those shown because of restricted market conditions and discounted the price–earnings computation. The court then accepted the $700 valuation established by the plaintiff.

IS THE FRANCHISE SYSTEM CONTRARY TO PUBLIC POLICY?

This case presented a problem of some importance in the automobile industry.

The automobile manufacturer had long felt that the effectiveness of dealers in selling new cars to the public was of vital concern. To insure a sound distribution system, the manufacturer surveyed potential marketing areas and established a separate independent dealership in each marketing area. By contractual agreement the dealer was required to maintain the new car warranties established by the manufacturer by providing service and parts departments to meet the repair needs of the customers. To manage the sale of new cars, the franchise dealers agreed to sell new cars only at the place of business defined in their contracts with the manufacturer.

Prior to the institution of the litigation, a small number of dealers in southern California decided to sell new automobiles to discount houses for resale as new cars. As the discount houses were located in many different marketing areas, this practice had the effect of establishing numerous selling outlets for each dealer selling through discount houses. The manufacturer considered this a violation of the dealership contract and insisted that the practice be discontinued. Representatives of the discount houses petitioned the government to compel the manufacturer to refrain from these actions on the grounds that such were contrary to public interest and were in violation of the antitrust laws.

As the manufacturer prepared for trial, it seemed that the government attorneys would attempt to prove public benefit through discount house sales. The manufacturer therefore had the problem of showing that the franchise system was endangered by discount house activities and that the franchise system was at least of equal or greater public benefit than selling through discount houses.

To illustrate how the public was served by the franchise system, a dealership was described as an economic unit consisting of a new-car sales department, a parts department, and a service department, for it was incumbent upon the dealer to supply parts and repair services. Several interesting questions were posed by the manufacturer's attorneys with particular reference to the fact that discount houses offered no parts and repair services. The key questions were:

1. Were the service and parts departments an adjunct to new car sales activities, or were they profit-making operations?
2. Would dealers continue to maintain the service and parts departments if discount houses made significant inroads into the sales of new cars by dealers and would the public be damaged if these activities were discontinued?
3. Did discount house activities threaten principally the small volume dealers? What reductions in sales of new cars and what

reductions in unit selling prices of new cars could be absorbed by low-volume dealers before incurring overall operating losses?

4. Did customers who purchased from a dealer through a discount house pay higher or lower prices for passenger cars than ordinary retail customers who purchased directly from that dealer?

The answers to these questions were determined by study and analysis of the operating records of more than 75 dealers and 7 discount houses in southern California. An expert accountant was called in by the manufacturer's attorneys and it was quickly concluded that, because of the large number of dealers and discount houses involved and the wide diversity of operating conditions and management methods, all types of logical though conflicting conclusions could be supported by individual situations and examples.

In view of this, mathematical and statistical methods to analyze and classify the operating data of the dealers and to establish the major overall characteristics of the data studied had to be used. To describe the group characteristics most precisely, the median situation for each type of data was developed. The median was described as the single most representative and accurate measure of individual members when considered as a group, particularly when there was a small number of extreme situations of individual members in the group.

The studies disclosed and testimony was given that:

1. For the fiscal years studied, 70% of the dealers whose operating records were reviewed suffered losses in their service and parts departments and the median losses exceeded $10,000 annually. These departments offered services to meet new car sales commitments and were not independent profit-making activities. The studies demonstrated that profits on new car sales were necessary to offset losses in these departments.

2. Profits of dealers were directly influenced by the volume of new cars sold and the prices paid by customers. For dealers selling from 300 to 700 new cars annually, reductions in the volume of new cars sold from 12% to 20% or reductions in prices paid for new cars from 1% to 2.9% would result only in breakeven operations. Charts similar to Exhibits 9 and 10, respectively, were presented as testimony to reflect the impact on profits of reductions in new car sales, as well as reductions in selling prices. The studies indicated that discount house sales of new cars threatened chiefly the small dealer and that the margin of profit for small dealers was not sufficiently large to withstand any appreciable volume losses or small price reductions. Thirdly, on the basis of numerous statisti-

Exhibit 9.   Effects of Reductions in Sales Volume For a Dealer in the
300-New-Car-Volume Class

Financial Item	Percentage Reduction			
		5%	10%	12%
	Number of New-Car Sales			
	300 (000's)	285 (000's)	270 (000's)	264 (000's)
Gross profit on new and used cars	$113.8	$108.2	$102.7	$100.5
Gross profit on parts and service	66.8	66.8	66.8	66.8
Miscellaneous net income	19.4	18.6	17.8	17.5
Total gross profit	200.0	193.6	187.3	184.8
Variable selling expenses	39.5	36.9	34.2	33.2
Semifixed new and used car expenses	48.9	47.9	46.9	46.5
Semifixed service and parts expenses	65.4	65.4	65.4	65.4
Fixed expenses	40.0	40.0	40.0	40.0
Total expenses	193.8	190.2	186.5	185.1
Net profit before bonuses and income taxes	$ 6.2	$ 3.4	$ 0.8	$ (0.3)
				Breakeven point

cal tabulations, testimony was given that the median prices paid by customers who purchased through discount houses were not appreciably different from prices paid by ordinary retail customers who purchased directly from the dealers.

The statistical and mathematical presentations that portrayed the situations most characteristic of the entire group of franchise dealers appeared to help reveal the underlying situation in a mass of evidence that otherwise could have been presented as conflicting and contradictory results of different dealers. These studies helped to clarify the position of the manufacturer and assisted the judge in reaching a decision.

SHOULD MARKUP BE INCLUDED IN DAMAGES?

The plaintiffs, representing a class of purchasers of pharmaceuticals from drugstores, alleged that defendants, manufacturers of drug products, conspired to unlawfully fix the prices of drugs sold to pharma-

Exhibit 10.   Effects of Reductions in Sales Prices

Line	Financial	Number of New Car Sales				
No.	Item	300	400	500	600	700
1.	Retail sales	$649.1	$867.5	$1,085.9	$1,304.3	$1,522.7
2.	Sales commissions	17.2	24.1	31.0	37.8	44.7
3.	Sales minus commissions	631.9	843.4	1,054.9	1,266.5	1,478.0
4.	Profits before bonuses and income taxes	6.2	12.2	30.8	22.9	38.8
5.	Percent price reduction to breakeven point	1.0%	1.4%	2.9%	1.8%	2.6%
6.	Reduction in selling price per car to breakeven	$27	$38	$77	$48	$69

cies. The plaintiffs established that pharmacies, in developing selling prices to their customers, normally computed these prices on the basis of a pricing formula: selling price equals cost of merchandise plus cost of merchandise times a percentage markup. The plaintiffs demonstrated that, if the costs of merchandise were inflated because of the alleged illegal price fixing by, say, $50 million, the actual injury suffered by the plaintiffs was not only that inflation in price, but also included the normal markup on this inflated cost of merchandise.

The defendants agreed that in the normal course of business, pharmacies applied a markup percentage to merchandise cost and computed a selling price as alleged by the plaintiffs. The expert accounting witness for the defendants testified, however, that while markup was computed as a percentage of merchandise costs, markup was not caused by merchandise costs and that the formula used was merely a convenient and simple method of establishing selling prices. The witness explained that the amount of money in the price of a drug product that represented the markup reimbursed the druggist for the operating and selling expenses of the pharmacy and contributed to the profit earned on the sale of pharmaceuticals. Also, the operating and selling expenses of the pharmacy, such as salaries, rent, depreciation, heat, and so forth, were not influenced by costs of merchandise, the witness testified, although the profit objective of the pharmacist might have some relationship to merchandise investments. The witness also demonstrated that operating and selling expenses far exceeded profits. It was also shown how the markup percentage (not markup dollars) was affected by merchandise costs and that if merchandise costs were lowered, the markup percentage would increase, provided operating and selling expenses and profit objectives remained constant. Thus, if merchandise costs were lowered, markup percentages of the pharmacies would increase and the dollar amounts of markup collected from purchasers would not change significantly. The defendant argued that markup thus should not be included in the damage formula as the plaintiffs, in paying for markup in the selling prices, merely reimbursed the druggists for their legitimate recovery of operating and selling expenses and their realization of a profit.

The plaintiff agreed that in those states where markup was a fixed-dollar amount for each prescription, markup should not be included in the damage base. For all other states, the concept of the recovery of markup in damages must still be litigated.

WHAT IS THE VALUE OF GOODWILL?

The plaintiff owned and operated a restaurant adjacent to beach properties and alleged that the defendant, as a result of the negligent operation of oil wells located in the nearby ocean floor, polluted the beaches as a result of oil seeping from the wells into the ocean. The beaches, polluted by the oil spill, were no longer attractive to residents and nonresidents, and the number of people visiting the area was substantially reduced. This resulted in a reduced clientele for the restaurant and a corresponding loss of profits by the plaintiff. To estimate damages as a result of the alleged negligence of the defendant, the plaintiff listed profits for each month of a five-year period prior to the oil spill in a graphic format and developed a statistical trend line through these profit figures. The trend line was extended through the damage period and damages were calculated as the sum of the differences between profit figures represented on the trend line and actual profits. In addition, the plaintiff demanded an additional $100,000 as compensation for the loss of goodwill suffered by the plaintiff as a result of the negligence of the defendant.

To support the claim for the loss of goodwill, the attorney for the plaintiff quoted the Business and Professional Code of the Annotated California Codes, which defines goodwill of a business as "the expectation of continued public patronage." The plaintiff's attorney continued by quoting the code that stated "goodwill of a business is a part of the owner's property which he is entitled to enjoy and which is protected by constitutional guarantees. Goodwill is the advantage or benefit which is acquired by an establishment beyond the mere value of the capital stock, funds, or property employed therein, in consequence of the general public patronage and encouragement which it receives from constant or habitual customers, on account of the local position or constant celebrity or reputation for skill or affluence or punctuality or from other accidental circumstances or necessities. It is the probability that the business will continue in the future as in the past, adding to the profits of the concern, and contributing to the means of meeting its engagements as they come in. In determining goodwill, the elements to be considered are the situation of the premises, the amount of patronage, the general conditions existing at the time, the personality of the parties engaged in the business, the length of time the business has been established, and the habits of customers who have been used to dealing at a particular place to continue to go there."

The attorney for the plaintiff presented a number of witnesses who testified that the restaurant was highly regarded by residents and tourists, that the owner was personable and an effective businessman, and that the operations of the restaurant prior to the oil spill were consistent with the requirements for goodwill as described in the code. The attorney for the plaintiff concluded by stating that the fact that the loss of profits and of customers cannot be accurately measured while the business was closed does not preclude compensation as damages, and that, in his opinion, $100,000 was fair compensation for the loss of goodwill.

The expert accounting witness employed by the defendant examined the profit figures used by the plaintiff and testified that the monthly profit figures used did not agree in total with the annual profit figures reported on the income tax returns filed by the plaintiff. By using monthly profit figures that agreed with the federal income tax data of the plaintiff, revised estimates of lost profits were developed following the methods employed by the plaintiff. In discussing goodwill, the expert accountant testified that while the plaintiff may have enjoyed goodwill because of the expectation of public patronage, the value of such goodwill was zero rather than the $100,000 claimed by the plaintiff. The expert accountant stated that the value of goodwill was determined as the current value of expected future income in excess of a normal return on the investment in net tangible assets, and concluded that for the period prior to the oil spill, the net return enjoyed by the plaintiff on this investment was less than the average returns on investments in restaurants nationally, in the state, and in the area in which the restaurant was located. As there was no excess return, the goodwill that existed was considered to have no value.

WHAT LOSSES WERE INCURRED FROM BUSINESS INTERRUPTION DUE TO FIRE?

Two fires had occurred within four months at a small manufacturer's main plant and the insurance company had paid the policy limit for the second fire. The manufacturing company sued the insurance company for losses due to the first fire, claiming that business interruption from the first fire had caused a large loss of profits, even though only a relatively minor production area was damaged. The manufacturer claimed that the part of the plant damaged by fire was a bottleneck production area, affected plant-wide operations, and inability to use the damaged production facilities resulted in plant-wide disruption of production.

The expert accounting witness for the defendant decided that the basic analytical problem was to determine when production would have been restored to normal levels had the second fire not occurred. To add to the complexity of the problem, nearly all the records had been destroyed. The manufacturer's business was highly seasonal and the first fire occurred just as production was being stockpiled for the season. By analyzing the time records that were available, the expert accountant determined the relationship between labor hours in the bottleneck area and total production value and constructed a production restoration curve. A forecast of plant-wide production capability for each week was also prepared, and with these data the expert witness demonstrated that the lost profits from the first fire amounted to only 5% of the lost profits claimed. These calculations were described to the plaintiff's attorney during the deposition of the expert accounting witness. Later, the case was settled on a basis favorable to the insurance company.

DID A LARGE AIRLINE UNFAIRLY DRIVE A SMALLER ONE FROM THE MARKET?

The plaintiff owned and operated a small airline for the transportation of passengers between two cities in California and alleged that the defendant had used its greater resources to operate below cost in the market area served by the plaintiff, thereby driving the plaintiff out of business with resulting loss of properties, profits, and goodwill. The defendant, a large airline, contended that this was not the case, but admitted that it had not maintained its accounting records on a route basis and did not have readily available data describing revenues, expenses, and profits for service between the two California cities in question. An expert accountant was requested to analyze available data in order to develop the required accounting information, and to be prepared to testify as to the work performed and the accounting results developed.

The expert accountant determined that three major tasks were required: (1) to define an appropriate revenue and cost allocation method; (2) to construct an accounting model to calculate route profitability; and (3) to collect whatever accurate data existed in sufficient quantities to allow the model to calculate route profitability. Two problems had to be overcome in completing these tasks: the airline industry did not follow a standard revenue and cost allocation method so that a cost allocation method had to be developed which would stand the rigors of cross-examination; and the defendant's operating records for the damage period were incomplete and of limited accuracy. Careful research and analysis of the records were needed to insure that the accounting and statistical information used in the revenue and cost allocation models were accurate. Accounting analyses were then developed to demonstrate that the defendant operated the route in question profitably during the damage period.

The attorney for the defendant communicated the results of the study to the plaintiff and described the credentials of the accounting experts who conducted the study. If was indicated that these studies would be used during the trial to prove that the defendant did not operate below cost on the contested route. Subsequently an out-of-court settlement was reached which was satisfactory to both parties.

DID MANUFACTURERS OF BROAD-SPECTRUM ANTIBIOTICS ILLEGALLY CONSPIRE TO FIX RETAIL PRICES?

A number of states, acting on behalf of their citizens, sued the defendant manufacturers of broad-spectrum antibiotic drugs, alleging that because of an illegally obtained patent the defendants were able to establish and maintain prices of tetracycline drugs at unreasonably high levels for an extended period of time. An expert economic witness for the plaintiff stated in a pretrial hearing that he had made a study of the pricing history of tetracycline drugs and had observed that after an initial decline in prices one year after introduction, the prices had

Exhibit 11.   Damage Model—Tetracycline.

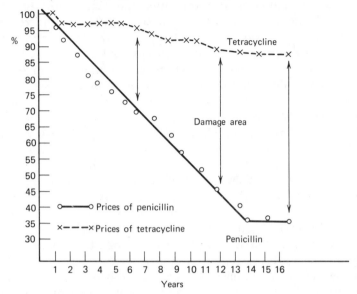

remained constant for seven years, followed by a modest price decline for a period of years. The expert economist also studied the price history of penicillin and stated that prices for penicillin had shown a continuous decline following entry and continued this decline for a number of years thereafter. The economist concluded that retail prices of penicillin had declined because the free forces of competition had been allowed to operate in the marketplace and that, had the forces of competition been allowed to operate on tetracycline, the retail price history of tetracycline would have been similar to that of penicillin. The expert economist declared that the different pricing histories for penicillin and tetracycline were evidence of an illegal pricing conspiracy in pricing tetracycline and could be used as a measure of damages arising from the alleged pricing conspiracy. To develop a damage model, the expert economist constructed a graph depicting retail sales prices of penicillin and tetracycline as percentages of their introductory prices, as seen in Exhibit 11.

Lines of best fit for the penicillin and tetracycline prices were developed and damages were calculated based upon the quantities of tetracycline sold each year during the damage period and the pricing differentials developed from the damage model.

To counter the arguments of the plaintiff's economic witness, the expert accounting witness for the defendant made a study of the trends and behavior of prices to retailers for major pharmaceutical products generally to compare these trends and tendencies with the pricing history for the products subject to litigation. The study covered major prescription products of large pharmaceutical manufacturers that were introduced and sold during the period in which the products in suit were introduced and sold. The manufacturers were included on the basis of market share, provided total sales of prescription products constituted 1% or more of the total ethical pharmaceutical market in any one year during the period in suit, as reflected in the Drug Store Purchase Audit compiled by Davee, Koehnlein, and Keating. On this basis, 25 companies were included in the study. Five leading products for each company were selected. The leading products for each manufacturer were identified by determining which products were most frequently among the top five for each company during the years in question. *Red Book*, a publication of Drug Topics Inc., was used to obtain data by dosage form, package size, and product strength. A data base similar to that included on Exhibit 12, was prepared for each of the 125 products selected.

Data contained in the data base were analyzed and the following testimony was developed to describe the pricing histories of leading pharmaceutical products not included in the suit.

A. In the 125 leading pharmaceutical products not included in the suit:

  1. The average number of years without a price change was 5.2.
  2. The average number of years without a price reduction was 8.2.
  3. The average number of years before the first price change was 7.6.
  4. The average number of years before the first price reduction was 10.3.

B. Excluding the defendant companies and for 100 leading pharmaceutical products:

  1. The average number of years without a price change was 5.4.
  2. The average number of years without a price reduction was 9.1.
  3. The average number of years before the first price change was 8.0.
  4. The average number of years before the first price reduction was 11.3.

Exhibit 12. Price Behavior: Major Products of Major Manufacturers (Red Book Prices in Dollars).

	Dosage Form	Strength	Size	1	2	3	4	5	6	7	8	9	10	11	12	13	14	15	16	17	18	19	20	21	22	23
																	Year after Introduction									
ABBOTT																										
Compocillin VK	Granule	125 mg/5 cc	80/cc																							
Desbutal	Capsule	5 mg	100						2.50				NL	NL	3.00		2.25	1.89				1.47		1.32		
Enduron	Tablet	5 mg	100												NL	NL	6.00									2.70
Erythrocin sterate	Tablet	100 mg	100						18.24		16.71	13.77														
Placidyl	Capsule	500 mg	100							NL	NL	3.25				4.00	11.70	9.96		4.40				5.00		5.55
AMERICAN HOME PRODUCTS																										
Bicillin	Suspension	300 mu/5 cc	2 oz					3.25										2.93			2.99		3.14			
Equagesic	Tablet		50							NL	NL	3.25					3.25								3.75	
Equanil	Tablet	400 mg	50												NL	3.86	2.90			3.50	3.57				3.10	
Pen-Vee-K	Tablet	250 mg	36										NL	10.80		10.40	7.80	6.63			5.21			3.84		
Sparine	Tablet	50 mg	50								NL	3.60					3.42				3.49					3.70

130

Exhibit 13. Price Stability—Five or More Years of Price Unchanged.

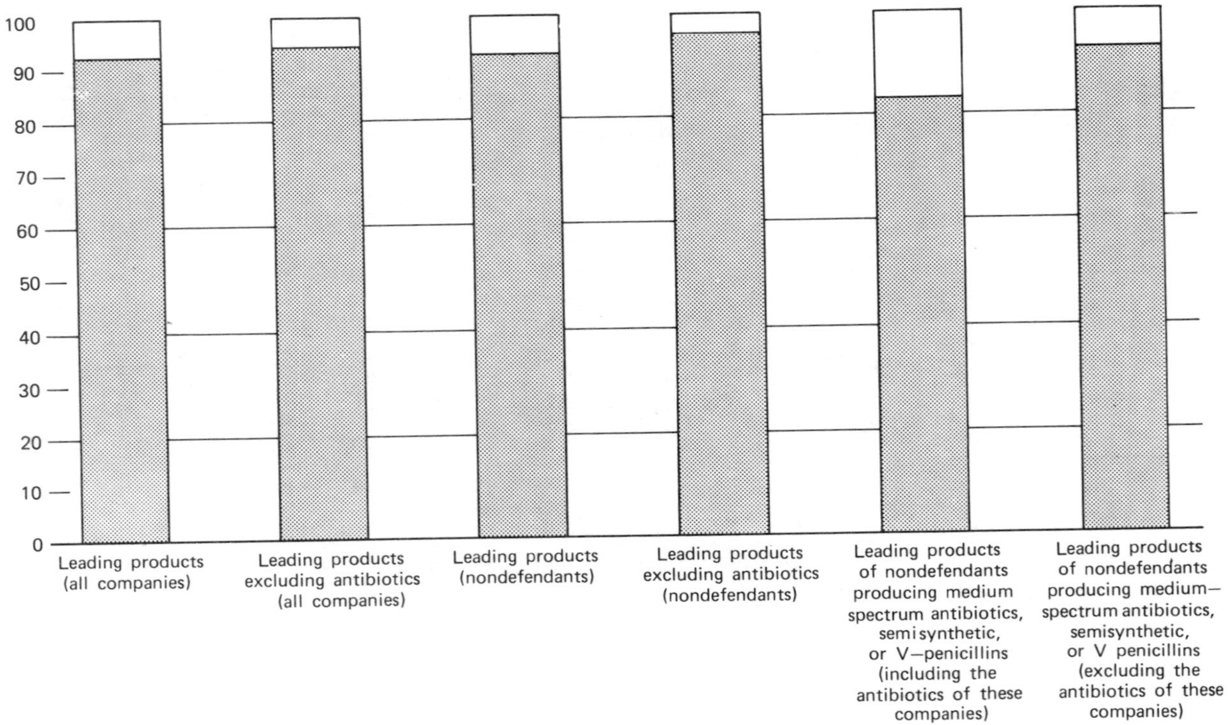

C. The number of years that elapsed before the first price change were:

Number of Years	Number of Products Having First Price Change
1	13
2	11
3	8
4	8
over 4	85
	125

Price stability charts as illustrated in Exhibit 13, that portrayed the percentages of product prices remaining unchanged for five, six, and nine years, were also presented as testimony.

Following the pretrial hearing, the case was settled to the mutual satisfaction of both parties.

8

Cross-Examination

Generally the testimony of the expert accountant is specific, directly related to monetary damages, and influential on the minds of the judge and jury. It is the type of testimony that presents a challenge to the opposing attorney and leads to extensive cross-examination of the witness. An understanding of the techniques of cross-examination and the attitudes of the attorneys towards this process will assist the expert accounting witness meet the rigors of this experience.

THE TECHNIQUES OF CROSS-EXAMINATION

The approaches to cross-examination seem to be as varied as the personalities, attitudes, and abilities of the cross-examiner. At no other time does the fact that a court trial is an adversary proceeding become more apparent than during cross-examination which is conducted under rules which seem to favor the examiner. Opposing counsel will do everything possible to discredit the witnesses' direct testimony by challenging their qualifications, knowledge of the facts, or the reasonableness of their conclusions. On the other hand, during cross-examination the objective of the witness is to gain the respect and confidence of the persons receiving the testimony, that is, the judge and/or jury, and to maintain the positions taken during direct testimony. At times, it may be possible during cross-examination to strengthen the points made during direct examination as facts, conclusions, and reasons brought out in cross-examination are frequently more effective than responses to prepared direct testimony. There is a tendency to give more weight to responses brought out during cross-examination than to prepared testimony.

Expert witnesses are subject to broader cross-examination than other witnesses. Once experts testify, they expose themselves to a probing which would have no place in the cross-examination of a factual witness. Experts may be cross-examined to the extent of any other witnesses, and in addition, may be fully cross-examined on the additional grounds that the expert lacks expert qualifications. By introducing independent evidence, or by cross-examining the expert, opposing counsel may show that the expert lacks the qualifications claimed on direct examination. Also, cross-examination may be based on an expert's prior inconsistent opinions in the same case, but not those given in another case. The opposing counsel may also cross-examine as to any monies or expenses which have been or are being paid to an expert witness by either side. This testimony is allowed so that the jury may determine whether the money received by the expert tends to bias that expert's opinion in the present case. Opposing counsel may refer to any textbooks or treatises of other experts on which the expert witness claims to have relied in forming an opinion. The cross-examiner attempts to use those books to show that they really do not support the expert's testimony. Counsel may be permitted cross-examination of any expert witness as to contrary views which have been expressed in a textbook or treatise, whether or not the expert claims to have relied upon or even read them, when such publications have been admitted in evidence. The expert witness will be carefully cross-examined as to the extent of that person's knowledge and the reasons for opinions, including the facts and other matters upon which they are based. The responses of the expert witness to questions of this type can identify the outstanding from the average witness.

In cross-examination, the examiner is not necessarily looking for information but may be trying to provide ammunition for the summation. Rarely will the cross-examiner ask a question without knowing what answer will be given by the witness. The more positive testimony given by a witness is likely to be probed, because to leave strong testimony unchallenged is to acknowledge its truth, from the viewpoint of the jury. Usually too many questions will not be asked and an attempt will be made to control the witness frequently by limiting the answers to a simple yes or no. This can cause considerable concern to the expert witness, particularly where the simple answer may lead to inappropriate inferences, but judges usually require a yes or no response on the premise that the other attorney will clarify the facts on redirect examination.

Accounting consists of rules, regulations, and techniques for recording, classifying, and summarizing the results of business transactions.
To a person not skilled in the use of accounting principles, methods,
and techniques, accounting has the appearance of a precise methodology with little room for judgment, difference of opinion, or doubt in the
proper application of the required rules and procedures. Accounting,
however, is a general discipline that is used by all forms of business
entities to record a multitude of different types of business transactions. The rules of accounting have been devised to handle a multiplicity of business situations. Analytical accounting methods have been
developed to meet various, and at times, conflicting business objectives. An analytical approach to a given situation may not be appropriate in a similar business situation, if the business objectives of each
situation differ. Thus, the selection of an analytical accounting method
can frequently depend upon the type of decision that must be made or
the objective of the party making the analysis, and as objectives differ
between parties in litigation, it is not unusual for equally competent
expert accountants to select different analytical approaches and to
arrive at different conclusions. Naturally, during cross-examination
opposing counsel will probe the analytical accounting methods used by
the witness and frame cross-examination questions to exploit the
weaknesses, questions, or lack of certainty associated with the
accounting methods adopted. The witness, during this period of cross-
examination, must be adroit in defending the accounting techniques
employed in direct testimony.

The cross-examiner will also attempt to take advantage of the
accounting ambiguities associated with direct testimony. Where an
analysis of cost behavior is included in direct testimony, challenges to
the cost accounting approaches will be established during cross-
examination. As noted in Chapter 4, the opportunities to challenge
cost accounting concepts are many. Any inconsistencies between the
testimony of the expert witnesses of the different disciplines will also
be fully exploited during cross-examination.

In addition to leading questions, the cross-examiner may use any
type of question which would have been proper on direct examination.
Compound questions that require one answer to more than one question, argumentative questions, and questions that assume facts not yet
in evidence are not permitted. Repetition of questions is frequently
allowed on cross-examination. Usually a witness can be cross-
examined on all relevant matters and the court may, in its discretionary powers, limit the examination.

Another purpose of cross-examination is to prevent a witness from giving carefully planned answers. Unpredictability in the questions is a means of revealing a witness's reactions without the armor of a contrived and prepared set of answers. The technique of cross-examination often produces responses, which are as significant for the inferences that can be drawn from them as for what is explicitly stated. This aspect of cross-examination is frequently frustrating for an expert witness who knows from the way the questions are framed that they are designed to give the jury an impression which, from the witness's point of view, is misleading.

The expert witness rarely knows the cross-examining attorney. Opposing attorneys constantly look for opportunities to make the jury distrust the expert or to make the expert admit to errors. Clever cross-examination by the opposing counsel can undo the good done during direct examination. On the other hand, the conduct of a witness during cross-examination can lend weight to the original testimony and make the expert witness much more valuable.

PREPARING FOR CROSS-EXAMINATION

Even those most confident of their facts worry about having their veracity more or less openly questioned. There is the fear of being caught in a contradiction or being embarrassed by a cunning strategem. Few people are so sure of themselves that they enjoy being cross-examined by an experienced lawyer. Pretrial preparation of the witness for cross-examination can do much to reduce tensions. Not every question put to a witness by opposing counsel is a trap for the unwary. The scrupulous regard for truth and knowledge of the facts are most persuasive upon the jury.

The rationale for positions taken during direct testimony and the facts upon which your expert testimony is based should be clearly in mind prior to the commencement of cross-examination. All exhibits used during direct testimony should be accessible, and you should be prepared to discuss these exhibits in the order selected by opposing counsel, which may not be the same as the order used during direct testimony. Working papers or other materials referred to during direct testimony should be available. Thus, as an expert accounting witness, you should be prepared to explain and defend the accounting theories and cost allocation methods described in your direct testimony.

A witness should carefully review any previous testimony presented during depositions and reconcile that testimony with the direct testimony given during the trial. All inconsistencies should be noted and explanations prepared to describe changes in testimony based upon new facts discovered after the deposition, or previous errors in deposition testimony that have been corrected. All prior writings of the witness should be read and if any statements inconsistent with the position taken at trial have been made, the witness should be prepared to explain such differences.

It is advisable to practice for cross-examination by having counsel act as the opposing attorney and cross-examine the expert witness. Many of the questions can be anticipated and a mock cross-examination demonstrates the readiness of the witness for this experience. This helps a witness in organizing responses to background questions and gives some experience in handling and referring to any of the exhibits, documents, or writings to be used on the stand. During the practice session, answers to technical questions can be reviewed for clarity and completeness. Responses to challenges to positions taken based upon statements obtained from learned treatises can be evaluated and refined as the rationale for distinctions between different positions is developed.

Cross-examination is not a debate or argument with opposing counsel. When an expert accounting witness is in possession of the facts and has reached conclusions based upon an objective assessment of these facts, the expert accountant should be able to withstand the most rigorous cross-examination. Cross-examination affords an opportunity to the witness as well as to opposing counsel, as effective responses in cross-examination are valuable in sustaining the position of the expert. This is the goal of the accounting witness during cross-examination and if this goal is reached, cross-examination will be an exhilarating experience.

BEHAVIOR OF THE EXPERT WITNESS DURING CROSS-EXAMINATION

There seems to be no correlation between the integrity of a witness and that witness's performance on the witness stand. It is far from easy to predict a witness's showing under stress. The skilled advocate makes a study of a witness's nervousness, mastery of the facts, and susceptibility to flattery, and the weaker the client's case the more the attorney will attempt to exploit the weaknesses of the opponent's expert witness.

During cross-examination, a witness should remain alert and not let one's mind wander, despite the frequent interruptions as the attorneys argue the admissibility of questions and evidence. One can easily be caught offguard and immediately get into trouble unless one is aware of everything occurring. Answers must be in response to the questions, straightforward, honest, and frank, and should be expressed in simple language clearly understandable to the layperson. Great patience is often required to communicate to nonaccountants the difficulties involved in the art of accounting.

When testifying, you should face the jury and speak loudly enough for the court and the jury to hear. Although you should demonstrate confidence in your testimony you should not appear to be arrogant. Losing one's temper during cross-examination, continually answering "I don't know," or making sarcastic replies makes one a pawn in the hands of the opposing counsel.

A certain amount of apprehension is to be expected as cross-examination approaches. The expert accountant should not count on a superior knowledge of the facts of a particular case or of the principles involved, because in most cases, opposing counsel has a competent staff who made a thorough investigation and may be even more aware of the type of admission that will influence the judge and jury than the witness. It is safe to assume that as long as opposing counsel continues to ask questions, counsel is getting answers believed to be beneficial. Opposing counsel will usually discontinue cross-examination when sensing that the opponents are benefiting more from the responses than the counsel's side. It is your function as an expert witness to cause opposing counsel to terminate cross-examination as quickly as possible.

Overconfidence may lead to overstatements in answering, and thus suggest new lines of inquiry to opposing counsel. As a general rule, it is safer to say too little rather than too much. However, where such answers are not required by the question, it is a mistake to confine answers to yes or no when supporting direct accounting testimony which is highly technical and replete with judgment decisions, for such answers can give opposing counsel control over the course of the testimony.

While the judge may give opposing counsel latitude in insisting that questions be answered with a simple yes or no, one way of improving the situation is for the witness to rephrase an unclear or deliberately suggestive question so there is no possibility of misconstruction from the record. Opposing counsel should have no ground for complaint, since one should not be required to answer a question one cannot understand. A witness is required, however, to answer all questions fully and honestly and cannot rephrase questions to be evasive. If testimony has the appearance of being evasive, the witness runs the risk of destroying the effectiveness of his direct testimony.

As an expert witness, you should avoid being drawn into arguments with opposing counsel. This situation can arise when the cross-examiner is trying to establish a point in contradiction to one established by the witness. Calmness is required unless you wish to risk creating an unfavorable reaction in the minds of the judge and jury. This does not imply, however, that if personal judgments or abilities are being questioned, an expert witness should submit placidly to any suggestions of lack of integrity. It is not unusual to be confronted with questions that assert or imply a lack of objectivity or independence or that tend to downgrade the accounting profession. In such instances, a strong but dignified answer is required.

To summarize, some of the more important rules of behavior to be followed on cross-examination are:

1. Before answering, every question must be understood; if it is not understood, the witness should ask that the question be repeated or explained.

2. The answer to the question should not be given until counsel has completed the question and no objection to the question has been raised.

3. Leading questions requiring only a yes or no answer should be carefully considered and if the answer could be misleading, the question should be clarified.

4. The witness must be careful to avoid debate or argument.

5. The opposing attorney must not be considered an opponent and hostility should be avoided; jurors expect that lawyers will be treated courteously.

6. A calm and collected appearance is of great importance, for jurors observe the demeanor of a witness, particularly during cross-examination, in order to determine the weight to be given to his testimony.

7. Confidently answering the questions adds to the professional stature of the witness.

8. Only the questions asked should be answered, for there is no benefit in adding to the lines of inquiry already developed by opposing counsel.

9. The accounting knowledge of opposing counsel should not be underestimated.

10. The facts of the case should be known thoroughly before taking the witness stand. All previous testimony given during depositions should be carefully reviewed to avoid the embarrassment

that can arise if inconsistent statements are made or previous testimony is forgotten.

11. The witness should never fall into the position of changing the facts by some exaggeration.

12. On the other hand, the expert should not be afraid to change an answer made during direct examination if subsequent knowledge proves the answer to be incorrect.

13. The expert witness should not try to base answers on whether the client will be assisted by the answer. The client has an attorney for protection.

14. All answers to questions calling for an opinion should be kept within the realm of reasonable accounting certainty.

15. Avoid the appearance of quibbling or being evasive.

16. Avoid attempts at humor.

17. Don't engage in personal exchanges with opposing counsel, no matter what the provocation.

18. Be patient in communicating to nonaccountants the difficulties involved in the art of accounting.

19. Guard against undue apprehension and avoid overconfidence and the accompanying risks of carelessness.

20. Maintain your pride in your profession and your integrity as a professional.

A professional has a right and is expected to be proud of one's profession and jealous of the standards required to qualify as a member of that profession. This is the posture you should take during cross-examination. However, you must also distinguish between slurs on your integrity and questions concerning your competence or judgment. You have a right to be indignant at the former, but must depend upon your stature in the profession and accomplishments to refute the latter. The latter test is one of the reasons for cross-examination and does not entitle an expert accountant to a defensive or testy attitude. Cross-examination can be physically taxing because of the high demands it places on mental alertness and professional judgment, but thorough preparation makes it easier to meet these demands.

PERSPECTIVES OF COUNSEL ON CROSS-EXAMINATION

Trial attorneys look upon cross-examination as a valuable right and seem to be stimulated as cross-examination begins and suspense in the courtroom rises. Under direct examination, the witness has been treated gently, and has been questioned in a friendly manner by an attorney who graciously accepts the witness's version of the facts. At the start of cross-examination, the conditions change and you must prepare yourself for a different type of exchange during which you may have to cross swords with a capable and resourceful opponent. The most apparently innocuous question may appear to be a dangerous trap to be handled only with the utmost caution.

The witness is not the only participant in the drama of cross-examination who feels apprehensive about it. The cross-examiner is also likely to have doubts when starting. Cross-examination is not so easily handled, the witness is an opponent, and the examining process is filled with risks. Success is by no means assured and the pitfalls are many, even for attorneys with many years of practice behind them. Only experience can teach where the line lies between a cross-examination that is helpful and one that is harmful. There are no set rules to guide the attorney in framing questions.

The important question for the experienced cross-examiner is: Should cross-examination be undertaken? There are many occasions in which counsel may refrain from cross-examination. If an adverse witness has said nothing on direct examination that is of value to the other side, it is pointless to cross-examine, for this may provide the witness a second chance to say something which could really hurt the opponents. For the same reason, it is dangerous to cross-examine a witness on some matter that has no bearing on the issues in dispute. If the expert witness has not made an impression on the jury, it is rarely necessary to cross-examine at all.

When counsel decides to cross-examine, effective strategies and tactics must be employed, for success is not the result of momentary inspiration. Cross-examination requires behavioral knowledge, logical thought, understanding, patience and self-control. It calls for ability to judge character, ability to act with precision, and a substantial knowledge of the subject matter. It requires caution and an analytical ability to discover the weak points of the witness under examination.

As a general rule, the successful cross-examiner comes to court prepared, as a result of long hours of work attempting to anticipate the types of witnesses that may be called for the other side and the testimony they may give. In order to avoid an aimless cross-examination, counsel will usually pursue a line of questioning directed toward a clearly defined goal. Counsel will probably attack the crucial and vulnerable parts of the testimony. By concentrating on a few major issues and the weak points, counsel will attempt to expose inconsistencies or omissions in the testimony. Under these circumstances, it is possible for counsel, in the summation, to cast doubt upon the entire testimony of the witness. Any line of questioning that succeeds in shaking the veracity or reliability of the witness may be enough to undermine the testimony of the witness completely.

Asking too many questions on cross-examination may elicit responses that are unfavorable to the cross-examiner's case. Prying into everything said by a witness on the stand gives the witness a chance to buttress statements and gives them added weight and credibility. It also gives the witness the opportunity to explain points not brought out thoroughly during direct examination. There is also the danger that the witness may take the opportunity to testify to matters that on direct examination would not be admitted as evidence.

Usually counsel will scrutinize an adverse witness carefully and follow the direct testimony attentively to discover a possible basis for cross-examination. The physical appearance of the witness may provide counsel with ideas for questioning the credibility or reliability of the testimony. Psychological traits exhibited by the witness while on the stand will also be observed. Counsel will attempt to judge whether the witness is overly confident, voluble, prone to digress, or nervous. The answers to these questions will direct the line of inquiry by the cross-examiner.

It is usually poor strategy for the cross-examiner to impose upon the witness, for it is the duty of the judge to keep cross-examination within proper bounds, and it is not effective strategy to give the jury the impression that the witness is being unfairly treated. Cross-examining attorneys have greater latitude with expert witnesses, however, because the jury does not identify with the expert in the same way as with the lay witness and the judge expects the expert to have the ability for self-protection more than the lay witness does. The more effective cross-examiners seem to disarm the witness with friendliness. The aim here is to put the witness at ease, and lead the witness from one admission to another.

The cross-examiner who succeeds in getting a witness to admit a material fact favorable to the examiner's client will frequently drop the point at once to eliminate any opportunity for the witness to clarify the point in the opponent's favor. On cross-examination, a witness will rarely be given a chance to explain previous testimony which is damaging. Frequently, an effective type of cross-examination consists of a series of starts and stops, twists and turns, backtracking and fresh beginning. Any signs of evasiveness, admissions of error, carelessness, or unethical conduct on the part of the witness are used for counsel's summation. This kind of cross-examination can be disconcerting to the witness. Where the witness is aware that some answers did not give a favorable impression and would like to explain, counsel does not provide the opportunity. The witness is forced to answer in a pattern not of his own making and finds it hard to anticipate what is coming next. Thus the witness is not always able to appreciate the point of a question before it is too late to take back or to qualify what has been said. The witness, under these conditions, has the feeling of not being in full control.

It is of no immediate importance that the jury may not appreciate the significance of some of the witness's admissions during cross-examination. Counsel's task during cross-examination is chiefly to collect ammunition for later use in addressing the jury. That will be the time for counsel to set everything in its place.

PERSPECTIVES OF JURORS

Cross-examination is a combat and the interest and attention of jurors are heightened as this combat begins. Generally the jury regards this combat between a lay witness and the opposing attorney as unequal because of the skill and experience of the lawyer. The sympathies of the jurors are with the lay witness. Very few of these sentiments are held for expert witnesses, as jurors usually feel that experts should be capable of protecting themselves. Furthermore, as conflicting opinions are usually presented by expert witnesses of both parties, jurors tend to search for weaknesses in the testimony of experts and feel that the cross-examiner is assisting them in their selection of which of the experts is more credible.

Jurors are apt to regard a witness as a whole: they either believe the witness or they do not. If jurors distrust a witness, they are likely to disregard that person's testimony altogether, though much of it may have been true. In their minds, the fact remains that the witness attempted to deceive or mislead them, or the witness left the stand taking unfair advantage of superior knowledge and consequently such testimony should be disregarded.

REDIRECT EXAMINATION

Once a cross-examiner has attempted to impeach a witness on the stand, the party that placed the witness on the stand will be allowed on redirect examination to rehabilitate that witness. Redirect examination follows cross-examination and the rules governing redirect examination are the same as those governing direct examination.

Moreover, counsel cannot on redirect examination ask questions which were covered on direct examination, nor ask a question forgotten on direct examination. The court has broad discretion in this matter, however, and can decide to allow counsel to reopen the direct examination and go into new material.

Redirect examination provides counsel with an opportunity to clarify any of the answers made by the witness during cross-examination. The witness will be asked to explain any admissions made during cross-examination so that the meaning and limitations to any admissions may be clearly brought forth. Where the witness had been forced to shift from one subject to another during cross-examination and as a result had difficulty in remembering certain details of his previous testimony, counsel will usually retrace this testimony in a logical pattern and reestablish the testimony as initially presented. Any failures of memory will be explained. Where cross-examination has brought to light an error made by the witness, redirect examination will be used to explain how and why the error occurred, and new testimony will be presented correcting any error previously made. Where any answers to questions of the cross-examiner were inconsistent with direct testimony or created doubt, counsel will provide opportunities for the witness to reconcile the two testimonies and to clarify the meaning of the entire testimony. Counsel will also attempt to anticipate how the cross-examiner will use the results of cross-examination during summation to the jury and will ask those questions of the witness needed to offset any apparent advantages gained through cross-examination.

IMPEACHMENT AND REHABILITATION OF WITNESSES

Impeachment of a witness means that the witness's statement has been discredited. *Rehabilitation* means that the discrediting information has been overcome and that the credibility of the witness's statement has been reestablished in the eyes of the jury. Usually a party does not impeach its own witness but it may do so: when the witness is one the law requires the party to call to the stand; when the witness is an adverse party; when the witness shows hostility on the stand; when the witness is biased, and when the party calling the witness is truly surprised by the testimony of the witness.

One method of discrediting the testimony of a witness is to reveal a prior inconsistent statement regarding the matter to which that witness has just testified. Prior to the introduction of an inconsistent statement, the witness must be given an opportunity to explain or deny the inconsistent statement previously made. The witness need not be shown the writing, if the prior inconsistent statement was in writing, nor need the contents be disclosed, although it will be necessary to show the writing to the opposing attorney upon request. The attorney seeking to impeach the witness need only ask if the witness has at any time made any written or contrary statement to the fact just testified to, and if so, the reason for the inconsistency. If the witness admitted making the statement, most courts would not admit the statement. If the witness denied making the statement or claimed a lapse of memory, counsel would be permitted to put the statement into evidence.

CROSS-EXAMINING THE OPPONENT'S EXPERT ACCOUNTING WITNESS

During the deposition of the opposing expert accounting witness, the deponent will be questioned as to education, experience, proposed testimony, past services as an expert witness, prior writings, speeches, and any other matter that will enable counsel to evaluate the witness and understand the proposed testimony. Copies of trial exhibits will be obtained, the source data for the opinions of the deponent will be identified, and copies of such data will be requested. The deponent will usually not be challenged at this time unless the errors in the testimony are apparent, or if it suits a strategic purpose of examining counsel. A major purpose of the deposition is to obtain the information needed to provide a basis for cross-examining the deponent during trial. The expert accountant for examining counsel will appear at the deposition to become acquainted with the testimony and manner in which this testimony is given by the opposing expert accountant.

The past testimony, writings, and speeches of the opponent's expert accountant will be reviewed to identify any inconsistent statements made previously, as compared with the testimony to be given at trial. The expected effectiveness by which such testimony will be given will be evaluated and the proposed testimony will be studied to establish an approach for challenging the opponent's expert accountant. Questions will be developed to be used by counsel in cross-examining the opponent's expert accountant, and frequently the expert accountant for examining counsel will sit with counsel during the cross-examination of the opposing accountant and suggest further questions to examining counsel as the cross-examination proceeds.

The opponent's expert accounting witness will be cross-examined on all the accounting work performed as a basis for his testimony. The accounting records used will be examined to insure that they relate to the issues at trial. Where estimates have been made, the source and reliability of the estimates employed will be examined. Analytical accounting methods followed will be evaluated and compared with the results of alternative methods and similar analyses will be made of the mathematical techniques adopted. All arithmetic calculations will be checked. Where accounting ambiguities exist, cross-examination questions will be developed to exploit any advantageous situations. Generally, the cross-examination experiences of the expert accounting witnesses on both sides will be somewhat similar.

Communicating with Interdisciplinary Team Members, Juries, and Judges

It has been said that "no one would talk much in society if only he knew how often he misunderstands others." If this is so in ordinary conversation and in routine business affairs, how much greater must the opportunities be for misunderstanding in litigation where the problems are complex, the facts are in dispute, and different conclusions are drawn from roughly similar circumstances. The opportunities for misunderstanding are increased where, as in major antitrust cases, teams of expert witnesses from such different fields of knowledge as accounting, economics, mathematics, and statistics are called upon to prepare coordinated testimony to explain their clients' positions.

THE CONCEPT OF COMMUNICATING

Communication is the perception of information, ideas, and attitudes by the recipient of the message. The transmitter of the message employs the technique that enables a recipient to perceive the symbols which have been exchanged between transmitter and recipient. These symbols reflect intellectual and emotional values and much of the meaning that comes from the messages seems to come from the listener's bias, experience, and need. Gestures, tone of voice, and social and cultural backgrounds cannot be disassociated from the spoken language in the search for meaning in the information transmitted. Communication can occur only when the recipient is capable of understanding what is being transmitted. Thus, one can only communicate in the recipient's language, terms, or understanding. To determine whether the information is within the understanding of the recipient, some type of feedback response is required of the recipient. This gives some validity to the following overly simplified schematic of the communication process, which is frequently illustrated as follows:

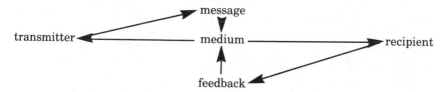

The transmitter, in sending a message to the recipient, employs a medium of conveyance. Accounting is one of the necessary communication mediums. The recipient's response constitutes feedback to the sender. Unless there is this interaction between the recipient and the transmitter of the message indicating that the message has been received and understood, there is no way of knowing whether the effort at communicating was effective.

All too frequently the recipients of messages hear what they expect to hear. There seems to be a natural inclination to resist any message which is contrary to the expectations of the recipient. Before communications can be effective, there is need for the transmitter to know what the recipient wishes to hear and is able to understand. The transmitter than must use some means to emphasize that new, unexpected information is being presented that requires effort on the part of the recipient to listen to, and not resist.

When listening ceases, communication ceases. When there is defensive listening, that is, the recipient is concerned with other thoughts or ideas, there is no listening. The most common results of defensive listening are confusion, hostility, or miscommunication. There are many other barriers to adequate listening, such as: (1) limitations of the recipient's capacity to absorb the information; (2) distractions created by competing stimuli for the attention of the recipient, or subjective stress; (3) assumptions which are unstated in the message on the assumption that what is obvious to the transmitter is known by the recipient; (4) the inclusion in the message of information which can mean different things to different people; and (5) confused presentations wherein the recipient ascribes a meaning to the message at variance with that intended by the sender.

Communication is one of the most complex of human tasks and this is especially so when the expert witness communicates directly with the jury. It is usually the function of the expert accountant to describe detailed, technical, and complex business situations in accounting terminology and format. This must be done without detailed knowledge of the backgrounds, interests, and abilities of the members of the jury, and under conditions that allow few opportunities for feedback from them. Where there is a nonjury trial, the communication problems are much simpler. Although trial judges may have no experience in accounting, their knowledge of accounting is generally far greater than that of the general public, as accounting information is frequently included in judicial proceedings. Furthermore, the judge has the opportunity to question the witness and does so with less restraint than when a jury is present. Thus, there is greater feedback between transmitter and recipient of information. Presenting accounting testimony effectively, however, frequently remains a formidable problem for the expert accounting witness.

Despite the difficulties involved, expert accounting witnesses must induce judges and juries to listen to their testimony, to hear what the witnesses wish them to hear, and finally to accept the messages they are communicating. How can an expert accountant become effective in inducing the judge and jury to listen when people rarely listen to others, when communications can be so easily misunderstood, and when improvements in personal communication abilities depend upon some understanding of recent research and experiments by psychologists, sociologists, and communication engineers, among others?

In this instance, it is somewhat fortunate that litigation is a combat between two parties, and that resolution of the combat is arrived at by the selection of the position of one party over the other by the judge and jury. Thus, while expertise in the communication process is desirable it may not be essential, and superiority over the adversary in this process may be sufficient. Appreciation of the problems inherent in effective communication, recognition of the importance to the expert witness of knowledge and integrity and the maintenance of these characteristics, and understanding of how easily people confuse assumptions, inferences and value judgments with facts, including the many ways in which meanings can be altered to conform with desires, whims, or subjective needs, can assist the expert accounting witness to attain superiority in the communication process over an adversary.

WHY EFFECTIVE COMMUNICATION IS IMPORTANT TO THE EXPERT ACCOUNTING WITNESS

The expert accounting witness usually appears on the witness stand toward the end of the client's case. When appearing for the plaintiff, your function as an expert witness is to supplement previous testimony with accounting data and to convert the alleged injuries, as described by the business, economic, mathematical, and statistical witnesses, into estimates of financial loss which become the damage claim. This claim is prepared before the trial commences and is the result not only of the thoughts of the expert accountant, but also includes the concepts of the other witnesses. As the plaintiff will usually state that the damage claim is a conservative statement of the financial impact of the alleged injuries, careful evaluations have to be made of the validity and acceptability of the proposed testimony which leads to the damage claim. Many meetings of witnesses will be held prior to trial to explain, analyze, and consider the concepts to be presented by the witnesses and to coordinate the testimony that is to be given. Decisions will be made on the strengths and weaknesses of proposed testimony, and the concepts that can withstand cross-examination will be accepted and quantified in the damage formula. During these meetings the problems of communicating in ambiguous situations will be experienced over and over again, and these problems can be overcome only when the participants recognize the difficulty of communicating under such circumstances and become effective in communicating in these situations. As an expert accounting witness, you will be better qualified to meet the rigors of cross-examination if you have been able to clarify and coordinate the earlier testimony of other witnesses with your own. While you are not responsible for the testimony of other experts, clever cross-examination can discredit an expert accountant who incorporates in the damage claim unsupported, easily discredited, or misunderstood concepts of other experts.

Prior to and during the trial, changes may be made in the position of the plaintiff through stipulations, motions, and orders of the court. The expert accountant must be aware of these changes and modify the damage claims accordingly. During the trial, concepts of the witnesses may be discredited and computational theories may be found unacceptable, thereby requiring changes in the damage claim. Communication lines with counsel must be open so that these situations may be quickly communicated to the expert accountant.

The expert accountant for the defendant faces the same types of communication problems as does the expert accountant for the plaintiff, needing to effectively participate in many interdisciplinary team meetings and master the skills of communicating in an environment of uncertainty. The expert accountants on both sides discuss technical matters which are difficult for the ordinary jury members to understand, and skill in communicating is an essential ingredient in presenting accounting testimony.

PROBLEMS IN COMMUNICATING WITH INTERDISCIPLINARY TEAM MEMBERS

Failure in communicating among members of different disciplines and with experts in the same field are not unusual. Each discipline develops its own vocabulary and there is no reason why the meaning of specific terms used by an accountant, for example, should be self-evident to an economist or mathematician. New terms are being brought into use but the most serious barrier is not the unfamiliar word but the common term where variations in meaning exist. Technical terms may provide a precise meaning or may, through careless usage or faulty understanding, lead to ambiguity. Information can mean different things to different people, and patience and tolerance are needed to avoid the disputes that can arise from different interpretations of similar data.

Difficulties can arise in communicating because of the vast amount of research in progress and the increasing tempo of discovery. The nature of experimental work in different disciplines is unique, and the special problems of evaluation in these research projects can lead to the development of new techniques which are familiar only to those performing the studies.

During the development of the economic and accounting strategies, particularly in large antitrust cases, meetings with interdisciplinary team members will be frequent and participants will be required to communicate their findings and conclusions. As a communicator, the expert accountant must have some knowledge of the educational and experience backgrounds of the team members so as to form an idea of how to communicate messages. There is a danger of withholding information on the grounds that what is so obvious to oneself must be self-evident to the other members, and the more knowledgeable the communicator, the greater the degree of care must be exercised to avoid this pitfall. Also, incorrect assumptions of proficiency of the receiver of information should be guarded against, for expertise in one discipline gives no assurance of proficiency or interest in other fields of knowledge. Statements should be as short and as simple as possible, for the less said, the easier and faster the message is received, and less room exists for misunderstanding. The sender of the message should test whether the receivers have gotten the same message that the sender thinks has been transmitted. The receiving of information usually requires far more interpretation than people are aware of, and when the presentation of information is overly technical, the barriers to effective communication will usually remain.

Listening is also part of communicating and is concerned with what is done with the data obtained from oral messages. It is a search for meaning, and good listening leads to questions. When one listens defensively, one doesn't listen at all. Defensive listening occurs when the listener takes the time to compose a rebuttal while another is still speaking. The listener has already decided that the speaker is wrong, and this is based on the assumption that the listener can predict what the speaker is about to say. Defensive listening occurs most frequently at meetings or conferences, and is present whenever there is a threat, disagreement, dispute, confusion, impatience, emotional involvement, or commitment to a point of view. As these conditions seem to permeate all phases of the litigation process, the expert accounting witness must make the effort to understand and practice the arts of effective communication.

COMMUNICATING WITH JURIES

The jury system is based on the belief that people evaluate things differently. It is one function of the jury system to bring these divergent evaluations to the trial process. If all people weighed trial evidence in the same manner, a jury of one would be as good as a jury of twelve. The jury brings into the courtroom the different perceptions that exist in the community. It is these many perceptions of the jury that add to the complexities of communicating with them by the expert witnesses.

Many people have come to the conclusion that juries are a good thing because they don't always apply the law. As a distinguished judge once stated, "A jury has its uses. You have to have something that does give a little, something to seal the law to the facts. There isn't any known way to legislate with an allowance for the right feeling. The jury protects the court. It is a question how long any system of courts could last in a free country, if judges found the verdicts. It doesn't matter how wise and experienced the judge may be. Resentment would build up every time the findings didn't go with current notions or prejudice. There is no focal point with a jury; the jury is the public itself. That is why a jury can say, when a judge couldn't, 'I don't care what the law is, that isn't right and I won't do it.' It is the greatest prerogative of free men."

In civil cases, the right to trial by jury has generally been preserved to the parties. Any party may demand a trial by jury of any issue associated with right of trial by jury by serving on the other party a demand in writing at any time after the commencement of the action and not later than 10 days after the service of the last pleading directed to such issue. The parties may specify the issues to be tried by the jury, otherwise the trial by jury of all the issues shall have been demanded. A demand for trial by jury may not be withdrawn without the consent of the parties. The court, in its discretion, may order a trial by a jury of any and all issues. The parties may stipulate that the jury in federal court shall consist of any number fewer than 12 or that a verdict or a finding of a stated majority of the jurors shall be taken as the verdict or finding of the jury. Not more than six alternate jurors may be selected.

The jurors are selected at random from a fair cross-section of the community where the court convenes. All citizens have the opportunity for service on the jury and have the obligation to serve as jurors when summoned for that purpose. Qualifications of the jurors are determined solely on the basis of information provided on the juror qualification form and other competent evidence. A person is unqualified or may be exempt from jury duty if the person is: (1) not a citizen, 18 years of age or older, and a resident of the district for one year; (2) unable to read, write, and understand the English language well enough to fill out satisfactorily the juror qualification form; (3) unable to speak the English language; (4) incapable by reason of mental or physical infirmity; and (5) has a charge pending against him or her or has been convicted of a crime punishable for more than one year, and civil rights have not been restored by pardon or amnesty. In civil cases, each party is entitled to three peremptory challenges, and all challenges for cause or favor are determined by the court.

Many expert witnesses have found the problems of communicating with juries to be difficult principally because of the wide disparity of knowledge, skills, and experience of jurors and because of the absence of feedback from the jury to the expert witnesses that would enable the witnesses to determine whether their testimony has been received as intended. To react to these problems as effectively as the situation permits and prior to preparing direct testimony, the expert accounting witness should obtain some description of the ages, work experiences, and educational backgrounds of the jurors, for it is their understanding of the testimony of the expert that will be influential in determining the decision on the facts of the case. In most instances, the expert accountant must have the ability to present complex accounting situations in simple terms and by simple examples, provided the judge approves the presentation of simple accounting examples as illustrative testimony. As an expert, the accounting witness will be permitted to give a dissertation or exposition of accounting principles, practices, and techiques relevant to the case and point out to the jury how these statements can be applied to the facts of the case. The expert accountant may also present opinion as evidence to fill gaps in the facts and to make testimony clearer for the jury when they ordinarily would not understand it or when there is no other way in getting the facts before the jury for deciding the case.

When opinion evidence is presented, the expert witness takes the further step of suggesting to the jury the inferences which should be drawn from applying the witness's specialized knowledge to the facts. The facts or data upon which an expert bases an opinion or inference may be those perceived or made known at or before the trial. If the facts or data are of a type reasonably relied upon by experts in the particular field in forming opinions or inferences upon the subject, the facts or data need not be admissible in evidence. Facts or data upon which expert opinions are based may be derived from three sources: (1) firsthand observations of the witness; (2) the presentation of data at the trial by hypothetical questions or by having the expert attend the trial and hear the testimony establishing the facts (the problems of determining what testimony the expert relied on need not be brought out in direct testimony unless the court requires such a disclosure or opposing counsel requires the disclosure of the underlying facts or data on cross-examination); and (3) the presentation of data to the expert outside the courtroom and other than by his own perception.

The expert witness, in order to assist the jury where specialized knowledge and experience is required, may testify in the form of answering hypothetical questions. Although the hypothetical question starts with the word *assume,* the jury knows that the question deals with the subject matter of the case. In answering the question, an expert witness must organize the reasons so that the answer is in good logical sequence, making it easy for the jury to understand.

The difficulty with opinion evidence is that it is speculative and there are no definite answers, as opinions of experts can differ. When opinion evidence is given, the expert witness is, in effect, deciding an issue or fact in the case, and this is the role of the jury. However, testimony in this form that is otherwise admissible is not objectionable because it embraces an ultimate issue to be decided by the judge or jury. When opinions of experts are excluded, however, it is because they are unhelpful and therefore superfluous.

OPENING AND CLOSING STATEMENTS OF COUNSEL

The trial attorneys have two opportunities to communicate directly with the jury. The trial begins with the opening statements by counsel, which deal with the facts of the case and not with issues of law. In civil cases the attorney for the plaintiff is usually called on first. Although the trial judge and counsel for the defendant will listen attentively to see if there is a prima facie case, the essential purpose of the opening statement is to permit counsel to communicate directly with the jury, to present to the jury the client's version of the facts, and to lay the foundation of the proof to be presented in substantiating the claim. The opening statement should include a forthright presentation of: (1) what happened that caused the dispute between the parties; (2) why the defendant was to blame; what the defendant did that should not have been done or should have done that was not done; (3) what injuries or damages the plaintiff sustained as a result of the defendant's blameworthy conduct; and (4) how the dollar value of these damages were calculated.

A clear word-picture in the opening statement of the chief events and circumstances involved will make it easier for the judge and jury to follow the main thread of the case as it moves through the details to be brought out later in the testimony. The attorney can also use this opportunity to strengthen rapport with members of the jury and to dispose them to be sympathetic to the client. The opening statement must be consistent with the complaint and the bill of particulars and should be correlated with every document, deposition, and exhibit that counsel intends to place into evidence. In civil cases, if opening statements are not normally recorded by the court reporter, either counsel may request that the opening remarks to the jury be made a part of the trial record.

In describing the facts, counsel will interpret the evidence in a manner favorable to his clients. Usually emphasis will be on facts, not surmises, suppositions, or opinions. Counsel will usually attempt this type of presentation without overstating the case, thereby avoiding promising to prove more than is possible. If counsel fails to provide the proof the jury was led to expect, the adversary attorney will have ammunition for a summation which could be quite harmful.

In the opening statement, counsel will attempt to avoid a disjointed monologue in which every detail of the case is included, for the effect of such tactics is to distract the members of the jury from the main line of argument and bog them down in irrelevant details. Counsel will attempt in the opening remarks to lead the jury along a direct line without any detours and irrelevant details.

The same general principles that make for an effective introductory statement by counsel for the plaintiff apply also to the defendant counsel in the opening remarks to the jury. Defense counsel may waive the right to make an opening statement to the jury, and may do so when an opening statement might result in premature disclosure of certain facts which would give the plaintiff a chance to obtain additional proof or to find rebuttal witnesses. Where this is done, the jury hears no answers whatsoever to the statements made by counsel for the plaintiff. In the opening statement, defense counsel will rarely attempt to disprove all the plaintiff's contentions but will, after presenting a clear, affirmative story of the defendant's position, seek and discuss those major issues in which the plaintiff's case seems to be deficient. The jury will be asked to follow the testimony on those issues with particular care. It will also be pointed out by defense counsel that the statements of the adversary are not evidence and that proof must come from witnesses, exhibits, or depositions.

The opening statements are the first of two opportunities the attorneys have during the trial to address the jury directly and at length. After all testimony has been heard, the attorneys have another chance to discuss the facts of the case and make their final appeals to the jury. This rounds out the presentation of the case and brings it to its conclusion, as the *summation* is the last opportunity for each counsel to address the jury. In the closing remarks, each counsel will attempt to persuade the jury of the justice of the client's position and of the interpretation of the facts which were brought out in the testimony. Counsel will marshal all arguments available in the client's favor and present them as convincingly as possible. The summation generally will concentrate on the strong points of the case. The chief weaknesses of the adversary case, gaps in evidence, illogical inferences, inconclusive data, inconsistencies, dubious data, and so forth, are described.

Summation usually follows the normal trial sequence: plaintiff, defendant, and plaintiff rebuttal. There are no limitations on eloquence, but both counsel are required to stay within the record. Counsel may not argue points of law, for this is the province of the judge, who supplies the jury with the necessary law of the case in the charge to the jury. The charge is usually given following the summations of counsel, and the jury then retires to consider its verdict.

If the summation is to serve its purpose, it must be clear and coherent. The essential ideas should be presented in an order that is logical and comprehensible. How effectively counsel has organized the materials in the summation will have an impact on the jury. Counsel should have a well organized outline of remarks and should have readily available at the counsel table, clear notes of the testimony, and all exhibits received in testimony. In the large, complex antitrust cases, this requirement alone is a major undertaking.

Counsel is permitted, at the court's discretion, to address the jury for a reasonable period of time. Usually the trial judge will ask counsel for both sides to agree on the length of time each will need. The summation should be frank and direct. All the knowledge gained concerning effective communication should be applied. The summation is counsel's last opportunity to make points that will stick in the minds of the jury. Thus, the summation should be convincing.

COMMUNICATING WITH AND BY THE TRIAL JUDGE

The adversary proceedings which characterize the court system leave the initiative in litigation to the parties. It is rare for a judge to ask questions directly of a witness. At every stage each side has the right to appeal to the judge to prevent a particular line of questions being put to the other side. The judge considers the objection and decides it at once in most instances. Sometimes the trial will be interrupted for the judge to hear legal arguments on the point. The judge will consider a point, if an objection is made by a party. Without an objection being made, there will be no intervention by the judge. The judge will act impartially to protect a party's rights, but only if the party requests this intervention. The concept of neutrality and impartiality in a judge is an ancient one.

A judge upholds the integrity and independence of the judiciary. While the rulings are subject to appeal, the judge is still supreme in the courtroom. A judge is expected, however, to respect and to comply with the law, to maintain professional competence in it, and to promote confidence in the impartiality of the judiciary. The judge maintains order and decorum in the proceedings before the court and affords to each person who is legally interested in a proceeding or that person's lawyer, the full right to be heard according to the law. Judges are expected to be courteous to litigants, jurors, witnesses, lawyers, and others with whom they come in contact and they require similar conduct from lawyers, court officials, and others subject to their direction and control. Judges are expected to avoid impropriety and the appearance of impropriety in all their activities. While a judge may engage in activities to improve the law, the legal system and the administration of justice, he should regulate his extrajudicial activities to minimize the risk of conflict with his judicial duties. A judge should regularly file reports of compensation received from quasijudicial and extrajudicial activities and should refrain from political activity inappropriate to his judicial office.

FEDERAL RULES OF EVIDENCE

In a jury trial, the witnesses communicate directly with the jury by giving testimony during direct and cross-examination while the judge listens. The trial judge controls this communication in federal courts, in accordance with the Federal Rules of Evidence, by ruling on objections made by opposing counsel to evidence being given or proposed. The state courts usually apply similar rules of evidence. The purpose of the rules of evidence is to secure fairness in administration, elimination of unjustifiable expense and delay, and promotion of growth and the development of the law of evidence so that the truth may be ascertained and proceedings justly determined.

Under the rules, evidence must be relevant, material, and competent. *Relevant* evidence means evidence having any tendency to make the existence of any fact that is of consequence to the determination of the action more probable or less probable than it would be without the evidence. Relevant evidence is generally admissible; irrelevant evidence is inadmissible. Yet, not all relevant evidence is admissible, particularly when such evidence creates unfair prejudice, confusion, or waste of time. Evidence is *material* if it has a direct effective bearing or influence on one or more pertinent facts at issue. Evidence is competent if it is given in the form of testimony by a properly qualified person, or if it was produced by such a person. Evidence of habit or routine practice of an organization is relevant to prove that the conduct of a person or organization on a particular occasion was in conformity with that habit or routine.

Hearsay is a statement other than one made by the declarant while testifying at the trial or hearing that is offered in evidence to prove the truth of the matter asserted. Hearsay evidence is generally excluded because it is not subject to the three conditions under which a witness is required to testify: under oath; in the presence of the trier of facts; and subject to cross-examination. The emphasis in the hearsay rule tends to concentrate on the condition of cross-examination, and as the hearsay statement was made by a declarant other than the one on the witness stand, there is no opportunity for cross-examination. Cross-examination is considered by many to be the great legal engine for the discovery of truth, as the hope in cross-examination is to expose imperfections of perception, memory, and narration.

Exceptions to the hearsay rule in civil cases deal with situations where the availability of the declarant is regarded as immaterial and where the unavailability of the declarant is made a condition to the admission of the hearsay statement. In criminal cases, the Sixth Amendment to the U.S. Constitution requires confrontation and the ability to cross-examine. In civil cases where the declarant testifies at the trial and is subject to cross-examination concerning a statement made, prior statements made by the witness are not subject to the hearsay rule where: those statements are inconsistent with his testimony and were given under oath subject to the penalty of perjury at a trial, hearing, or other proceeding or in a deposition; or the statements are consistent with his testimony and are offered to rebut an express or implied charge against the witness that the statements are of recent fabrication, or improper influence, or motive. Prior inconsistent statements are admissible to impeach but not as substantive statements. A memorandum, report, or record, in any form, of acts, events, conditions, or opinions made at or near the time by a person with knowledge or from information transmitted by a person with knowledge, if kept in the course of regularly conducted business activity, and if it was the regular practice of that business activity to make such record, all as shown by testimony of the custodian or other qualified witness, will be treated as an exception to the hearsay rule, unless the source of information or the circumstances of preparation indicate lack of trustworthiness.

A presumption imposes on the party against whom it is directed the burden of going forward with evidence to rebut or to meet the presumption, but does not shift to such party the burden of proof in the sense of the risk of nonpersuasion that remains throughout the trial upon the party on whom it was originally cast. A judicially noted fact must be one not subject to reasonable dispute in that it is either: generally known within the territorial jurisdiction of the court; or is capable of accurate and ready determination by resort to sources whose accuracy cannot be questioned. In civil cases, the court instructs the jury to accept as conclusive any fact judicially noted; in criminal cases, the jury may, but is not required to accept any fact judicially noted. Privilege is governed by common law as interpreted by the courts or in accordance with state law where the state law supplies the rule of decision. Federal courts must observe privilege in: required reports; lawyer–client communications; psychotherapist–patient relations; husband–wife relations; communications to clergymen; political vote; trade secrets; secrets of state and other official information; and in the identity of an informer.

Every person is qualified to be a witness except as otherwise provided in the rules of evidence. No mental or moral qualifications are specified. A witness may not testify to a matter unless evidence is introduced sufficient to support a finding that he has personal knowledge of the matter. The judge presiding at the trial may not testify in the trial as a witness. A juror in any given trial may not testify as a witness before the jury in that trial. The credibility of a witness may be attacked or supported by evidence in the form of opinion or reputation subject to these limitations: evidence may refer only to reputation for truthfulness or untruthfulness; and evidence for truthfulness is admitted only after character for truthfulness has been attacked.

For a witness not testifying as an expert, testimony in the form of opinions or inferences is limited to those opinions or inferences which are: rationally based on the perceptions of the witness; and helpful to a clear understanding of that person's testimony on the determination of a fact in issue. The court usually recognizes that witnesses often find it difficult to express themselves in language which is not that of an opinion or conclusion. Leading questions should not be used on the direct examination of a witness except as may be necessary to develop the testimony. Ordinarily, leading questions will be permitted on cross-examination. When a party calls a hostile witness, an adverse party, or a witness identified with an adverse party, interrogation may be by leading questions.

If a witness in a civil case uses a document to refresh the memory for the purpose of testifying, either while testifying or before testifying, and if the court determines that it is necessary in the interests of justice, the adverse party is entitled to have the document produced at the hearing, to inspect it, to cross-examine the witness concerning it, and to introduce into evidence those portions which related to the testimony of the witness. If it is claimed that the documents contain matter not related to the subject matter of the testimony, the court shall examine the document *in camera,* excise any portion not so related, and order delivery of the remainder to the party entitled to it. If a document is not produced, the court shall make any order that justice requires.

If scientific, technical, or other specialized knowledge will assist the trier of fact to understand the evidence or to determine a fact in issue, a witness qualified as an expert by knowledge, skill, experience, training, or education may testify to it in the form of an opinion or otherwise. On a trial judge's own initiative, or on the motion of any party an order may be entered to show cause why one or more expert witnesses should not be appointed to assist the court. The trial judge may request the parties to submit nominations and may appoint the expert witnesses agreed upon by the parties or those based upon the judge's own selection. The expert witnesses so appointed shall advise the parties of their findings, if any, their depositions may be taken by any party and these experts may be called upon to testify by the court or by any party. The court-appointed expert witnesses are subject to cross-examination by each party, including a party calling them as witnesses. The court may, in the exercise of its discretion, authorize disclosure to the jury of the fact that the court had appointed the expert witness.

The court-appointed expert witnesses may also represent the trial judge in pretrial hearings dealing with reports and findings of the expert witnesses of the parties. In these meetings, the court-appointed experts may acquire an aura of infallibility to which they are not entitled. This power can exert a sobering effect upon the expert witnesses of each party and upon the clients utilizing their services.

The trial judge is empowered to exercise reasonable control over the method and order of interrogating witnesses and presenting evidence so as to: make the interrogation and presentation effective for the ascertainment of the truth; avoid needless consumption of time; and protect the witness from harassment or embarrassment. Detailed rules describing the order and mode of interrogating witnesses have not been developed. However, the ultimate responsibility for the effective working of the adversary system rests with the judge.

FEDERAL RULES OF CIVIL PROCEDURE

In federal courts the trial judges, from a procedural standpoint, are guided by Rules of Civil Procedure and Rules of Criminal Procedure. These rules are intended to be construed to secure the just, speedy, and inexpensive determination of every action and to give notice of claims and defenses, complemented by a scheme that would permit parties to discover in advance of trial, facts and issues underlying the controversy. These innovations were intended not only to eliminate the technical rigidity associated with previous practice, but also to mitigate the sporting quality of adversarial litigation. The state courts have similar rules governing court procedures.

Discovery under the federal rules is extremely broad in scope, encompassing any unprivileged matter that is relevant to the action before the court, even if the information requested would not be admissible at trial, provided it appears reasonably calculated to lead to the discovery of admissible evidence. Discovery generally proceeds at the initiative of the parties without requiring the involvement of the court.

The breadth of and reliance on party initiatives make discovery susceptible to abuse. To protect against unwarranted and vexatious use of discovery, protective orders and sanctions were included in the procedures. The protective order excuses the moving party from answering excessive discovery demands. A party whose discovery request has not been satisfied may seek relief from the court through an order to compel discovery. If that order is disobeyed, the court may exclude claims or defenses, strike the pleadings, dismiss the action, or enter a default judgment. The court may also treat the failure as contempt.

Also under the Rules of Civil Procedure, the court may, in its discretion, direct the attorneys to appear for a pretrial conference. A pretrial conference can accomplish much in the way of speeding trials and reducing litigation costs. At a pretrial conference the parties will consider: (1) the simplification of the issues; (2) the necessity or desirability of amendments to the pleadings; (3) the possibility of obtaining admissions of facts and of documents which will avoid unnecessary proof; (4) the limitation of the number of expert witnesses; (5) the advisability of a preliminary reference of issues to a master for findings to be used as evidence when the trial is to be by jury; and (6) such other matters as may aid in the disposition of the action.

Class actions are permitted under these rules and one or more members of a class may sue or be sued as representation parties on behalf of all only if: (1) the class is so numerous that joinder of all members is impractical; (2) there are questions of law or fact common to the class; (3) the claims or defenses of the representative parties are typical of the claims or defenses of the class; and (4) the representative parties will fully and adequately protect the interests of the class. Class actions will be maintained if, in addition, the prosecution of separate actions by or against individual members of the class would create a risk of inconsistent or varying adjudications with respect to individual members of the class that would establish incompatible standards of conduct for the parties opposing the class or adjudications with respect to individual members of the class, which would, as a practical matter, be dispositive of the interests of the other members not parties to the adjudications or substantially impair or impede their ability to protect their interests; or the party opposing the class has acted or refused to act on grounds generally applicable to the class, thereby making appropriate final relief or corresponding declarative relief with respect to the class as a whole; or the court finds that the question of law or fact common to the members of the class predominate over any questions affecting only individual members and that a class action is superior to other available methods for the fair and efficient adjudication of the controversy. Matters pertinent to the findings permitting a class action include: (1) the interest of members of the class in individually controlling the prosecution or defense of the separate actions; (2) the extent and nature of any litigation concerning the controversy already commenced by or against members of the class; (3) the desirability or undesirability of concentrating the litigation of the claims in the particular forum; and (4) the difficulties likely to be encountered in the management of a class action.

Facts known and opinions held by expert witnesses are discoverable under these rules. A party may, through interrogations, require any other party to identify each person whom the other party expects to call as an expert witness at trial, to state the subject matter on which the expert is expected to testify, and to state the substance of the facts and opinions to which the expert is to testify with a summary of the grounds for each opinion. A party may discover facts known or opinions held by an expert, who has been retained or specifically employed by another party in anticipation of litigation in preparation for trial, and who is not expected to be called as a witness at trial upon a showing of exceptional circumstances under which it is impracticable for the party seeking the discovery to obtain facts or opinions on the same subject by other means.

Rules of evidence and rules of civil procedures are similar in jury and nonjury trials. Where a nonjury trial is agreed upon, the trial judge becomes the adjudicator of both the facts and the law. A nonjury trial is likely to be completed much sooner and more efficiently than a jury trial. Under these circumstances, the expert witness may present to the court evidence which is more technical and less detailed than if a jury were present. Although trial judges usually are not experts in many different disciplines, they frequently have directed many trials dealing with economic, accounting, and mathematical matters and have acquired knowledge in these fields and an ability to absorb technically detailed information. While many of the communication problems remain when an expert discusses one's own specialty with an expert in a different endeavor, the communication problems are far simpler than those that arise when an expert must educate a layman in that same field of specialty. Furthermore, the expert witness in a nonjury trial is communicating with one person rather than 12 jurors, and the judge is in a position to ask questions whenever the evidence presented to him is unclear. This closes the communication cycle more effectively than when a jury is present. Where the judge is the trier of facts, accounting testimony need not be supplemented by simplifying, hypothetical examples of accounting evidence, and technical descriptions of accounting events can be used rather than attempting to describe complicated technical situations in common words to enhance understanding by the jury at the risk of less precise descriptions of the events discussed in the testimony.

MOTIONS BY ATTORNEYS

Aside from the evidence given by the witness, most of the communications during trial are between the trial judge and the attorneys. These discussions are conducted in both a formal and informal manner. Throughout the trial the judge is asked to rule on a variety of *motions* presented by the attorneys or on requests to admit or reject evidence. These motions can be ruled upon by the court with or without agreement by the trial lawyers. The judge will frequently interrupt the proceedings to hold informal conferences with the attorneys in his chambers, or at the bench, but beyond the hearing of the jurors, and these discussions will usually be off the record. Such discussions give the trial attorney a clearer understanding of the thought processes of the judge and not only facilitate the judicial proceedings but strengthen the communication process during the remainder of the trial.

At the conclusion of evidence, in civil cases, motions are frequently made by the attorneys for a directed verdict by asking that the judge direct the jury to render a verdict as ordered by the judge. When this motion is asked for by defendant counsel, the defendant asserts that the plaintiff has not established all the evidence necessary to make a case. The authority of the judge to direct a verdict by the jury developed at the common law. It has been held that such authority of the trial judge flows from the judicial function of determining the sufficiency of the evidence. It has been determined that the right to a trial by jury does not include a right to a verdict based upon jury deliberations. The questions that a judge should consider in reaching a decision on this motion are: (1) do the facts brought out by admissible and substantial evidence and all the proper inferences derived from them establish a legal case; and (2) do the facts so clearly fail to present a pertinent issue of fact that reasonable men could not disagree? The judge usually excludes the jury from the courtroom while the lawyers argue these questions before the bench. If the answer to either or both these questions are favorable to the defendant, the judge can immediately take the case from the jury by directing the jury to render a specified verdict for the defendant. However, if there is any doubt, the trial judge can delay ruling until after the jury has delivered a verdict. This occurs frequently because, if the judge is later to be shown to be wrong in directing a verdict, or if an upper court reverses the case, it is not necessary to have another trial but only to reinstate the verdict of the jury. However, if it is clear that the motion should be granted or denied, the judge has a duty to grant it or deny it at this time. Actions on this motion are separate and apart from the functions of the jury. The judge has found as a matter of law that there is no issue which calls for jury action. If the judge grants the motion he will order the jury to return a specified verdict. This is done without the jury leaving the courtroom. If any of the jurors refuse to render the directed verdict, they can be held in contempt of court.

In civil and criminal cases the defendant is usually the party who makes this motion. In a civil case involving several counts, the result can be that certain counts can be stricken from jury consideration, or the entire case can be disposed of. Where there are multiple defendants, the motion can be granted to some and denied to others. The motion can also be made by the plaintiff in civil or criminal cases. In a civil case, the motion can be granted on the basis that the defendant has produced no substantial evidence to support a defense. The jury would then determine an amount of damages to be awarded the plaintiff. In criminal cases, the use of a directed motion by the prosecutor is restricted. If the motion is denied, the case will proceed to a jury verdict.

At the conclusion of the trial the attorneys for each party present to the judge, in written form, their conclusions on how the law or laws apply to the case on hand. The trial judge then discusses the case with the jury prior to asking them to retire to consider their verdict. In the charge to the jury, the judge: explains the issues involved in the case; explains the positions taken by each side; discusses the principles of evidence and their application; describes the rule or rules of law which will be applicable to any factual situation which may be found in the evidence; and presents specific instructions applicable to the case at hand.

The jury is then asked to retire and render a verdict.

It is the privilege of the lawyer for the losing party to request that the jury be polled: that each juror separately report a verdict. In that case, the clerk of the court calls each name and asks each juror for an individual verdict. If all render the same verdict, the verdict will be accepted. If any juror gives a contrary verdict, the judge sends the jury back to the jury room for further deliberation.

CHAPTER

10

Negotiating Settlements and Disbursing Awards

To litigate a claim, a person must have: patience and endurance; an ability to withstand frustration and uncertainty; adequate financial resources; a competent attorney; an understanding judge; and more than average good luck. Judge Learned Hand once told the Bar of New York, "as a litigant I should dread a lawsuit beyond almost anything else short of sickness and death." The frustrating delays of dispute resolution through formal, legal means, and the excessive costs are primary causes for the crisis in the American system of civil justice. The pretrial paper wars and the extended trials clog the dockets of the state and federal courts.

Most business executives feel that it is preferable to avoid litigation by investigating and resolving disputes on a businesslike basis as promptly as possible. They generally prefer the uncertainties of private settlement procedures to the uncertainties of a trial. It is common for corporate management to schedule meetings at which responsible employees from each company appear and present both sides of the dispute. At these meetings, the business executives act as lawyers, jury, and judge. By contrast, once litigation is initiated such simple and informal attempts at dispute resolution rarely occur. Instead, settlement discussions generally involve the more direct discussion of what it will take to settle the case, and court approval of the proposed settlement must usually be obtained.

It can be disastrous for a company to be sued. Resolving the dispute may be far more costly than paying a large settlement to the plaintiff. Acting upon this concept, many attorneys institute litigation as a mechanism for forcing settlements. On the other hand, the defendant usually is in possession of the money or property that is the subject of the dispute. The defendant thus has a reason for delaying the litigation and can place discovery hurdles in the path of the plaintiff. Either party can use discovery as a means of gaining substantial settlements to avoid years of involvement, enormous expenses, attorneys' fees, and the inordinate drain upon corporate time and energy.

The judicial process is not only time consuming and expensive, but in certain cases adverse decisions can come close to destroying or severely dismembering a corporation. There seems to be at least two possible sets of facts, legal precedents, rules, and possible outcomes of each case. Even after judgment is awarded in the lower courts, there is no certainty that higher courts will uphold the judgment. Judges have a habit of dissenting in their opinions. If a case comes to court at all, there is always some doubt as to what rules apply. Since no two cases are ever exactly alike, in case law, strictly speaking, there are few controlling rules or situations. Litigants also take advantage of superior financial resources to overwhelm their opponents. Under the circumstances, settlement often looms as an attractive alternative, and more than 90% of federal civil cases are settled.

The Federal Rules of Civil Procedure, which provide for extensive pretrial discovery of the strengths of both parties' positions, and pretrial conferences, which add to the mutual knowledge of the case, increase the frequency of settlements. Meetings between lawyers and hearings before judges in advance of the trial result in many negotiated compromises. At the pretrial conferences, while settlement is not a deliberate objective, it is often the result. While the trial judges attempt to protect the interests of both parties, they usually will look favorably upon settlements negotiated between competent attorneys. Evidence of furnishing, or offering to furnish, or accepting, or offering to accept a valuable consideration in compromising, or attempting to compromise a claim which was disputed as to either validity or amount is not admissible to prove liability for or invalidity of the claim or the amount. Evidence of conduct and statements made in compromise negotiations are likewise not admissible.

The federal trial judge for the Southern District of New York in 1969 when discussing the desirability of a proposed settlement in the broad-spectrum antibiotic cases with all but six nonsettling states indicated: "A careful study of the records leads to a conclusion that the chances of recovery in any of these cases are no better than 50–50 and probably should more realistically be called slight. Not only is it uncertain that any plaintiff can secure a jury verdict, it is also uncertain whether judges or justices will find the evidence sufficient to support any such verdict. There is no direct evidence of any price fixing or of any conspiracy. Such evidence as there is must come almost entirely from the defendants themselves and as the Court of Appeals noted the facts may be said to be virtually undisputed. Before the first Hearing Examiner and at the criminal trial, executives of the defendants testified. They denied the existence of any conspiracy or any price fixing. Even if a jury chose to disbelieve such testimony, it is at least questionable whether there is other evidence to support a verdict for the plaintiff. At the same time, it has to be considered that California, six other states, two counties in California, and Kansas City, Missouri, have rejected the offer of settlement. These rejecting plaintiffs are represented by able and experienced counsel whose opinions about the proposed compromise must also be taken seriously into account. Even among the best lawyers, however, opinions may, and often do, differ. It is felt that in this instance a misplaced optimism about a highly problematical result has led to the exercise of questionable judgment. The rejection of the settlement occurred, of course, before the criminal conviction of three of the defendants had been reversed by the Court of Appeals. It must also be recognized that ultimately a larger recovery may possibly be obtained by the rejecting plaintiffs than the amount presently available in the settlement. However, the chances of this occurring do not seem to be very great. It is known from past experience that no matter how confident one may be of the outcome of litigation, such confidence is often misplaced. Merely by way of example, two instances in this Court may be cited where offers of settlement were rejected by some plaintiffs and were disapproved by this Court. The trial in each case resulted unfavorably for plaintiffs; in one case they recovered nothing and in the other they recovered less than the amount which had been offered in settlement."

In this case, the nonsettling states rejected an initial settlement offer of $14,851,600. Despite the foregoing comments of the federal judge and after further negotiations, these states later agreed to a settlement offer of $39,616,000 although very little favorable to the plaintiff had intervened between the two settlement offers. However, one of the states refused the second settlement offer and sued in a federal district court in North Carolina. Judgment on all issues was rendered in favor of the defendant and the plaintiff received no monetary damages. Such examples reflect the uncertainties involved in litigation, the high risks undertaken, and the basic rationale for attempting to negotiate settlements.

Handling settlement negotiations is an art and not a science. It should only be practiced by the most skilled of the trial attorneys, who are able to assess objectively the strengths and weaknesses of the positions of both parties. Systematic approaches dealing with the use of logical analyses and the use of mathematical techniques are useful adjuncts to the skilled application of negotiating instincts by the trial attorney.

THE ART OF NEGOTIATING

Negotiating settlement agreements is the responsibility of the trial attorney. Brilliance as a litigator, however, does not automatically confer upon the trial attorney capability in the difficult art of negotiation. The expert accountant who has an understanding of the art of negotiating and experience in the application of logic and mathematical procedures to problem solving can become a valuable member of the negotiating team.

In litigation, negotiating is a decision-making process largely concerned with the establishment of a monetary value to settle a dispute. Success is the value attained in the agreement as compared with the value of a deadlock in which no agreement is reached and the parties are required to continue the litigation. In negotiating, a deadlock should not be considered a failure, but should be looked upon as an alternative in litigation planning. Deadlock can be treated as a tactic in litigation, for it tests the strength and resolve of both parties. During negotiations, a sense of timing is extremely valuable. As discussions evolve there is a time to get involved and a time to remain aloof. There is a time to be expansive and a time to be inscrutable. There is a time to probe or to accept, a time to give, and a time to refuse. There is a time to enter negotiations after all necessary preparations have been made and a time to delay when preparations are inadequate.

It appears that the more successful negotiators combine a number of personal traits. Usually they possess keen minds, exercise good business judgment, know when to talk and when to listen openmindedly, and have the wisdom to be patient. They are willing to get involved with the opposing party, possess an ability to tolerate conflict, and the ability and courage to commit themselves to high targets and take the risks that go with these high aspiration levels. They are stable, articulate, and self-confident people who are willing to work with other experts, have reputations for integrity, and are unafraid to reach agreements that are mutually satisfactory or to accept deadlocks. An effective negotiator has the power to persuade, the ability to motivate, an understanding of human behavior, and the ability to perceive and exploit advantageous situations.

A number of negotiating tactics have been developed to provide an arsenal of ideas and a realistic sense of confidence for the negotiator who attempts to analyze the strengths of the two opposing positions; to make concessions without weakening one's own position; and to set goals. Some of the more interesting negotiating tactics follow.

1. Never undertake negotiations unless you are fully prepared and are armed with a complete understanding of the issues involved, the possible alternatives, your strengths and goals, and you are ready to accept and deal with the demands, concessions, threats, deadlines, and delays of the opponent.

2. Attempt to control or at least be fully comfortable with the agenda, for the agenda formulates the questions and establishes rules that are fair or biased in one direction.

3. Establish high aspiration levels and recognize that aspiration levels, risk taking, and success are interrelated.

4. Do not trust your assumptions about the opposing party until they are proven and do not reveal your strengths or intentions prematurely. Do not assume that the opponent knows how strongly you desire to settle the case.

5. Start the negotiation discussions on easy-to-settle issues rather than on controversial issues. Stress similarity of positions rather than controversies, and stress the desirability of agreement. Tie controversial issues to issues on which agreement can be reached.

6. Do not set your initial demands near your final offer and rarely accept the first offer of your opponent. Never give a concession without receiving one in return and do not make the first concession on important issues. When an opponent makes a concession accept it and keep a record of the concessions you have made. Do not make concessions until you know all the demands and do not exhibit your concession pattern too freely.

7. Discuss both sides of the issues and explicitly state your conclusions. Present your viewpoints last.

8. Do not underestimate the strength of your position and do not be intimidated by the opponent. Do not forget that the opponent believes that he has something to gain by negotiating. Do not be intimidated by the "last and final offer."

9. Listen as carefully as you talk, and be patient.

A PRAGMATIC APPROACH TO SETTLEMENT NEGOTIATIONS

As noted previously, the goal of settlement negotiations is the successful conclusion of a lawsuit without the necessity for trial. The attainment of this goal starts with the objective assessments of: the strengths and weaknesses of the positions of both parties; the uncertainties of the outcome of the trial; the benefits of settlement for the client; the strength of the opponent's desire for settlement; the attitude of the trial judge toward settlement; and a range of monetary values under which settlement will be acceptable. Settlement negotiations bring to the attention of both parties the fact that there are many competing alternative courses of action and provide the environment in which assumptions on many of the foregoing points can be tested.

Decision theory has general application in the selection of a course of action among competing alternatives. It deals with an analytical framework for deciding how decision makers can make their decisions more rational in the context of the relevant information and criteria available. Decision theory attempts to use both objective data and intuition, and aggregates both into an overall preference measure that is meaningful to the decision maker and others involved in the decision. The decision becomes an integration of logic and intuition.

A systematic approach to decision making can be attained by adopting the following thought processes.

1. Define the problem–Clearly specify the nature of the lawsuit and the strengths and weaknesses of each party, distinguish between causes and symptoms and between the way things are and the way they ought to be. Identify the claims and defenses that most likely will be accepted by the judge and jury, the various alternative courses by which the trial may proceed, and the possible outcomes if the trial is continued to completion.

2. Define the goals established for settlement negotiations. This should narrow the focus of general concern. What range of settlement values are acceptable to the plaintiff and affordable by the defendant? What nonmonetary dangers may result for the defendant if the outcome of the trial is unsuccessful for the defense and what actions must be taken to guard against such risks?

3. State the criteria or subgoals as specifically as possible to determine if monetary values can be assigned so that some type of general measurement system can be applied in evaluating alternatives.

4. Identify any possible constraints associated with each alternative

settlement possibility. Settlement alternatives which do not meet the constraints should be excluded from consideration.

5. List all possible alternatives for a negotiated settlement of the lawsuit. These decision alternatives can be evaluated according to the criteria and subgoals established in step 3, after weights or some set of values are assigned to each of the criteria. The assignment of weights can be accomplished by subjectively estimating the relative importance of each attribute.

6. Evaluate each alternative against the scale of measurement for each attribute so that the total value of each alternative reflects the proper utility benefit or desirability of the alternative.

7. Select among the various alternative courses of action that action which provides the greatest benefit. Enter settlement negotiations with an understanding of the relative weighted values of the various alternative courses of action.

This logical approach to settlement negotiations provides the following benefits:

1. It assists the negotiator in coming to grips with the important issues of the negotiations as embodied in the criteria, rather than responding to the initiatives of the opponents.

2. It allows the combined intuition and experience of the negotiator to be brought to bear selectively on different parts of the negotiations.

3. It provides a springboard for augmentation of hard data with intuitive feelings concerning the nature of the litigation, the relative strengths of each party, the attributes involved in the decision alternatives, and their relative importance.

4. It forces the negotiator to break down the decision-making problems into smaller components.

5. It provides a rationale for selection among various alternatives and a basis for communicating the decision factors involved in the settlement strategies.

6. It facilitates communication among the parties involved in the development of settlement strategies.

7. It provides a thought process that allows separate judgments about attributes and alternatives that are aggregated into overall preference scores for each prospective alternative settlement approach under consideration.

A MATHEMATICAL APPROACH TO SETTLEMENT NEGOTIATIONS

Decision making can occur either under conditions of certainty, where all the facts are known, or under conditions of uncertainty, where the events that will occur are not known, but probabilities can be assigned to the possible occurrences. Decision making under conditions of uncertainty requires that the decision maker use judgment and experience in determining which outcomes are more likely than others, and combine this knowledge with the consequences associated with the various decisions. Lawsuit settlement negotiations are generally conducted under conditions of uncertainty.

Quantitative analysis is frequently helpful in judging the effectiveness of different possible decisions and, in general, the quantitative solution process common to most decision situations occurs as follows:

1. Establish the criteria that will be used. In settlement negotiations the objective is to quantify the value of the plaintiff's allegations and the defenses of the defendant and to establish a probable monetary value of the lawsuit.
2. Select a set of alternatives for consideration.
3. Determine the mathematical model that will be used and the values of the parameters of the process.
4. Determine which alternative optimizes the criteria established in step one above.

In establishing a possible range of monetary values for conducting settlement negotiations, the Bayes Decision Process appears to be a logical methodology for bringing together the negotiator's judgment and the economic consequences of a given action, and having both conditions bear upon the decision. As settlement negotiations are complex, this decision process will not consider all the facts, but only those factors which are most relevant to the problem. The mathematical model used will be relatively simple, and after the model has been constructed, certain conclusions may be derived about its behavior by means of logic. The negotiator can then base actions on these conclusions.

The Bayes Decision Rules as applied to settlement negotiations may be presented as follows:

1. Describe the possible outcomes of the lawsuit and the monetary value associated with each possibility.
2. Assign a probability weight to each of the possible outcomes; the

probability weights may be subjective weights, although the reasoning in developing the weights should be as realistic as possible and the attorney who establishes the weights will be required to adopt the perspectives of the judge and jury rather than those of the advocate.

3. Compute for each possible outcome its probability value.

4. Multiply for each outcome its probability value and add the sum of all these products for all the possible outcomes; the total is the expected value of the lawsuit.

5. Identify which of the possible outcomes is the most likely result of the lawsuit and consider both the most likely outcome and the expected value of the lawsuit in developing settlement strategies.

An example of how these rules were applied in negotiating the settlement of a difficult case follows.

WHAT IS A SETTLEMENT WORTH?

During the periods of trial preparation and at any stage of the trial, settlement negotiations may be instituted, frequently at the insistence of the trial judge. Settlement negotiations are one of the more difficult aspects of litigation strategy that the trial attorney encounters. Counsel must consider all the legal, factual, and emotional aspects of the case, and, if it seems preferable, suggest to the client that the case be settled for an award or a course of action that is generally contrary to the client's hopes and wishes. In this environment, a logical organization of the rationale followed in reaching the conclusion is needed, and many times a quantification of the risks undertaken by trial of the issues is beneficial in considering the desirability of conducting settlement negotiations.

Many lawsuits involve complex legal and factual issues. The purpose of the trial is to decide upon these issues of law and fact and to assign a monetary award to each issue decided against the defendant. Testimony can be voluminous where the issues are complex and interrelated. In this environment, an orderly array of the damage alternatives allows counsel to concentrate on the specific implications of testimony and other available evidence, and to relate such evidence to possible damage awards. In a recent case, an array of damage alternatives, in the form of a Damage Matrix, Exhibit 14, allowed counsel to demonstrate the significance of the issues and the testimony directed toward each issue.

Exhibit 14. Damage Matrix.

Damage Alternatives	Initial Damage Year			
	1976	1977	1978	1979
Plaintiff's methods and assumptions	$5,000,000			
Defendant's challenges				
a. Damage period originated in 1977, 1978, or 1979		$4,900,000	$4,000,000	$3,000,000
b. Corrections of statistical assumptions and statistical plan of plaintiff expert witness		(450,000)	(400,000)	(350,000)
c. Revised method of estimating sales volume	(700,000)	(600,000)	(500,000)	(400,000)
d. Revised method of estimating prices under competitive conditions		(1,050,000)	(700,000)	(600,000)
e. Excluding certain persons from class action	(200,000)	(200,000)	(150,000)	(100,000)
f. Other issues	(100,000)	(100,000)	(50,000)	(50,000)
Total defendant challenges	(1,000,000)	(2,400,000)	(1,800,000)	(1,500,000)
Damage alternatives (Plaintiff – $5,000,000)	$4,000,000	$2,500,000	$2,200,000	$1,500,000

As the damage matrix revealed, there were several issues of fact to be resolved by litigation. It was not clear what year the alleged violations occurred. Analysis of the plaintiff's evidence raised questions about the adequacy of the statistical plan designed to estimate sales allegedly lost because of the asserted anticompetitive behavior of the defendant. Also challenged were the plaintiff's methods for estimating what prices would have been, if the alleged violations had not occurred. This demonstration of the impact and range of the available challenges to the plaintiff's methodology was useful in beginning possible settlement studies.

Exhibit 15.   Probabilistic Settlement Value Worksheet.

Outcome of Trial	Award	Probability (Per Counsel)	Probability Value	Cumulative Probability
Verdict for defendant	–0–	10%	–0–	10%
Verdict for plaintiff	$1,500,000	5	$ 75,000	15
Verdict for plaintiff	2,200,000	10	220,000	25
Verdict for plaintiff	2,500,000*	55	1,375,000	80
Verdict for plaintiff	4,000,000	10	400,000	90
Verdict for plaintiff	5,000,000	10	500,000	100
		100%	2,570,000	
Expenses of trial			300,000	
Total			$2,870,000	

* Most probable award.

Counsel was then asked to assign probability values to the success of each of the challenges to the plaintiff's assertions and a Probabilistic Settlement Value Worksheet, Exhibit 15, was developed.

The probability percentages as estimated by counsel represented the best judgment on the odds for different outcomes of the trial based upon the weight of available evidence, attitudes and opinions of the court, abilities of witnesses, and many other factors which lead to a court decision. In this example, the most likely outcome of the trial had a probability of 55% and an award value of $2,500,000. The expected value of all probable outcomes of litigation was $2,570,000. As the cumulative probability column indicates, there was a 10% chance of a decision in favor of the defendant, a 25% chance of an award in favor of the plaintiff of $2,200,000 or less, and a 20% probability of a damage award in excess of $2,500,000. Thus, a settlement offer in the amount of $1,000,000 was considered an appropriate starting point in deciding upon settlement strategy.

The ability of the defendant to sustain a $5,000,000 damage award as opposed to a settlement of between $1,000,000 and $2,500,000 can be important. If a $5,000,000 award would be financially catastrophic to the defendant, while an award of $2,500,000 or lower could be handled, additional impetus may be given to settlement negotiations.

Naturally, the defendant's counsel will attempt to settle at the lowest possible figure and the plaintiff's attorney will strive for the highest; the ensuing debate tests the negotiating abilities of the trial attorneys. The foregoing methodology, however, has the advantage of establishing a basis for communicating the logic behind complex issues involving whether settlement negotiations should be undertaken and what range of values are appropriate in considering settlements.

USING ACCOUNTING SERVICES IN DISBURSING CLASS ACTION AWARDS

Under the Federal Rules of Civil Procedure, a class action can be maintained if, among other requirements, the difficulties likely to be encountered in the management of a class action are not unmanageable. One of the management problems associated with large-scale class actions is the development of methods and procedures to assure a fair distribution of the settlement funds to class members. Until recently, it had not been shown by example that a fair distribution to members of a consumer class was manageable. There was an absence of conclusive precedent and many practical difficulties existed. No techniques had been established to permit very large numbers of claimants to apply for refunds based on actual events during a time period beginning many years prior to the litigation. The possibility that records upon which refunds would be based would not be available had to be handled in a manner that gave reasonable assurance that settlement funds were fairly distributed. Also during the time between the events sued upon and the conclusion of the litigation, large movements of population could occur, a number of potential claimants would die, and there would be many name changes through marriage or divorce. These and other conditions increase the difficulties of locating the members of a class.

Recently, the special master appointed to administer the distribution of a $39,600,000 settlement fund to consumers of allegedly price-fixed antibiotics in six states reported the successful accomplishment of this task. The report described how the techniques of project organization, claim form development, selection of computer consultants, claim form pretesting, blanket mailings, mass media publicity, and other educational efforts were coordinated to establish nearly a million claims from consumers. The special master described the auditing and verification procedures followed and concluded that a high degree of honesty among the claimants was evidenced even though records of purchases were generally unavailable. Refund checks were mailed to 885,000 members of the class action. The conclusions reached by the special master were that the distribution of the award monies was completed successfully and that the total administrative costs involved were only slightly greater than the monies earned in interest by the settlement fund. The special master also reported that very large numbers of consumers can be compensated for relatively small injuries, even where the identities of class members are unknown at the outset and records documenting purchases are unavailable; consumer class actions involving millions of class members are not unmanageable; and a fluid recovery establishing an aggregate class damage fund is a prerequisite to successful distribution of damages to class members.

Where an accounting firm has expertise in consulting activities and has staff skilled in the design and processing of computer systems, members of that firm can play an important role in the organization, planning, and design of systems for the disbursing of class action awards. Where such work is undertaken, the objectives of the assignment generally are:

1. To achieve within a satisfactory time frame a distribution of the settlement funds to valid class members of the class action whose numbers may be in the hundreds of thousands or millions.

2. To provide the highest degree of awareness among potential fund recipients of the distribution program so that every member of the consumer class is notified in a clear and comprehensible way of the right to file a claim for refund even under conditions where it is not possible to obtain or collate a definitive list of such consumers, nor calculate precisely the numerical size of the class, or the exact percentage of the population as class members during the relevant period.

3. To organize the project to insure that it proceeds in a planned and orderly sequence of events to completion. For this purpose the use of planning network diagrams has been found to be beneficial. (Two examples of these networks used to administer the nationwide distribution of the monetary settlement resulting from a class action lawsuit against a federal agency and describing the organization and pilot testing of the program, and the national distribution of forms, are presented as Exhibits 16 and 17. Claims processing and evaluation and completion efforts follow the two activities for which network diagrams have been presented.)

4. To adopt methods and procedures which are cost-effective, so as to permit the maximum amount available for distribution.

5. To design procedures for distributing the funds which emphasize controls that minimize the risk of distribution to nonqualified recipients. Procedures should be carefully documented to insure that fair and equitable treatment is accorded all parties and that

Exhibit 16. Planning Network Diagram Organization and Pilot Test (Numbers in Parentheses Indicate Working Days).

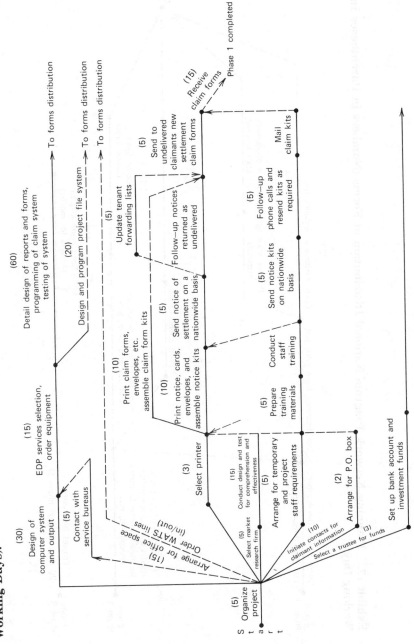

Exhibit 17. Planning Network Diagram National Distribution of Forms (Numbers in Parentheses Indicate Working Days).

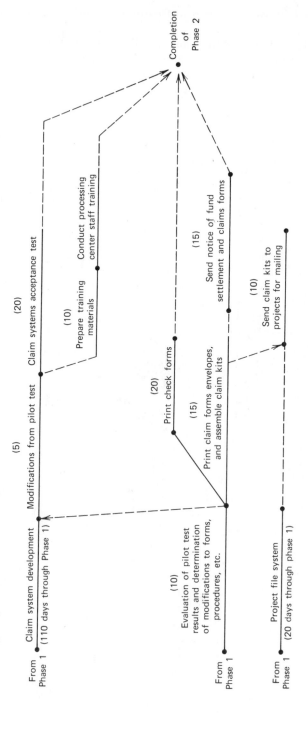

sufficient documentation of all action taken is prepared and maintained. Every reasonable effort should be made to prevent false or exaggerated claims. Although it is unreasonable to expect that all claimants may have retained proof to support their claims, claimants' estimates may have to be accepted and procedures established to avoid abuse of this situation. A system of checks and safeguards should be established to ensure that claimants do not, through mistake or fraud, overstate the amount of their injury. The refunds should be in direct relation to the extent of the injury despite the difficulty of producing proof of such injury. To ignore this difficulty would be a disservice to members of the class.

6. To develop a computer system which provides for effective and efficient claim evaluation and disbursement. (An overview of an initially proposed data processing system for handling claim evaluation and disbursements for the nationwide distribution of claims referred to in step 3 is presented as Exhibit 18. In addition, the key systems files, the detailed systems design, and the input forms must be designed.)

7. To prepare the required forms and ensure maximum comprehension and response from a population which is difficult to reach. (In one case, it was decided by a special master that the only way to insure that each consumer was notified was to mail the notification forms to every household in the states where refunds were being made. It was necessary to mail a claim form in which the rights of consumers under the settlement were explained accurately and in such a manner as to be readily comprehensible to individuals of the most diverse backgrounds and levels of education. It was believed that no other publication or publicity could substitute for the coverage of such mailed publication to the total population. It was recognized that an undeterminable number of claimants who had resided in the state during the period covered by the settlement had left the state and would not be reached by mailed notifications. It was concluded, however, that in the search for these claimants, it was not economically feasible to mail notifications to every household in the country, and that this group would have to be reached by a program of publicity that was national in scope.)

8. To establish a claims processing center to answer questions received from claimants, to resolve incomplete or rejected forms, and to support mechanisms to locate claimants.

Exhibit 18. Claim Evaluation and Disbursement System Design Overview.

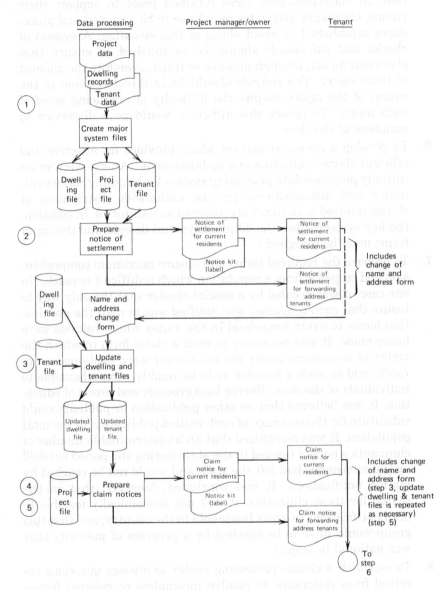

Exhibit 18   (Continued)

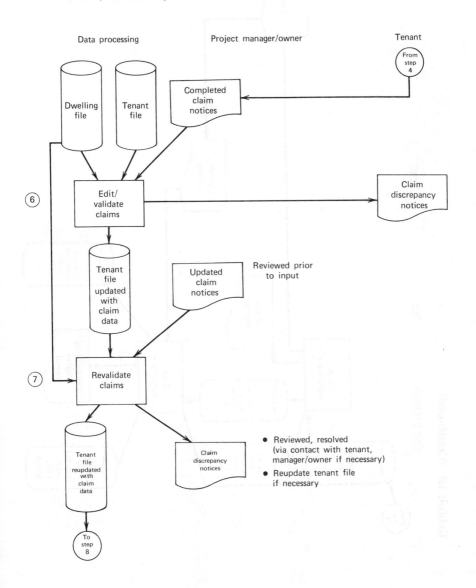

183

Exhibit 18 (Continued)

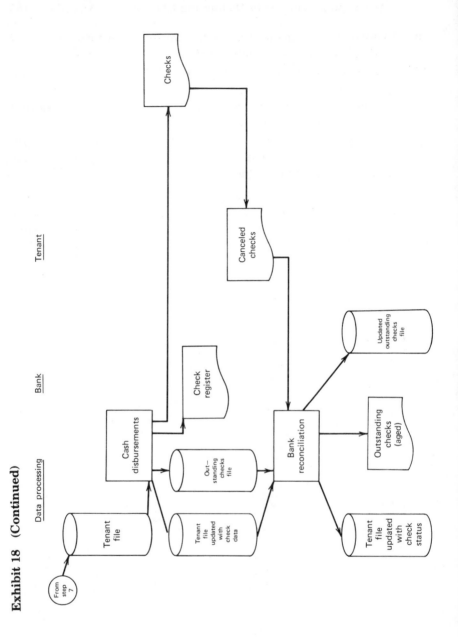

9. To appoint a trustee for the settlement fund, a printing company for the forms, and an electronic data processing center.

10. To process the approved forms and to distribute monies to qualified claimants.

11. To complete the foregoing at a carefully controlled total cost that does not unreasonably diminish the fund.

12. To maintain the right of each individual claimant to procedural due process, clarity, timely notice, and to appeals procedures despite the magnitude of the project.

Systems such as the foregoing have demonstrated that the requirements for fair distributions of awards to participants in large-scale class actions are manageable and do not constitute barriers to such class actions.

CHAPTER

11

The Trial

A trial is a search for truth in accordance with the statutes, legal precedents, and customs of the day. It is an exciting contest between attorneys who are skilled in the use of words as a means of attacking their opponents and exercise intellect and wit as defenses. The main actors in a trial are the attorneys and witnesses. In complex and important cases, preparation for trial may take many months or years and is the supreme test of the attorney, for cases are won or lost on the basis of the effectiveness of preparation for trial. Businessmen rarely anticipate litigation and thus have no reason to concentrate on events that are subject to litigation. It is the task of the attorney to reconstruct the past by assembling the facts from those who should know but have vague memories and records.

In reconstructing the past by assembling and interpreting the facts, the attorneys frequently work closely with experts of different disciplines. Throughout the entire judicial process, the trial attorney is in complete charge of the legal and strategic development of the case. The trial attorney will not only research statutory law and past cases similar to the present one to identify the judicial theories, case law, and types of factual situations that are favorable to the position of his client, but will also be required to supervise and coordinate the work and proposed testimony of the witnesses.

During the preparatory phase of the trial, all discovery is completed and depositions of the expert witnesses are taken. In complex cases, pretrial conferences are held in an attempt to explain, clarify, and agree upon as much evidence as possible between the parties. During these conferences, the experts of both parties explain the studies they have conducted and their conclusions. Where the facts used by experts and their conclusions are contested, the judge may employ experts as special masters to conduct the pretrial hearings and to report their evaluations of the proposed testimony of the parties' experts. Where a trial is held before a jury, the judge may require the special masters to testify during the trial. Usually the testimony of the special masters is given a great deal of weight by the judge and the jury, for they have no connection with either party. The preparatory period of the trial ends with the submission of trial briefs to the judge by each party.

Prior to opening the trial, there are many opportunities for a negotiated settlement; businessmen rarely enjoy the prospects of a long and arduous trial, and the vast majority of cases are settled. Settlement negotiations call for special skills in the art of negotiation, and settlements are usually based upon the future expectations of both parties and the adroitness by which the trial attorney deals with the opposing party. When all efforts at pretrial settlement of the issues have failed, a trial of the issues is the remaining remedy available to both parties. Usually, neither party is completely satisfied with this alternative, for trials are expensive, time-consuming, and demand the time and attention of key businessmen. The outcome is in doubt until the verdict is rendered and the penalties of an adverse verdict can have a destructive impact upon the welfare of the losing party.

Antitrust cases are the largest, most complex, costly, challenging, and time-consuming of the cases brought to trial. Antitrust litigation requires an elaborate use of government legal forces. There seems to be an antagonism toward large, successful companies supported by the belief that success and size have wrongdoings somewhere in their origins. Antitrust litigation is based on a set of continually evolving theories about the economics of industrial organization, as decided primarily by judges. Antitrust cases, however, have a validity, for monopoly is rarely a blatant affair.

Antitrust cases demand the attention of the most capable trial attorneys and require the testimony of leading businessmen, economists, mathematicians, and accountants. Not only does there seem to be uncertainty about the meaning of the antitrust laws, but there is confusion about whether or not this ambiguity is desirable. On the one hand, it is generally believed by businessmen that clear-cut and specific rules make it possible for men to accomplish in their business dealings the legal results they intend. President Woodrow Wilson, the father of the Federal Trade Commission Act said, "the business of the country awaits, has long awaited and has suffered because it could not obtain further and more explicit legislative definition of the policy and meaning of the existing antitrust laws. Nothing hampers business like uncertainty. Nothing daunts or discourages it like the necessity to take chances, to run the risk of falling under the condemnation of the law before it can make sure what the law is."

On the other hand, leading members of the U. S. Department of Justice seem to have taken the view that the law should not be too specific, on the premise that it would be a disadvantage to businessmen generally if we tried to write hard and fast rules, for business practices are constantly changing and the generalities of the laws make them adaptable to new and different circumstances. A former chairman of the House Judiciary Committee, Emanuel Celler, once stated that he vigorously opposed any antitrust laws that attempted to particularize violations, giving bills of particulars to replace general principles. He explained that the law must remain fluid, allowing for a dynamic society. Otherwise, he continued, the process would become a rat race between the monopolist seizing upon omissions and the Congress trying to fill them into the law, always eighteen steps behind.

Complex antitrust cases place heavy burdens upon the expert accounting witnesses who participate. Such cases call for the exercise of the knowledge, traits, characteristics, and abilities described in the previous chapters. To focus upon the activities of the expert accounting witness in such cases and to coordinate the information presented in previous chapters, the role of the expert accounting witness in two antitrust cases is described below. Expert accounting witnesses who successfully handle assignments during the preparatory phase and the trial of complex antitrust cases can reasonably assume that they have the abilities required to participate in many different types of litigation assignments.

THE PLAINTIFF GOES TO TRIAL

The attorney for the plaintiff prepares the complaint and serves the complaint and a summons upon the defendant. The court obtains jurisdiction of the defendant through the serving of the summons and the defendant has a specified time to answer the complaint. If there is no reply, the plaintiff has the right to have judgment entered by default. The defendant's attorney usually enters an appearance by filing a paper indicating the attorney's representation of the defendant and that henceforth all papers may be served on the attorney.

Usually the expert accountant is not hired as a witness until it becomes apparent that these services are needed. As a general rule, the sooner the expert accountant becomes a member of the litigation team the better, for many important decisions are made early in the judicial process, such as: the types of financial and accounting information that should be obtained during the discovery process; how the information data base will be managed; what financial and accounting questions should be included in the interrogatories; how discovery of financial and accounting information will be undertaken at the defendant's premises; and how damage theories will be developed. Much time can be saved and needless work and duplication of efforts can be avoided when the expert accountant participates with the attorney in the numerous decisions made during the discovery period.

The complaint and the answer establish the broad, general outlines of the legal proceedings, such as the alleged offenses, the products involved, the time period during which damages are claimed, and the markets served. After reading these documents, the expert accountant should become familiar with the industry, the position of the client in the industry, the defendant's position, the products involved, the geographical market served, and the economic conditions in the market. The financial position of the client, the general and cost accounting records, as well as the annual and monthly financial reports should be studied. At this early stage of the proceedings any information that the trial attorney may be in a position to furnish, including the names and backgrounds of other expert witnesses, the major areas that require investigation, initial thoughts on what types of financial and accounting information will be useful, and broad concepts describing how the trial will be pursued can be of significant value.

Decisions should be made with reasonable promptness on the type of data base to be maintained for the information developed, data furnished to opponents, and data obtained from opponents during discovery. If the trial attorney decides to use computer facilities to build this data base and to retrieve data from it, the expert accountant frequently can assist in establishing and maintaining the computer data base information system.

As the key issues in monopoly cases deal with power over prices and power over market entry, and as an infinite variety of quantitative analyses can be undertaken to support or refute the existence of such power, the expert accountant obtains from the client's accounting records sales data describing for each product-in-suit: the dollar volumes of sales, the number of units sold, and the selling prices by geographic market. Similar data for the industry are obtained from government and industry statistical sources. If the suit alleges that the plaintiff was deprived of unit sales, it is necessary to study and understand the cost accounting system used by the plaintiff, for an accounting model is needed to estimate lost profits on lost sales.

The expert accountant participates with the trial attorney in preparing interrogatories to be served on the defendant to obtain financial and accounting data on the sales volumes, prices, and profits of the defendant's competitive products-in-suit. Copies of annual financial reports to stockholders, monthly accounting reports to management, and descriptions of general and cost-accounting procedures are requested of the defendant. The names of accounting executives and the location of accounting and sales records, as well as a description of what sales statistics are produced and what types of accounting equipment are used to develop sales statistics, are asked. The answers to the interrogatories are analyzed carefully by the plaintiff's expert accountant.

After reviewing the answers to interrogatories with the trial attorney, the expert accountant develops a plan for further discovery of defendant's accounting records. When discovery is undertaken, the mechanical facilities that are made available for copying the records, and the accounting and statistical records to be copied are determined. These conclusions are discussed with the defendant's representatives. Discovery usually takes place on the opponent's premises and the atmosphere is formal but reasonably cooperative. When discovery has been completed, the expert accountant analyzes the data obtained to insure that the information needs have been satisfied, as discovery is only allowed for an agreed time period. If discovery is later found to be inadequate, information sources other than those of the defendant may have to be relied upon.

The establishment of the damage claim is the major function of the accounting expert for the plaintiff. If illegal power over prices is alleged and if this power resulted in reduced prices for the plaintiff's products, it is necessary to develop a reasonable estimate of this lost revenue and the lost profits thereon. The estimates need not be exact, for the plaintiff will not be deprived recovery of a reasonable estimate of profits on lost revenue because the illegal act of the defendant made it impossible to state exactly the amount of the loss. However, the plaintiff must develop a method that establishes reasonable proof of such loss.

A number of different approaches can be used to establish lost profits on products sold in reduced quantities and/or at lower prices because of the alleged illegal acts of the defendants. Several of the more common approaches are described below:

1. Sales forecasts prepared by the plaintiff prior to the alleged injury for the period of the injury can be used to demonstrate what the sales would have been but for the alleged illegal acts of the defendant. By comparing forecasted revenues with actual revenues, an estimate of lost revenues can be developed. Usually it is necessary to subtract from the lost revenues the variable costs that would have been incurred on any quantities of products unsold as a result of the alleged illegal acts of the defendants to obtain the lost profits on such sales. The expert accountant should be prepared to demonstrate that the sales forecasts prepared by the plaintiff have a history of reasonable reliability.

2. Budgetary systems used by the plaintiff in planning and controlling company activities may provide valuable information for estimating lost profits resulting from the alleged illegal acts of the defendant. Such systems usually include methods for estimating sales under alternative economic conditions and identify the variability of costs under different operating conditions.

3. Statistical regression techniques can be used to establish trend lines for sales in the predamage period and such trend lines can be carried forward into the damage period. By comparing sales or revenues developed from the trend line with actual sales during the damage period, estimates of lost revenues can be made. By subtracting the variable costs from the lost revenues, estimates of lost profits can be developed.

4. Where sales forecasts and budgetary data do not exist, it may be necessary to quantify the testimony of sales executives describing how sales were affected by the alleged illegal acts of the defendants to arrive at a figure for lost revenues. If the cost-accounting system of the plaintiff is inadequate, a method must be devised to estimate the total costs that would have been incurred on the lost revenues. Anticompetitive acts of the defendant can result in a loss of revenue by the plaintiff through reduced prices or through both reduced prices and volumes of products sold. Different types of cost analyses are required in each situation. Where prices alone were depressed, it is necessary to analyze costs and expenses in order to identify those disbursements which increased or decreased as a result of the amount of sales revenues. For example, selling commissions are usually based upon the total sales revenues, and some rents are a function of sales revenues, as are certain taxes. To compute damages in those cases where volume was not af-

fected, such variable expenses as selling commissions, rents, taxes, and so forth, must be subtracted from the estimate of lost sales to arrive at an estimate of lost profits on lost sales.

Where volume of sales as well as sales prices were affected by the alleged illegal acts of the defendant, the cost-accounting studies are usually quite difficult, for it is necessary to establish the manufacturing, distribution, and administrative costs that would have been incurred on the unsold products. Generally, this will require an analysis of costs by the variable, semivariable, and fixed components, and an assessment of variable and semivariable costs to the unsold product quantities. Prior to eliminating fixed costs, it is necessary to determine that capacities were available to handle the additional quantities that would have been sold. Programmed costs such as advertising would be examined to determine if increased advertising would have been needed to reach the higher sales volume levels. If programmed and/or fixed costs would have increased with increased volumes of items sold, estimates of such costs allocable to the unsold units would be included in the damage claim as a deduction from lost revenues.

5. In another type of antitrust case where the plaintiff represents a class of consumers alleging that illegal power over prices by the defendant resulted in excessive pricing, it is necessary to develop what the sales prices of defendant's products would have been but for the illegal pricing by the defendant. The records of the defendant or published market price statistics can be used to illustrate what the actual prices were. The cost-accounting records of the defendant can be researched to provide product costs, product profitability, and estimates of what the prices would have been but for the alleged illegal price control by the defendant. If profits appear excessive when measured by the rate of return on investment, industry profit statistics, or nonmonopoly profits, the profits determined to be excessive may be used as a measure of damages. Frequently the prices of similar but nonmonopolistic products can be established and compared with the prices of the alleged monopoly-controlled prices. The price differentials can be multiplied by the estimates of units sold to the plaintiff class to establish the damages claimed.

At times, the plaintiff trial attorney may request the expert accountant to develop proposed testimony on the liability aspects of the case, as well as on damages. Examination of the cost records of the defendant may show that products were sold at prices below cost to strengthen an established market position or to bar entry to the market by others. As noted above, the cost accounting records may also illustrate unfair pricing in a controlled market. Such data are frequently found to be effective in establishing liability under the antitrust acts.

Upon completion of the initial damage studies, the expert accountant prepares a report to the trial attorney describing the studies made to establish the damage figure, the methods used, the initial conclusions reached, and any proposals for further investigations. This report is stamped *Attorney Work Product* and as it is used by the attorneys in developing trial strategies, the contents of the report are considered as privileged information, not subject to discovery by the opponents. The working papers of the expert accountant will be available for discovery, however, and care must be taken not to include in the working papers commentary dealing with trial strategies. This report to the attorneys prepared by the expert accountant will usually be delivered, with the approval of the trial attorneys, to the other plaintiff experts. It will be the subject of frequent meetings, not only to explain the contents but to review and analyze the data included therein and to test alternative approaches, particularly as perceived by members of the interdisciplinary team. When the studies by the other interdisciplinary team members are completed, their reports will be reviewed and analyzed. These meetings may lead to further studies, refinements, or changes in the positions taken, and at the conclusion of these meetings, a coordinated interdisciplinary approach to the trial should result.

The expert accountant then delivers a list of proposed questions to be asked on direct examination. After the attorney reviews these questions and makes the additions, changes, or deletions deemed necessary, a practice session is held during which a simulated direct examination of the expert accountant is conducted. This experience is useful to both the trial attorney and the expert accountant because it helps each get acquainted with the other's style and mannerisms, and identifies questions that are weak or not posed correctly, and answers that are not as effective as expected. At this time the need for hypothetical questions is evaluated, and if used, the types of simplifying examples that are needed are determined. Also, areas where opinion questions may be asked are discussed and the types of opinion questions are reviewed. Proposed exhibits are prepared, the facilities that will be used during testimony, such as blackboards, charts, view-graphs, motion pictures, and so forth, are agreed upon and any proposed rules for testifying that the trial attorney wishes to follow are reviewed.

The damage claim is sent to the defendants and the expert accountant should then prepare to give a deposition which will be taken at a mutually agreeable time as established by the plaintiff and defendant attorneys. During the deposition the defendant attorney attempts to learn as much as possible about the proposed testimony of the expert accountant. How the damage claim was established, the information relied upon, the calculations made, the people involved in the study, the exhibits to be used, the testimony intended, what working papers were developed, the opinions of the expert, and the background, education, experience, writings, and professional attainments of the expert are all discussed. The defendant attorney is usually assisted by the expert accountant employed for the defense and this expert prepares in writing suggested questions to ask the deponent. The interrogation is conducted in a relaxed manner, but a stenographic record is made and answers are given under oath. The attorney for the plaintiff is present to insure that the deposition is conducted without harassment of the deponent, and at times may object to the questions asked and instruct the witness not to answer. The arguments as to the propriety of these questions are later resolved by the judge.

Shortly before the beginning of the trial, the opposing trial attorneys send to the judge and to each other trial briefs, which describe their position on the legal issues involved, and the evidence they will present at the trial to support their conclusions. The expert witnesses play a significant role in furnishing the economic, mathematical, statistical, accounting, and financial data included in the trial briefs. The attorneys deal with the laws involved and the relationships of the facts and proposed testimony in the case to the laws on which the case is tried. This concludes the preparatory phase of the judicial process, although positions and evidence can be updated throughout the trial.

The trial starts with the opening statement of counsel for the plaintiff followed by the defendant attorney. Usually the expert accounting witness for the plaintiff does not present testimony until the damage issues are handled toward the end of the plaintiff's case. Prior to taking the witness stand, the expert accountant should review the testimony given during the deposition. If subsequently acquired information has led to any changes in this testimony, or if errors were made and included in the deposition, corrections should be made and explained during direct testimony. The questions asked during direct examination should have been discussed with counsel prior to taking the stand, and the witness should have within easy reach, while on the stand, such exhibits as charts, graphs, tables, financial statements, hypothetical examples, and so forth, intended for use. Effective and convincing testimony is the objective of all the work that preceded the act of testifying. All the behavioral knowledge that the witness has acquired concerning the act of testifying can be used at this time.

Cross-examination follows immediately upon the conclusion of direct examination. Opposing counsel is an adversary, but nevertheless may not unduly harass or embarrass the expert witness. Knowledge of the subject matter testified to is the most important preparation for cross-examination, but understanding and applying the characteristics and the behavioral traits required to handle direct and cross-examination is of great value at this time. On cross-examination, the opposing counsel need not bring out any facts other than those needed to reinforce the client's position.

As expert witnesses, accountants are subjected to a broader cross-examination than other factual witnesses. The purpose of opposing attorneys during cross-examination is to destroy the effect of the testimony given by the witnesses during direct examination. Expert accountants who believe that their greater education and training in accounting give them a considerable advantage over the cross-examining attorneys may be acting under a misapprehension. The witnesses' greater knowledge and training may induce them to take a superior attitude, becoming lax in their thinking, which is the advantage that the cross-examining attorneys seek. Trial lawyers know that accounting is not an exact science, which of itself leads to different conclusions by experts in the same field. During years of experience in presenting cases in court trial attorneys have had the opportunity to do considerable reading on many accounting subjects and frequently have had opportunities to discuss accounting with leading accountants. Expert accountants probably have been hired to give the attorneys advice on what questions to ask. Consequently it should be assumed by witnesses that the opposing attorney has considerable knowledge in the field of accounting.

After the cross-examiner has attempted to impeach the expert accountant on the stand, counsel for the plaintiff may desire to rehabilitate the witness and restore credibility to any part of the testimony that was weakened by cross-examination. The rules on redirect examination are liberally applied in most instances, and the attorney is given appreciable latitude in questioning the witness. After redirect examination, at the discretion of the judge, recross-examination of the witness may be allowed. The purpose of this is to overcome the opposing attorney's attempts to rehabilitate a witness, or to rebut evidence which is damaging.

THE DEFENDANT GOES TO TRIAL

The judicial process employs the adversary system to attain justice. Civil cases are determined on the basis of the evidence presented in court and the judge does not supplement the evidence presented by either side, regardless of how obvious it is that counsel has failed to present significant evidence. It is the function of the expert accountant employed as a witness for the defendant to develop testimony which refutes the accounting and financial assertions of the plaintiff, weakens and casts serious doubt upon the financial claims of the opponent, and if approved by counsel, suggests alternative damage possibilities beneficial to the defendant. In many cases, testimony of the expert accountant can be used in the liability and proximate-cause phases of the trial, as well as for damages.

The expert accountant for the defendant follows many of the procedural steps described for the plaintiff accounting expert, including reading the complaint and the answer, and learning as much as possible about the industry and the position of the plaintiff and defendant in the industry, the products involved, the geographical markets served, and the economic conditions in the market. The accountant observes how the products involved are manufactured and requests explanations of the general and cost-accounting procedures of the client, particularly if it is apparent that it will be necessary to understand the cost accounting procedures of the plaintiff. The defendant expert accountant assists the trial attorney in deciding how the data base for the trial is to be developed and managed and obtains from counsel the names and backgrounds of other witnesses, the names of the interdisciplinary team members, initial thoughts on the major areas that require investigation, the types of financial and accounting information that will be useful, and broad concepts on how the trial will be pursued.

At the outset, the expert accountant for the defendant should recognize that the damage claim is prepared predominantly from the general and cost accounting records of the plaintiff and that to evaluate this claim effectively, one must have a thorough understanding of the accounting procedures followed by the plaintiff for each year of the damage period. Thus, the interrogatories prepared by the defendant expert accountant and discovery procedures adopted will generally be far more detailed and time-consuming than similar activities adopted by the plaintiff expert accountant.

The defendant expert accountant provides the attorney with the accounting questions to be included in the interrogatories. In addition to the types of questions asked by the plaintiff expert accountant, copies of annual reports to the Securities Exchange Commission, copies of federal income tax returns, product profit-and-loss statements, cost-accounting manuals, departmental budgets, departmental expense reports, and explanations of changes in general and cost-accounting procedures during the damage period are requested. The names of accounting executives and the location of general accounting, cost accounting, and sales records as well as a description of the sales statistics produced and accounting equipment used are asked. The answers to the interrogatories are carefully evaluated and provide the basic rationale for the discovery program.

When the answer to an interrogatory may be derived or ascertained from the business records of the party served, or from an examination, audit, or inspection of such business records, or from a compilation, abstract, or summary based thereon, and the burden of deriving or ascertaining the answer is substantially the same for the party serving the interrogatory as for the party served, it is a sufficient answer to such interrogatory to specify the records from which the answer may be derived or ascertained and to afford the party serving the interrogatory reasonable opportunity to examine, audit, or inspect such records and to make copies, compilations, abstracts, or summaries. Many of the questions included in the defendant's interrogatories deal with descriptions of cost-accounting methods and procedures, and request detailed explanations of how the cost accounting records were used in compiling figures included in the damage claim. The plaintiff usually takes advantage of the foregoing rule and requires the defendant expert accountant to undertake discovery on plaintiff's premises. During discovery, the plaintiff's accountants usually comply with the basic requirements of the rules governing discovery but will not be as cooperative as auditors expect client's personnel to behave. For discovery to be useful, the expert accountant must possess a good knowledge of cost accounting systems, methods, and procedures, and have a clearly defined program of investigation prior to commencing discovery at the opponent's premises.

The analysis and evaluation of the damage claim prepared by the plaintiff is the major responsibility of the expert accountant for the defendant. Thus the damage theories adopted, the data used, the mathematical and statistical formulas applied, and the accounting computations made are rigorously examined. Where sales forecasts or budgetary data are used in the damage claim, how effectively the plaintiff prepared such forecasts or budgets in the past is tested and the applicability of such data to the damage claim is evaluated. Where estimates of expenses attached to lost revenues are made by the plaintiff, how fairly such expenses are identified and computed is tested. Where lost revenues on products unsold as a result of the alleged illegal acts of the defendant are claimed, extensive knowledge of the manufacturing and distribution operations and the cost and general accounting procedures used for each year of the damage period is required. How accurately cost behavior was identified, computed, and applied in the damage claim must be established, for the incorrect classifications of variable costs as fixed can have significant impact on damage claims, particularly when damages suffered are trebled under antitrust laws.

The expert accountant for the defendant may be asked to refute allegations of the plaintiff that monopoly profits were earned by the defendant. Studies of profits made by other companies in the industry and by other industries may establish fair rates of return at far different levels than those claimed by the plaintiff. Product pricing studies developed by the plaintiff may be reviewed and challenged by the expert accountant for the defendant if errors or inconsistencies are noted.

During the liability phase of the trial, the defendant expert accountants may be called to testify where they have investigated prices of products recognized as not established under monopoly conditions and where such products have pricing patterns similar to the products-in-suit. The results of such studies may also challenge the but for prices used by the plaintiff in the damage model.

The plaintiff is required to prove that the illegal actions of the defendant were the proximate cause of the injury suffered. Accounting analyses of the plaintiff's activities, evaluations of the financial statements, commentary in the annual report to stockholders, speeches of executives, reports of loan officers, and comments of stock analysts made prior to the institution of litigation may assign many reasons other than the activities of the defendant for the problems complained of by the plaintiff. Where the results of these situations can be quantified, formidable obstacles may be established for the plaintiff to overcome in meeting the requirements of proximate cause.

As a result of the many different studies made by the defendant expert accountant, a number of different damage scenarios may be developed. Mathematical errors and obvious theoretical challenges are usually accepted by the opponents when counsel advises plaintiff representatives of such challenges. The more debatable damage scenarios provide a basis for estimating alternative damage possibilities and are useful in settlement negotiations.

Upon completion of the initial damage studies, the defendant expert accountant prepares a report for counsel describing the studies made, where and how the information developed may be useful, the conclusions reached, and proposals for any further investigations to be made.

This report is stamped *Attorney Work Product* and is not subject to discovery, as it contains information dealing with trial strategies of counsel. However, the accountant's working papers are available for discovery and precautions must be taken not to include anything dealing with trial strategies.

With the approval of counsel, the accounting report is delivered to the other members of the interdisciplinary team. Frequent meetings are held to review the work of all members of the interdisciplinary team where knowledge is interchanged, conclusions are examined critically, and a coordinated interdisciplinary approach to the problem is established.

Proposed questions to be asked on direct examination are reviewed with counsel and a simulated direct examination is conducted. Plans will then be made for how exhibits will be prepared and presented at the trial and arrangements made for the deposition of the defendant expert accountant. Usually the plaintiff expert accountant will assist plaintiff counsel during this deposition by furnishing questions to be asked the deponent. Any deposition may be used by any party for the purpose of contradicting or impeaching the testimony of the deponent as a witness. If only part of a deposition is offered in evidence, the other party may require opposing counsel to introduce any other part which in fairness should be considered.

At trial, the defendant's case is started at the conclusion of the plaintiff's presentation. The format for testimony of the defendant expert accounting witness is substantially similar to that followed by the plaintiff expert accounting witness and the knowledge, expectations, and behavioral traits expected of both expert accounting witnesses are substantially similar. Both expert accountants listen to the trial testimony of each other and provide their counsel with suggested cross-examination questions of the opposing accounting expert.

The trial of an antitrust case is time-consuming, burdensome, and costly. The potential damage to the defendant is great, for companies can be restricted as to size, market power, product and geographical coverage, and profitability. Heavy financial damages can be awarded to the plaintiff. The difficulty of reaching a jury conclusion, the uncertainty of results, the probability of almost automatic appeal of the judge's decision, the severe burden placed on the judge in attempting to properly handle these huge, complex cases, and the crowded court calendars create heavy problems. All these conditions establish a favorable atmosphere for out-of-court settlements. By establishing alternative damage scenarios, and by attempting with counsel to quantify these alternatives, the expert accountant for the defendant can play an important role in a satisfactory conclusion to these complex issues.

ROBINSON-PATMAN CASES

The expert accountant who serves as a witness in Robinson-Patman cases is generally employed by the defendant, who is attempting to prove a cost-justification defense to an allegation of unfair price discrimination. The cost-justification defense arises from the economic premise that a seller should not be compelled by law to charge an artificially high price to a particular buyer, if the seller can show by facts and figures that it costs less to sell to a particular buyer than the other buyers. If the seller were to make more money selling to one buyer than another when the price is the same, the act allows the seller to reduce the price to the purchaser to whom it is more profitable to sell, to the extent that the reduction in price is based on the lower cost of selling. Such cost savings might result from the purchasing practices by the low-cost buyer, savings in shipping costs, reduced sales expenses, different warehousing costs, less expensive crating, and other distribution cost factors.

It has been difficult for the expert accountant to demonstrate cost justification on the basis that cost economies arising from the volume of one customer are great enough to permit lower prices. Production volume is considered to be a function of all orders and all products and not the result of the incremental order or the last production quantities. Also, special treatment for new customers or discounts based on the cumulative volume of business each year which have no relationship to the size of individual shipments have not been accepted as cost justification for lower prices.

The burden of proof of a cost differential is on the seller. Any cost differential is presumed to be unjustified unless the Federal Trade Commission finds to the contrary. The procedural requirements are such that a cost differential must be disregarded unless it is certain and precise. But since cost differentials are inherently uncertain and imprecise, most cost differentials cannot exist in the contemplation of law. This situation exists because of the hostility of the commission to cost justification, with the result that even costs that are reasonably estimable often fail to be taken into account.

In developing direct testimony, the expert accountant must be prepared to recognize that distribution cost accounting is not an exact science and that the client may have no precise idea at all of the exact cost of selling a certain quantity of goods to a certain customer. Where one of several accounting distribution techniques is applied to determine the approximate cost of different parts of the manufacturing and distribution process, the expert accountant must be able to justify the selection and defend the rationale on cross-examination. Typically, the inexact nature of these cost figures, together with the strict requirements of the Federal Trade Commission in proving cost justification, has made this defense a difficult and expensive one to prove. Guidelines for making use of the cost-justification defense are scarce and the hazards are many.

Where the defendant sold products subject to a quantity discount schedule, evidence should be maintained that the cost studies to establish the quantity discounts were made with care and that the studies were substantially complete. The seller, whose first attempts to cost justify an otherwise unlawful price discrimination occur after a charge under Section 2 is made, operates under a psychological disadvantage in the ensuing legal proceedings. The expert accountant should advise the client that usually a prudent businessman will make some realistic cost justification appraisals to support the price concession before this type of allowance is given to a particular buyer. Good faith efforts to comply with Section 2(a) before the pricing practices are challenged puts a seller in a much better initial position.

If it is not possible to develop an adequate defense claiming cost justification, but if evidence demonstrates that prices were lowered to meet competitive prices, the defendant has a defense against a violation of Section 2(a). This defense is limited by the following restrictions:

1. The seller cannot claim this defense if the seller knows, or should know, that the competitor's price that was met was itself unlawful.

2. The seller's price discrimination must be a temporary measure to meet competition and not part of a permanent price schedule whereby some customers are systematically charged higher prices than others.

3. An equally low price of a competitor means an equally low price for a given quantity. The seller is not meeting competition by selling smaller quantities than a competitor at the same price.

4. The seller's price discrimination must be limited to meeting a specific individual competitor's price to specific individual customers.

5. The seller must meet, not beat, the competitor's price to the particular customer.

Price changes made in response to changing conditions affecting the market for, or the marketability of the goods concerned, may not be illegal. This category embraces actual or imminent deterioration of perishable goods, obsolescence of seasonal products, distress sales under court process, or sales in good faith in the course of discontinuing business in the products concerned.

COURTROOM DECORUM

A courtroom battle is unique, as it combines all the elements of a theatrical drama with the seriousness of real life in society. The courtroom is the stage for the judicial process and the performers are the trial lawyers and the witnesses. The critics and decision makers are the judge and jury. Courtroom procedures, such as standing when the judge enters and leaves, and the wearing of black robes by the judges establish an aura of dignity, and the judges will insist that the decorum and dignity of the court be maintained. The judge controls the courtroom; and the attorneys, as officers of the court, are expected to assist the judge in maintaining the established practices of the court.

Lawyers occupy a strategic role, for we have been a legalistic society from the beginning. Trial lawyers will generally act honorably in court, and will rarely bully a witness if they wish to make a good impression on the court and the jury. The attorneys have an obligation to be as courteous and as respectful of the court as possible; and, if bullied by the court, lawyers are unwise to respond in like manner. They can demonstrate to the jury the fact that they are being treated unfairly and can convert this disadvantage to an advantage. Judges prevent trial counsel from bullying witnesses, although expert witnesses may be subjected to somewhat harsher treatment on the grounds that the expert witnesses are more capable of taking care of themselves.

Relationships between opposing trial counsel are governed by the same rules that apply to relationships of attorneys with the court. Commenting upon the other attorney, criticizing, or taking note of that attorney personally are rarely done. If attacked by opposing counsel, an attorney must guard against anger, which can cloud clear thinking and is a luxury that a trial attorney can rarely afford. The importance of the relationship of the lawyer to the jury cannot be overemphasized: all that the trial attorney does is aimed at the jury, and the attorney must think of the jury as twelve distinct individuals.

An expert witness must act honorably in the courtroom despite any provocation by opposing counsel, must respect the dignity of the court, comply with any instructions issued by the judge, and answer all questions asked by the judge and the trial attorneys in a courteous manner. Rarely is it wise for the expert witness to respond to opposing counsel in jest or in an angry manner. The expert witness must be punctual for all court appearances and demonstrate a desire to expedite the trial. An expert accounting witness must maintain the dignity of one's profession while participating in the judicial process. If confronted with questions which imply a lack of objectivity or independence, or which tend to downgrade the profession, the expert accounting witness need not submit placidly to such suggestions. Emotion is to be expected when answering challenges to professional integrity, but such answers must be presented in dignified terms.

CHAPTER

12

A Time for Reflection

The trial ends for the expert witness when final cross-examination has been completed and the opposing attorney states that there are no further questions. Usually the initial reaction of the expert witness is one of relief that a difficult experience has been concluded. As an expert witness, you have developed, discussed, and defended your studies and conclusions and have responded under the probe of cross-examination with no opportunity for extensive deliberation or consultation with others. There is also a feeling of elation after presenting your understanding of the facts in clear and concise direct testimony and sustaining your position during cross-examination. This elation is heightened when you have demonstrated your professional abilities against opponents who obtained the best of professional expertise to challenge you. In the quiet of your office, you have the opportunity to reflect upon your participation in the case, the effectiveness of your efforts, the lessons you have learned, and the quality of the professional services you have rendered. There is little equal in professional life to the joy of contributing to winning a hard fought but fair litigation proceeding.

The trial does not end for the attorneys when all evidence has been presented and the judge completes the instructions to the jury. Usually after a brief rest, the attorneys review the record of the trial to insure that it contains the necessary documentation for an appeal, if an appeal is needed. Motions for a directed verdict will be prepared stating that the opposing party has not sustained its position and thus there are no issues of fact for the jury to decide. If an unfavorable jury verdict is rendered, the attorneys may challenge the validity of the verdict. Finally, after the jury is released, the attorneys may interview selected jurors to determine how the jury arrived at the verdict and to identify the evidence that was most convincing in arriving at a decision. The attorneys can then evaluate the effectiveness of the strategies they selected in presenting their case and perhaps reflect upon what would have happened if alternative strategies had been adopted.

ADDITIONAL ACCOUNTING SERVICES TO TRIAL ATTORNEYS

Where expert accounting testimony is not needed, the expert accountant can, nevertheless, perform many valuable services for the trial attorney. Sir Edward Coke, the sixteenth century English jurist wrote, "reason is the life of law; nay, the common law itself is nothing but reason." There is no doubt much truth to this observation when the law is viewed in the abstract. When it is viewed as a reality, however, it must be observed that the law's reason can at times be somewhat limited in scope. Indeed, to attain full scope, the power of reason must have the opportunity to consider all relevant information. Accounting experts can, by using accounting insights and perspectives, view business and economic facts and make available for consideration by the trial attorneys information that might not be otherwise evident, thereby broadening the scope of the law's reasoning through more complete and effective analysis of the facts.

Expert accountants can also serve trial attorneys as instructors of accounting methods and procedures. Prior to the detailed preparation of their cases, the trial attorneys may find it of value to employ expert accountants to conduct intensive training courses in the accounting areas that are being contested. Prior to the trial, lawyers must prepare their cases in a meticulous manner and become familiar with every significant detail. Much can be lost in the early fact-finding stages of the judicial process, if lawyers are not aware of the significance of the information obtained during discovery. To obtain an appreciation of the types of accounting information that may be needed, accounting training courses specifically designed to meet the case requirements can be developed and presented to trial attorneys by expert accountants.

Computers are playing an increasingly important role in litigation, in legal research, in developing litigation data bases, and in managing the legal practice. Where litigation data bases are developed, accounting consultants can perform an essential role in controlling the cost and quality of a computer data base and help bridge the day-to-day communication gap between the computer and litigator by translating the needs of the litigator into a language the systems analyst understands, and by explaining the work of the systems analyst to the lawyer. Skilled accountants can identify the computerized legal research systems that are available to legal firms, assist in the selection of the computerized legal research system, and train attorneys in the use of the system. Accounting consultants can also develop courses to train trial attorneys in how mathematical model building and computers can be used in legal problem solving.

Where the law firm decides to acquire or to rent a computerized data processing system, accounting consultants can be of valuable assistance in helping the attorneys to negotiate a computer contract. It is extremely difficult for the unsophisticated user of computer services to anticipate and to protect against contingencies arising during the use of computer services. Also, the contract negotiation process should be used as a means of discovering and evaluating competitive system capabilities. Where the user is inexperienced in computer negotiations, the vendor can make the acquisition seem painless by presenting a form agreement ready for execution at an affordable price. The form agreements generally are drafted by the vendor's legal counsel, to provide maximum protection to the vendor. The form contract is usually brief, and where ambiguous, generally works out to the advantage of the vendor. Under these circumstances, the accounting consultant can act as a balancing force in the contract negotiations to help insure that the requirements of the law firm are correctly stated and that the contract protects the user as well as the vendor.

To optimize the acquisition of a computerized data processing system, it is advisable for the law firm to deal with potential vendors through an interdisciplinary negotiating team made up of a member of administrative management, a leading staff attorney, a representative of the financial department, a data processing specialist, and the accounting consultant. It is important for administrative management to insure that the acquisition is consistent with both the long- and short-term goals and objectives of the firm. Most computer acquisitions result in substantial changes in methods and procedures of the law firm, and such changes are more readily accepted and implemented when it is apparent that the proposed computer systems have the acceptance of administrative management. The data processing agreement is a legally binding contract and should never be signed without prior review by competent legal staff, who should be made aware of all aspects of the acquisition so that one can maximize coverage of each item in the agreement and avoid ambiguities or omissions in the formal contract. Many of the proposed computer acquisition agreements provide for complex financial arrangements, which should be analyzed in detail by the team member skilled in such financial concepts as discounted cash flow, the determination of present and future values, investment tax credit regulations, depreciation alternatives, and lease capitalization rules. The data processing specialist and the accounting consultant are needed to evaluate the systems concepts, computer operating capacities, and software characteristics. The team should play a significant role in the implementation of the system that is selected.

Expert accountants can also be used by trial attorneys in the role of devil's advocate, to review proposed cases in detail and to evaluate their strengths and weaknesses from an accounting perspective. If this review is effective, trial attorneys will be better prepared to present and defend the lawsuits. Expert accountants can also evaluate the cases of opponents and provide counsel with accounting challenges to be used during the ensuing trials.

Where the accountant is employed as an expert witness, the ideal situation is to be employed as early as possible in the judicial process, for only then can one be of maximum assistance to the trial attorney. At times, however, trial attorneys may not anticipate the requirement for an expert accounting witness but as the trial proceeds, the attorney may realize that there is need for the expression of accounting thought on certain aspects of the factual situation. Where there is no time for the accounting expert to study the facts at issue, the accountant may be asked to respond to a series of hypothetical questions. When hypothetical questions are used, the trial attorney presents to the expert witness, in question form, certain facts at issue, asks that for purposes of the question only, the facts are assumed to be accurate, then asks that the expert accounting witness answer the question based upon the assumed facts and the specialized knowledge of accounting. Where the hypothetical question is permitted, the expert witness need have no personal knowledge of the facts under discussion. In answering a hypothetical question, the expert witness is not establishing an ultimate fact which must be determined by the jury. Use of hypothetical questions can also provide a fertile field to imaginative attorneys during cross-examination.

Putting hypothetical questions to expert witnesses is an exception under the general rules of evidence. Generally, witnesses are permitted to testify to anything they have actually seen or experienced which is material to the issues at trial. They can testify to anything they have heard in the presence of the opposing party; they can testify as to statements made by one of the parties to a lawsuit which may be against the interests of the party making the statement, or to anything within their knowledge which concerns the issues. However, they are not permitted to testify to anything heard from a third party or to facts learned from someone other than the parties to the case, as such is hearsay evidence. When witnesses try to give opinions they are deciding one of the issues of the case and this is the role for the jury. The exception occurs when an expert witness is allowed to express an opinion to fill any gaps in the facts and to make testimony clear for the jury when they ordinarily would not understand it or where there was no other way to get the essential facts before the jury for deciding the case.

Restricting the activities of an expert accounting witness to answering hypothetical questions provides a service to trial attorneys, but in view of the extensive assistance that can usually be provided by the accountant, such limited participation in a trial usually is not satisfactory to the expert accounting witness. Opinion evidence can be speculative in nature and for some hypothetical questions there may be no definite answers. Also, opinions of experts can differ and opinion evidence can be abused. This has led to the uncomfortable situation of experts in the same profession taking directly conflicting positions when answering similar hypothetical questions. Trial circumstances, however, are unpredictable; trial attorneys are usually under tremendous time pressures and, where no time is available to acquaint the expert witnesses with the facts, some benefits can be derived by asking expert accountants to answer only hypothetical questions.

IMPLEMENTING WORD PROCESSING SYSTEMS

Law firms have also found that word processing technology has placed significant cost reduction and administrative efficiencies within the reach of all types and sizes of legal practices. There are a great many approaches to obtaining these objectives, but it has been found that the promised performance levels are not easily reached. In implementing word processing systems, the following program has been useful in obtaining the benefits of this technology:

1. Define the requirements of the word processing system. The scope of the requirements definition study should include all phases of the document production process, such as: typing and transcrip-

tion; reproduction and photocomposition; mail, messenger, and interoffice communications; and filing, storage, and document retrieval. The form and content of the documents should be reviewed, as well as document production flows, in order to determine the required changes in procedures and organization which a revised word processing system would dictate. The requirements definition study should produce recommendations for: the determination of proper administrative staffing levels; the development and implementation of effective procedures and operating guidelines; the measurement and evaluation of service levels; and the performance of administrative functions.

2. The team approach used in negotiating computer systems acquisitions should be adopted for selecting word processing systems, as well. Proposals should be sent to a number of vendors in order to improve the opportunities for satisfying the largest number of word processing requirements; to expand the negotiating team's knowledge of the available features and benefits of competitive offerings; and to gain the advantages of a competitive bidding and negotiating process.

3. The implementation process should provide for: the installation of the selected word processing equipment and the training of the equipment operators; the documentation and implementation of the revised organization structures, work flows, operating procedures, and management techniques to assure proper functioning of the new system; and monitoring the performance of the equipment and staff and making the adjustments to the procedures that are needed for effective performance.

Word processing is a method of organizing offices around functional specialties rather than the traditional executive–secretary relationships. One of the primary innovations in making word processing available was the development of sophisticated typewriters, or text-editing devices, which make use of electronics and computer technology. These typewriters have memories that record text on magnetic cards and tapes and can display whole pages of material on cathode ray tubes. In word processing, first-draft document production is no faster than a regular electric typewriter; however, text editing and playback capabilities are faster. When you wish to edit and revise a long document or to send out several originals, and if you wish to be assured that there are no errors or erasures in the final document, the equipment provides many advantages. The use of these devices always takes more time than simply typing the first original because it must be played back from the tape or cards after these have been originally produced. These devices are excellent for reports, legal briefs, and other documents that are carefully edited and must appear in high quality form. Under the word processing concept, all or most of the typing is removed from the secretary and concentrated in the word processing center where typing specialists do nothing but type. The secretaries are thus free to assume added duties or to serve a larger group of executives.

The word processing organization is usually more efficient than the traditional executive–secretary type of organization because it provides specialization by function and greater ability to manage and control activities. The organization of the office into groups of specialists (correspondence and administrative secretaries) creates a more manageable organization and provides more opportunities for the use of professional managers who can train and supervise on a full-time basis.

A GLANCE TOWARD THE FUTURE

So far little progress has been made in meeting the quantitative burdens imposed upon the courts. Minimum standards of judicial administration have been formulated by the American Bar Association, and modernized court systems have been established in several states. Career administrators have been provided for the major courts in a number of states. Although trial attorneys and administrators of large law firms are making effective use of modern management techniques, little has been done in this area by the courts. Xerox machines are used, but office machines have had little effect on judicial operations. In a large number of courts, longhand entries concerning cases are made in cumbersome ledger-type record books. Ideas for curing the ills of the trial courts through better planned administration, modernized procedures, and a reduction of the workload of judges go unheeded. The great mass of lawyers often keep aloof from such reforming efforts.

Attorneys are, however, officers of the court, and have a responsibility to participate in improving the efficiency and effectiveness of judicial procedures. Many attorneys are also familiar with the impact of computers on the administrative practices of their law firms, the effectiveness of computers in legal research, the automation of litigation data bases and the use of computers in model building and decision making. It does not seem too remote a possibility that attorneys with such knowledge and experience, in the near future, will combine their expertise with that of the accounting computer consultants to participate in extending computer practices into the judicial process so that judges, as well as attorneys, can become proficient in the use of computers to expedite the judicial process.

In the future, substantial progress will continue to be made in reducing the size and cost of computer equipment, expanding its memory, increasing processing speed, reducing data transmission costs, and in simplifying the languages needed to communicate with electronic data processing equipment. Substantially, all information available to humans will, in the future, also exist in computer-available form. Memories in information processing systems will be of sizes comparable to the largest memories now used by humans. It will become feasible and economical to use English or another natural, noncode language to interrogate and command the memory of an information processing system. Any program or information that has proven useful in one information processing system will be copied into another part of the same system or into another system at very low cost and without severe problems of standardization. Information processing systems will become increasingly capable of learning. In particular, they will be able to develop their own indexes as new information is added to memory. Computers will become more useful in planning and scheduling activities and in receiving, classifying, storing, comparing, sorting, analyzing, evaluating, and retrieving vast quantities of information.

Presently available computer equipment, together with the improvements promised in the future, seem to offer potential opportunities for reducing some of the quantitative burdens imposed upon the judiciary. It would appear that judges will soon find the means for using the potentials of computer equipment to reduce much of the clerical effort associated with their functions so that more time can be spent in managing their cases. Some of the areas in which computers are used presently, or may be used more extensively in the future, include the following.

1. Simple reporting forms could be developed for preparation by the judges to report significant case developments. The data on these reports could be converted into electronic form and simple computer procedures could be designed to prepare all the case reports presently required by the judiciary. This would eliminate the cumbersome ledger-type record books, and perhaps could lead to the development of more significant information for the management of lawsuits.

2. Professional firms and industry use critical path scheduling, short interval scheduling, and computer procedures to plan, monitor, and control the working schedules of their personnel. The applica-

tion of these techniques has resulted in more effective use of these key human resources and may have some value for planning, monitoring, and controlling the trial calendars of judges within a judicial district to maximize the use of the available time of these key legal resources. Procedures could be developed whereby milestones, or key events, could be established for each trial in terms of the number of trial days required for the accomplishment of each milestone. Time reports could be prepared by the judges to report periodically the time consumed on each milestone, and the estimated time required to complete the remaining milestones. Computer procedures could be designed to report for each judge: the current status of the caseload; estimated completion dates for each case; and the workload of each judge. Such information would be useful in identifying at an early date unacceptable backlogs of cases for each judge, the need for rescheduling trials, and the need for more or less judicial assistance.

3. Judges are the key human resource in the judicial process and any improvements in their working habits, methods, or procedures can make this resource more available to the public. Industry has found that productivity studies, wherein work procedures are charted, studied, and analyzed, have usually resulted in the development of significant work simplification recommendations which consolidate, combine, reduce, or eliminate many activities and thereby provide additional time to accomplish the more important job requirements. It appears that application of these techniques to the judicial work practices could result in the saving of valuable time of the judges.

4. Based upon the huge appetite for discovery, complex lawsuits result in massive documentation. As a result, trial attorneys' burdens in marshalling the relevant evidence and preparing the legal and factual arguments are impressive. They must not only wade through the documents produced during discovery, but must also examine memoranda, pleadings, motion papers, briefs, and transcripts that seem to multiply with the size of the case. The courts' task is also magnified, since the record on an important motion or a trial can be overwhelming. Anything that can be done to speed the courts' and the attorneys' handling of this paperwork will reduce the workload of the courts and speed the progress of trials.

In large-scale litigation, paper-document depositories have become common. By a pretrial order, the court can establish a document depository and provide for the protection of those documents designated confidential. The documents can be made available to the judge and, if made available to both parties, counsel can copy anything in the depository. Since document production orders can be satisfied by delivering one copy to the depository, compliance can be checked readily. Document depositories have improved the efficiency of discovery and have provided better judicial control over the lawsuit.

Because of their size, document depositories provide little assurance that relevant information can be found when needed. By computerizing the files in the document depository and developing a litigation data base for the files, considerable success has already been achieved in storing, searching, and retrieving information. However, at present each side operates independently on data in the depository. Many attorneys feel that under judicial supervision, information technology could be extended to document management of both sides of the case and the results made available to all those participating in the case.

A joint document depository with joint computer-assisted litigation support systems would facilitate the judicial process. An electronic depository eliminates the problem of geography, as information stored in magnetic form in a computer can be accessed from anywhere through the use of a communications terminal. The trial judge or any authorized attorney would be able to use the electronic depository through a telephone line. Any number of lawyers or judges would be able to examine the same materials and print copies of selected materials at the same time. The problem of loss of confidentiality can be controlled, as document security and magnetic file security systems can be established which are as extensive as those established for the paper depository. The use, modification, withdrawal, or change of any document can be controlled by a preestablished set of rules. An attorney's work product could be protected as parts of the depository may be made available to any judge or lawyer involved in the case, other parts could be made available only to restricted persons and these restrictions could be changed or modified as desired. The use of the data base by each side could be maintained in confidence from all other parties.

The judge usually does not have access to separate litigation support systems developed by each party. A cooperative electronic depository could be of substantial value to a judge. In dealing with pretrial or trial motions, for example, the judge could rapidly obtain the relevant discovery or trial testimony on an important point by researching the depository, with confidence in the completeness of the information obtained. The electronic depository could also be used to determine whether discovery requests and orders have been complied with through a computer-assisted check on the contents of the depository.

The electronic depository would provide a capacity for searching available files for required information. A vast body of information can be examined with incredible speed and the desired information retrieved in many different and unique ways. In a paper depository, the required information might prove impossible to find despite huge time-consuming efforts. Many other possibilities exist for the imaginative use of an electronic depository by the court and counsel.

5. Many attorneys use computers for legal research and employ computer services such as the Mead Data Central's Lexis Litigation Support Service. A number of other computerized legal research systems are also used. Numerous judges understand the use of computer terminals and how computerized legal research systems can be applied. It appears that this trend will continue into the future and the computer terminal may become familiar equipment in the courtroom. With the expanding application of computer procedures in the courtroom we may soon find that in large, complex cases, testimony and evidence will be recorded in electronic form and computer procedures developed to file, analyze, and retrieve selected information. Copies of evidence and transcripts of testimony could then be retrieved from the file and recorded upon a screen for reading and examination when called for by the judge and counsel during and after the trial.

Decision making will probably remain a highly individualized practice by the jury and the judge. However, with the growing familiarity with computer systems by the judiciary, it may not be far into the future before judges make some use of computerized business decision-making techniques for analyzing the business problems presented during the trial and for testing and evaluating various alternative decision possibilities.

A CONCLUDING THOUGHT

Participation in the judicial process is an exciting and interesting experience. The judges and attorneys involved often possess high-level intellectual abilities and articulate their views with precision and clarity. The business problems being litigated frequently demand the attention of experts from a number of disciplines and arguments among experts as to the proper application of their knowledge to the facts at hand enliven many meetings and court hearings.

The effectiveness of the judicial process is determined by the acceptance of its results by the public. We live in a complex business environment and society has become more and more demanding upon our legal institutions. More and more people are organizing into groups, identifying legal spokesmen, and demanding redress of their grievances, both real and imaginary. More and more quantitative burdens are being imposed upon our trial judges.

It doesn't matter much to the litigants if, despite the capabilities of judges and attorneys, court calendars become so congested that it takes years to start trial of litigated issues. The long delays not only postpone the redress of just grievances but add to the costs of litigation. Whatever can be done to lighten these quantitative burdens on the courts can be an important element in preserving the judicial system.

Expert accounting witnesses can make a contribution toward strengthening the judicial process by recognizing that their responsibility to the trial judge and jury is to analyze facts and to present testimony and evidence in an unbiased manner, so that understanding of the facts will be enhanced in the minds of the judge and jury. By diligent study of the issues and the facts being litigated, and by an articulate presentation of testimony, expert witnesses may not only provide valuable services to their clients, but can help to speed the process of the trial. In addition, expert accountants who are skilled in modern management practices and the development and application of electronic data processing procedures can, working with judges and attorneys, help to reduce the time required for litigation. To the extent that this use of accounting assistance helps to relieve some of the time burdens upon trial judges, the expert accountant will have performed a valuable service for the community in addition to providing professional services to his client.

Legal Lexicon for Accountants

Accountant privilege—The protection afforded to a client from disclosure by the accountant of material submitted to or prepared by the accountant.

Adjudication—The formal giving or pronouncing of a judgment or decree in a cause.

Admission—A written request served upon any other party for the admission, for purposes of the pending action only, of the truth of any matters set forth in the request that relate to statements or opinions or facts or the application of law to fact, including the genuineness of any document described in the request. Any matter admitted is conclusively established unless the court on motion permits withdrawal or amendment.

Admission against interest—A statement made by one of the parties to an action which amounts to a prior acknowledgment that one of the material facts relevant to the issues is not as now claimed.

Adversary proceeding—A practice for adjudicating disputes in which the essential elements are an impartial tribunal of defined jurisdiction, formal rules of procedure and governing substantive law, and assignment to the parties of the tasks of presenting their own best cases and of challenging the presentations of their opponents.

Affidavit—A written or printed declaration or statement of facts, made voluntarily and confirmed by oath or affirmation of the party making it, taken before a party having authority to administer such oath or affirmation.

Affirmative response—In pleading, it is matter constituting a defense. It can be new matter which, assuming the complaint to be true, constitutes a defense to it.

Answer—The document filed in reply to a complaint. The answer denies that certain allegations or parts of them are true, denies other allegations for lack of information or belief, and admits those that are true.

Arbitration—The submission for determination of a disputed matter to a neutral person (the arbitrator) chosen by the parties involved in a controversy, in a manner provided by law or agreement.

Bankruptcy trustee—One appointed by the bankruptcy court to take charge of the bankrupt estate, to collect the assets belonging to the bankrupt, to bring suit on the bankrupt's claims, and to defend actions against the bankrupt. The trustee has the power to examine the bankrupt and to initiate actions to set aside preferences.

Best evidence rule—Prohibits the introduction into evidence of secondary evidence unless it has been shown that the original document has been lost or destroyed or is beyond the jurisdiction of the court without the fault of the offering party.

Bias—The concept that incoming impressions are slanted off so that the impressions do not follow a clear path to the mind.

Bifurcated trial—The trial of liability issues in a civil case separate from the damage issues.

Cautionary instruction—That part of a judge's charge to the jury in which he instructs them to consider certain evidence only for a specific purpose.

Caveat emptor—The buyer must take the risk of his purchase.

Certiorari—A writ commanding inferior courts to certify proceedings for review by higher courts. The writ is issued in order that the court issuing the writ may inspect the proceedings and determine whether there have been any irregularities. Now used as the normal method for obtaining review by the United States Supreme Court.

Churning—Occurs where a broker who exercises control over the volume and frequency of trades abuses the customer's confidence for personal gain by initiating transactions that are excessive in view of the character of the account and the customer's objectives as expressed to the broker.

Complaint—The legal document which commences the lawsuit and in which is set forth the facts upon which the suit is brought and the grounds for the complaint. These grounds are set forth in allegations, which are numbered.

Constructive notice—Such notice as is implied or imputed by law. Notice with which a person is charged by reason of the notorious nature of the thing to be noticed, as contrasted with actual notice.

Contempt of court—Any act which embarrasses, hinders, or obstructs the court in the administration of justice, or which lessens its authority or dignity. Direct contempts are committed in the immediate view and presence of the court or so near the presence of the court as to hinder the due and orderly course of proceedings. Constructive contempts arise from matters not near the presence of the court but which tend to obstruct or defeat the administration of justice.

Cost bills—The party that obtains judgment is usually entitled to recover the costs of the action from the other party.

Cross-complaint—The purpose of the cross-complaint is to allow the defendant to settle all matters of controversy between the parties in one action and avoid a multiplicity of suits. A defendant who files an answer must include by way of cross-complaint any related cause of action against the plaintiff, or that party cannot thereafter in any action assert such related cause of action.

Damages—Every person who suffers detriment from the unlawful act or omission of another may recover from the person in fault a compensation thereof in money.

Demurrer—A pleading objecting to defects appearing on the face of a complaint or answer which creates issues of law only. A special demurrer enumerates specific grounds. A general demurrer states that the complaint does not give facts sufficient to constitute a cause of action against the defendant.

Deposition—Testimony taken under oath in writing. A notary public or other authorized person administers the oath to the person whose deposition is being taken. Counsel for the parties are present and opposing counsel asks questions of the witness. A reporter takes the questions and answers verbatim in shorthand or stenotype and later transcribes the notes. The witness reads and corrects the deposition and signs it. By written stipulation, the parties may agree to take the deposition before any person, at any time or place, and upon any notice.

Dictum—A gratuitous or voluntary statement, remark, or observation made by a judge in pronouncing an opinion upon a cause concerning some rule, principle, or application of the law but not necessarily involved in the case or essential to its determination.

Discovery—The prescribed legal procedures by which each attorney attempts to find out before the trial everything possible about the case, such as who the witnesses are, what they know about the facts of the case, and upon what facts they are relying to prove the case. The principal devices for discovery are: depositions, interrogatories, and requests for admission. In addition, by means of motions for production of documents and *subpoenas duces tecum,* evidentary documents may be inspected.

Efficient cause—The cause of an injury to which legal liability attaches; that cause which produces effects or results; the proximate cause.

Equity—Justice based on a system of rules and principles which originated in England as an alternative to the rules of common law and which was based on what was fair in a particular situation. Affords relief where the courts of law are incompetent to give it.

Evidence—Includes every means by which facts are established or disproved, whether by oral testimony, writings, photographs, or objects.

Ex-party hearing—A hearing during which the court listens to only one side of the controversy.

Expert testimony—Evidence of persons skilled in some art, science, profession, or business, whose skill and knowledge is not common to the average man and which is possessed by the expert by reason of special study or experience.

Fellow servant rule—A common law doctrine permitting an employer to allege that the negligence of another employee was partly or wholly responsible for the accident resulting in the injury, thus reducing or extinguishing liability. Now generally abrogated by workers' compensation acts and the Federal Employers' Liability Act.

Findings of fact and conclusions of law—These are the findings of the court after a trial has been held. From the findings of fact are drawn the conclusions of the law by the judge.

Forensic—Belonging or having application to courts of justice.

Goodwill—The favor which management wins from the public. The ability of a business to generate income in excess of a normal rate on assets due to superior managerial skills, market position, product acceptance, new product testing, and so forth.

Government of laws—A fundamental principle of American jurisprudence which requires that decisions not be based on the character or influence of the litigants and the personal predilections of the judge, but on statutory and common laws.

Habeas corpus—Writs having for their purpose the bringing of a party before a court or a judge. The function of the writ is not to determine guilt or innocence but to determine whether the prisoner is restrained from liberty by due process.

Hearsay—Evidence not based on personal knowledge of the witness and which rests mainly on the veracity and competency of others.

Impeachment—The discrediting of a witness's statement.

In camera—In chambers.

In pan delecto—In equal fault.

Interlocutory injunction—Issued during the pendency of the litigation for the short-term purpose of preventing irreparable injury to the petitioner prior to the time that the court will be in a position to grant or deny permanent relief on the merits.

Interrogatories—Each attorney will develop, with the aid of the client, a group of questions to propose to the adverse party. Interrogatories are prepared with the title of the court and the cause followed by a list of questions.

Intervenor—A person who voluntarily interposes in an action with the permission of the court.

Judicial notice—The notice that a judge will officially take of a fact although no evidence to prove the fact has been introduced in trial. It is a doing away with evidence because there is no real need for it.

Jurisprudence—The science or philosophy of law which ascertains the principles on which legal rules are based in order to classify those rules in their proper order, to show the relationship in which they stand to each other, and to settle the manner in which new or doubtful cases should be brought under the appropriate rule.

Law—The body of rules or principles prescribed by authority or established by custom which a state, community, society, or the like, recognize as binding upon its members. The science of law is the study, recognition, and interpretation of these rules and principles. The interpretation of the law is a function of the judge. The law is applied to the facts by the jury.

Law of the case—If an appellate court has passed on a legal question and remanded the case to the court below for further processing, the legal question determined by the appellate court may not be determined differently in the same case where the facts are the same.

Lis pendens—Jurisdiction, control or power which courts acquire over property in suit during the proceedings and until final judgment.

Mala fides—Bad faith.

Mandamus—Command.

Mitigation of damages—Duty imposed on the injured party to exercise reasonable diligence and ordinary care in attempting to minimize the damages after injury has been inflicted.

Monopolization—The act, or the planned or attempted act of monopolization. Monopolization is the possession of monopoly power coupled with the attainment of that power by unfair means or the use of that power unfairly for the purpose of excluding competition.

Monopoly power—The power or ability to fix or control prices or to exclude competition from a relevant market.

Monopsony—A condition of the market in which there is but one buyer of a particular commodity.

Motion—An application to the court for an order of the court. A motion may be made at any time during the pendency of the action or proceeding, when the relief sought would be appropriate.

Ninety-day letter—Statutory notice sent by the U. S. Internal Revenue Service to a taxpayer stating tax deficiency. During the 90-day period, the taxpayer may either pay the tax and seek a refund or not pay the tax and challenge such alleged deficiency by petition to the U. S. Tax Court.

Nuisance—That activity which arises from unreasonable or unlawful use by a person of one's own property, working injury to the rights of another or the public and producing such material annoyance that the law will presume resulting damage.

Nunc pro tunc—Applied to acts allowed to be done after the time they should have been done, and giving them the same effect as if they had been done at the regular time.

Oath—A form of attestation by which a person affirms the truth of a statement, which renders one willfully asserting untrue statements punishable for perjury.

Obiter dictum—Words of an opinion entirely unnecessary for the decision in a case and not binding as precedent.

Offer of proof—When an objection to a question has been sustained at a trial or a hearing, the party aggrieved by the ruling may indicate in the record what would have been given, if the question had not been excluded. The answer is given outside the presence of the jury and the appellate court is then in a position to determine from the record the correctness of the ruling and the prejudice in its exclusion, if any.

Oligopoly—An economic situation in which a few sellers supply a standardized product.

Opinion evidence—Evidence of what a witness thinks, believes, or infers in regard to the facts in dispute as contrasted with the witness's personal knowledge of the facts themselves. A witness qualified as an expert by knowledge, skill, experience, training, or education may testify thereto in the form of an opinion. If a witness is not testifying as an expert, opinion testimony is limited to those opinions or inferences which are rationally based on the perception of the witness, and helpful to a clear understanding of the testimony in the determination of a fact in issue.

Order *nisi*—A provisional or conditional order allowing a certain time within which to do a required act, failing which the order will be made absolute.

Parole evidence rule—Prohibits contracting parties from altering the import of their written contract through the use of contemporaneous oral declarations.

Pendente lite—During the litigation.

Per se doctrine—In antitrust law if an activity is blatant and its intent is pernicious in effect, a court need not determine the reasonableness of the act before determining it to be in violation of the antitrust laws.

Pleadings—Written statements of the claims and defenses of the parties to a court action.

Predatory intent—Under the Robinson-Patman Act, the alleged price discriminator must sacrifice present revenues for the purpose of driving competitors out of the market with the hope of recouping losses through subsequent higher prices.

Prejudice—The idea that a mental block exists against incoming ideas which conflict with fixed ideas.

Pretrial conference—An informal conference of counsel and pretrial judge, either in the courtroom or judge's chambers, for the purpose of determining the matters upon which the parties agree and the genuine issues. By means of these conferences, the time spent by attorneys in preparing for the presentation of evidence is materially reduced and time for the trial is lessened. The attorneys are required to prepare and to submit to the pretrial conference judge at or before the conference a joint written statement of the matters agreed upon and a joint or separate written statement of the factual and legal contentions to be made as to the issues remaining in dispute. At the pretrial conference or within five days thereafter, the judge makes a pretrial order, which is a statement of the nature of the case, and the matters agreed on. The clerk serves the pretrial order upon the attorneys and once filed, the pretrial order becomes a part of the record in the case and where inconsistent with the pleadings controls the subsequent course of the case.

Price leadership—An economic condition of the marketplace wherein the leader in the industry establishes a price and the others in the market follow by establishing similar prices for their competitive product. Such practices have been held to not be in violation of the antitrust laws in the absence of showing an intent to monopolize.

Proximate cause—That cause which, in natural and continuous sequence, unbroken by an efficient intervening cause, produced the injury or damage complained of, without which such injury or damage would not have occurred.

Quasi contract—An obligation which the law creates in the absence of an agreement and which is invoked by the courts where there is unjust enrichment.

Ratio decidendi—The underlying principle of the case without which no judgment could have been given.

Rebuttal evidence—Evidence which tends to explain, contradict, or disprove evidence offered by the adverse party and also includes evidence given in opposition to a presumption of fact or a prima facie case.

Referee—A person appointed to exercise judicial powers, to take testimony, to hear parties, and to report the findings.

Rehabilitation—The discrediting information has been overcome and the creditability of the witness' statement has been reestablished in the eyes of the jury.

Relevant market—The geographical market composed of products which have reasonable interchangeability for purposes for which they are produced, considering their price, use, and quality. It excludes products whose "cross-elasticities of demand" are small.

Res ipsa loquitor—The thing speaks for itself and is a rebuttable presumption or inference that defendant was negligent, which arises upon proof that the instrumentality causing the injury was in the defendant's exclusive control, and that the accident was one which does not ordinarily happen in the absence of negligence.

Res judicata—The higher norm (the statute or a norm of common law) determines to a greater or lesser extent the creation and content of the lower norm (the decision of the court). This term represents an authority whose decision cannot be annulled or changed anymore.

Respondeat superior—The principal is responsible for an agent who is acting within the course and scope of employment by the principal.

Restatement of Law—A series of volumes authored by the American Law Institute that tells what the law is in a general area, how it is changing, and what the authors think should occur.

Scienter—Refers to a mental state embracing an intent to deceive, manipulate, or defraud. It is a term frequently used to indicate the defendant's guilty knowledge.

Settlement conference—Held informally before a judge if one or more of the parties advises the court of an acceptance of the invitation.

Stari decisis—Court decisions which stand as precedents for future guidance.

Stipulation—An agreement entered into by the parties, usually through their respective counsel. Counsel may stipulate as to agreed facts, evidence, to file an amended complaint, to extend the time to answer, and many other matters incidental to the case.

Subpoena—An order of the court directing a witness to appear in court.

Subpoena *duces tecum*—An order of the court commanding a witness who has possession or control of some document or paper that is pertinent to the issues of a pending controversy, to produce it at trial.

Testimony—Evidence presented as oral statements made under oath during a trial.

Tie-in arrangements—The market power of one product is used to increase the market power of another product.

Tort—A private or civil wrong or injury other than a breach of contract for which the court will provide a remedy in the form of an action for damages. There must be a violation of duty owing to the plaintiff which arises by operation of the law and not by agreement between the parties.

Ultra vires—Without power, or beyond the power.

Venue—The county or geographical area in which a court with jurisdiction will hear and determine a case.

Verdict:

　Contrary to law—A verdict which the law does not authorize a jury to render because conclusions drawn are not justified thereby.

　Directed—Verdict ordered by the judge as a matter of law when he rules that the party with the burden of proof has failed to make out a prima facie case. Under these circumstances, the judge orders the jury to return a verdict for the other party.

　General—A verdict whereby the jury finds either for the plaintiff or the defendant in general terms.

　General, with interrogatories—The court may submit to the jury, together with the appropriate forms for a general verdict, written interrogatories upon one or more issues of fact, the decision on which is necessary to a verdict. When the general verdict and the answers are harmonious, the appropriate judgment upon the verdict and answers will be entered. When the answers are consistent with each other, but one or more is inconsistent with the general verdict, judgment may be entered in accordance with the answers notwithstanding the general verdict, or the court may return the jury for further consideration of its answers and verdict and may or may not order a new trial. When the answers are inconsistent with each other, and one or more is likewise inconsistent with the general verdict, judgment shall not be entered, but the court shall return the jury for further consideration of its answers and verdict, or shall order a new trial.

Special—The special verdict is a statement by the jury of the facts it has found and the court determines which party, based on those answers, is to have judgment.

Verification of pleading—A pleading is said to be verified when it has appended to it an affidavit sworn to before a notary or a declaration made under penalty of perjury as to the truth of the pleading.

Voir dire—A preliminary examination to determine the competency of a witness.

Accounting Glossary

Accounting—A discipline which establishes rules, regulations, and techniques for recording, classifying, and summarizing the results of business transactions and presenting these data to the user in the form of financial reports.

Accounting evidence—Proof obtained by any of the various devices employed by the public accountant in the examination or review of accounting records.

Accounting principles—The body of doctrine associated with accounting, serving as an explanation of current practices and used as a guide in the selection of conventions and procedures.

Accrual accounting—A system of accounting which records transactions as assets and liabilities when obligations are incurred rather than when cash is paid or received, and assigns income and expenses to the periods to which they are related rather than to the periods in which they are settled in cash. Cash accounting is another system of accounting where assets, liabilities, income, and expenses are recorded when the receipt or payment of cash takes place.

A *posteriori*—Pertaining to the process of reasoning whereby principles or other propositions are derived from the observations of facts.

Average deviation—A measure of variability; the arithmetic mean of the differences between each item and the arithmetic mean of the data, where the differences are added without regard to the sign.

Basing point—A geographic location at which the quoted price of a commodity serves as the foundation for the price of the same product in another location.

Bill of materials—A list of the materials, parts, and assemblies or subassemblies, and the quantity of each required to make a product or to build the items specified by a particular order.

Breakeven chart—A chart showing the relationship of costs, prices, volumes, and profits under varying conditions.

Burden—Same as indirect cost or overhead. Consists of manufacturing expenses other than direct materials and direct labor incurred in manufacturing a product or rendering a service.

By-product—A secondary product obtained during the course of manufacture, having a relatively small importance compared with that of the chief product or products.

Capital coefficient—The average cost of acquiring an additional unit of productive capacity.

Common cost—The cost of facilities or services employed in the output of two or more operations, commodities, or services.

Consumed cost—Any cost, the benefits from which have expired, been lost or destroyed.

Contribution costing—The sales of commodities or services provide a source of funds from which direct costs are paid. The balance remaining is applied to the absorption of fixed costs, the payment of taxes and dividends, and the retention of profits.

Controllable cost—a cost which some person in the organization is responsible for controlling and which that person has the authority and ability to control. Such costs vary with volume, efficiency, choice of alternatives and management determinations.

Cost—An expenditure or an outlay of cash, other property, capital stock, services, or the incurring of a liability therefor, identified with goods or services acquired, or with any loss incurred and measured by the amount of cash paid or payable, or the market value of other property, capital stock, or services given in exchange.

Cost absorption—The expensing of a cost incurred, either at the time incurred and first given expression in the accounts, or at a subsequent point in time.

Cost of by-product—The costs directly identified with a secondary product that resulted during the production of the primary product or products. The joint costs of production of both the primary and secondary products are usually charged only to the primary product, since it is not possible to determine separately the cost of production for the secondary product. The only costs that can usually be identified directly with the by-product are those occurring after production, such as handling and storage, packaging, shipping, and selling costs.

Critical path—The most time-consuming sequence of operations of any of a series of operative stages contributing to a given end-product; or any stage in which a possible obstruction in performance would delay the programmed time.

Direct cost—The cost of any good or service that contributes to and is readily identified with a specific product or lot of production.

Economic lot size—The number of units to be ordered in a single purchase, or to be produced in a single run before machines are reset for another item and which will minimize costs.

Ergonomics—The matching of men and machines in such a manner as to increase efficiency.

Expired cost—An expenditure from which no further benefit is anticipated.

Full cost or total cost—The inclusion of all costs, fixed, variable, semi-fixed, and programmed.

Historical cost—The cost to the present owner at the time of acquisition.

Idle capacity cost—The variance attributable to the failure to utilize facilities at projected rates.

Incremental cost—The change in aggregate cost that accompanies the addition or subtraction of a unit of output or a change in factors affecting cost, such as style, size, or area of distribution. Also called marginal or differential cost.

Indirect cost—A cost which need not be directly attributed to the production of a specified good or service, but can be identified with an activity associated with production, such as supervision, building depreciation, factory rent, and so forth.

Joint costs—Costs incurred in the concurrent production and/or distribution of two or more closely related products.

Macro accounting—A composite of accounts maintained for an industry or for the entire economic activity within a region or a country.

Noncontrollable cost—A cost that does not fluctuate with volume and is not assigned to someone in an organization for control on a day-to-day basis.

Oligopoly prices—The price that prevails in a market of a few sellers and many buyers.

Oligopsony price—The price that prevails in a market with few buyers and numerous sellers.

Out-of-pocket cost—A cost paid directly in cash. Also used to imply variable costs for which payment is normally made currently as compared to fixed costs for which payment has usually been made in an earlier period.

Period cost—A cost that is consumed by the passage of time rather than by the amount of activity or output.

Prime cost—The cost of direct labor and direct materials associated with a particular product.

Product analysis—A study of products to develop new ones, adapt old ones to new uses, or determine product characteristics most valuable to the consumer. Also, the study of how to provide the greatest value per dollar of cost or sales price.

Production control—The scheduling and controlling of the use of men, materials, and machinery in order to produce goods on time and in an efficient manner.

Program cost—A cost directly connected with a program of activities aimed at accomplishing a particular goal such as an advertising program, a maintenance program, and so forth.

Quality control—A system, based in part on inspection, which is used to assure the uniform and acceptable compliance of a product with its specifications.

Responsibility costing—A method of accounting in which costs are identified with persons assigned to their control rather than with products or functions.

Statistical inference—The use of a limited quantity of observed data as a basis for generalizing on the characteristics of a larger, unknown universe or population.

Sunk—A past cost arising out of a decision that cannot be reversed.

Variable cost—An operating expense that varies directly with sales or production volumes, or with other measures of activity.

Variance—A deviation from a standard forecast.

Index